DEBITS, CREDITS, FINANCE AND PROFITS

AUSTRALIA
The Law Book Company Ltd.
Sydney : Melbourne : Brisbane

CANADA AND U.S.A.
The Carswell Company Ltd.
Agincourt, Ontario

INDIA
N. M. Tripathi Private Ltd.
Bombay

ISRAEL
Steimatzky's Agency Ltd.
Jerusalem : Tel Aviv : Haifa

MALAYSIA : SINGAPORE : BRUNEI
Malayan Law Journal (Pte) Ltd.
Singapore

NEW ZEALAND
Sweet & Maxwell (N.Z.) Ltd.
Wellington

PAKISTAN
Pakistan Law House
Karachi

WILLIAM THREIPLAND BAXTER

Debits, Credits, Finance and Profits

Edited by

Harold Edey and B.S. Yamey

London
Sweet & Maxwell
1974

Published in 1974 by
Sweet & Maxwell Limited
of 11 New Fetter Lane, London
and printed in Great Britain by
Richard Clay (The Chaucer Press) Ltd, Bungay, Suffolk

SBN 421 17530 3

PREFACE: W. T. BAXTER

This collection of papers by some of William Baxter's friends is presented to him on the occasion of his retirement from his chair of accounting at the London School of Economics, University of London. The presentation is made as an act of respect and friendship and as a mark of recognition of his signal services to the academic study of accounting, in his teaching (successively at Edinburgh, 1934–36; Cape Town, 1937–47; and the L.S.E., 1947–73) and his numerous and important contributions to the literature of accounting.

Former students and others who have benefited from Baxter's example and guidance are to be found in many countries in the practice of professional accounting, in public and private business, on the staffs of universities and colleges, and in other occupations. His published work covers all major fields of accounting, but he has not limited himself to that subject, as is shown by the contents of the selected list of his publications which is appended. He has looked both backwards and forwards in time. In his writing and teaching he has treated accounting, not as an isolated subject, but as a branch of knowledge related to studies in other disciplines.

W. T. BAXTER: SELECTED LIST OF PUBLICATIONS

"An Investigation into the Dissolution of a Medieval Italian Partnership," *Accountants' Magazine*, July 1932.

"Daniel Henchman, a Colonial Bookseller," *Essex Institute Historical Collections*, January 1934.

"Daniel Henchman" and "Christopher Kilby," in *Dictionary of American Biography*, XXI, Supplement One, London: Oxford University Press, 1935.

Income Tax for Professional Students, London, Pitman, 1936.

"The Treatment of Oncost in Cost Accounts," *The Accountant*, October 23, 1937.

The House of Hancock: Business in Boston, 1724–75, Cambridge, Mass., Harvard University Press, 1945.

"Credit, Bills, and Bookkeeping in a Simple Economy," *Accounting Review*, April 1946.

Accountants and the Inflation, Manchester Statistical Society, February 1949.

(Editor) *Studies in Accounting*, London, Sweet and Maxwell, 1950.

"The Study of Balance Sheets," *Accountancy*, February and March 1951.

(With B. S. Yamey) "Theory of Foreign Branch Accounts," *Accounting Research*, April 1951.

"A Colonial Bankrupt: Ebenezer Hancock, 1741–1819," *Bulletin of the Business Historical Society*, June 1951.

"Inflation and Accounting Profits," *Westminster Bank Review*, May 1952.

"Recommendations on Accounting Theory," *The Accountant*, October 10, 1953.

(With L. C. B. Gower) *Shares of No Par Value*, The Incorporated Accountants' Research Committee, 1954.

"The Accountant's Contribution to the Trade Cycle," *Economica*, May 1955.

"Accounting in Colonial America," in A. C. Littleton and B. S. Yamey (eds.), *Studies in the History of Accounting*, London, Sweet and Maxwell; Homewood, Illinois, Irwin, 1956.

"British Transport Commission *v.* Gourley," *The Modern Law Review*, July 1956.

"Partnership Rights – The Valuation Problem," *Accounting Research*, July 1958.

"Inflation and the Accounts of Steel Companies," *Accountancy*, May and June 1959.

(With Alfred R. Oxenfeldt) "Approaches to Pricing – Economist *v.* Accountant," *Business Horizons*, Winter 1961.

(Editor, with Sidney Davidson) *Studies in Accounting Theory*, London, Sweet and Maxwell; Homewood, Illinois, Irwin, 1962.

"Inflation and Partnership Rights," *Accountants' Magazine*, February 1962.

"Inflation and Accounts," *The Investment Analyst*, December 1962.

"The Future of the Accountant," *The Accountant*, July 11 and August 1, 1964.

"Accounting Values: Sale Price versus Replacement Cost," *Journal of Accounting Research*, Autumn 1967.

"General or Special Index—Capital Maintenance under Changing Prices," *Journal UEC*, no. 3, 1967.

'Valuation of a Practising Accountant's Work-in-progress," *Accountancy*, March and April 1968.

Depreciation, London, Sweet and Maxwell, 1971.

"Depreciating Assets: The Forward-looking Approach to Value," *Accountants' Magazine*, April 1971.

(With N. H. Carrier) "Depreciation, Replacement Price, and Cost of Capital," *Journal of Accounting Research*, Autumn 1971.

Contributed to the finance chapters in Henrietta M. Larson, Evelyn H. Knowlton and Charles S. Copple, *History of the Standard Oil Company (New Jersey) 1927–50*, New York, Harper and Row, 1971.

"Current Developments in Accounting," *Accountants' Magazine*, August 1972.

CONTENTS

viii *Contents*

STANDARD ACCOUNTING PRACTICE

Peter Bird

IN 1970 the British and Irish Institutes of Chartered Accountants began to prepare and approve a series of Statements of Standard Accounting Practice. Few would quarrel with the expressed purpose of this development: "to narrow the areas of difference and variety in accounting practice."[1] Almost identical words appear in the charter of the Accounting Principles Board of the American Institute of Certified Public Accountants.[2] Yet there is profound disagreement between the advocates of "uniformity" and of "diversity" within the American accounting profession, both accepting the Board's terms of reference. In Continental Europe uniformity in accounting has long been a topic of major professional concern, now being reflected in the drafting of EEC directives on company law; but the points of principal Continental concern are quite different from those of English-speaking accountants.

The present purpose is to develop a preliminary assessment of the British programme of preparation, publication and approval of Statements of Standard Accounting Practice. Before it is sensible to make any assertion as to whether they have got off on the right foot, they must be seen in their historical and their international setting. Even before that it is worth searching for some analytical tool with which to examine the attitudes of various times and countries to standardisation in accounting.

ANALYTICAL MODEL

The purpose of accounting statements is to communicate knowledge of the financial affairs of some entity from those who possess this knowledge to others interested in the entity who did not previously possess it. This proposition is as true of "management accounts" within an organisation as it is of the "financial accounts" with which this study is principally concerned. Problems of communication are studied within a variety of disciplines including electronics, computer science, biology, psychology and linguistics. A broad general model of the communication process used by students in some of these fields may cast some light on the particular problems of accounting statements[3]. It may thus help us to get the

[1] Institute of Chartered Accountants in England and Wales, "Statement of Intent on Accounting Standards in the 1970s," reproduced in *Accountancy*, January 1970, 2–3.
[2] AICPA Special Committee on Research Program, "Report to Council (1958)," reprinted in *Journal of Accountancy*, December 1958, 62–63.
[3] This approach has been suggested by N. M. Bedford and V. Baladouni, "A Communication Theory Approach to Accountancy," *Accounting Review*, 37 (1962), 650–659, and by D. H. Li, "The Semantic Aspect of Communication Theory and Accountancy,"

discussion of uniformity away from "the tendency of each group to characterise members of the other as fools or knaves."[4]

Shannon and Weaver[5] distinguish three levels at which communications problems arise:

Level A, at which the problems are technical
Level B, at which the problems are semantic
Level C, at which the problems relate to effectiveness

The distinction between these three levels will be explained by considering them individually but in the reverse order, starting with Level C.

The objective of communication is to generate in the "receiver" of a series of signals the same response (feeling and/or action) as would be aroused in him if it had been he, and not some other person who acts as a "transmitter," who had direct experience of a situation. Clearly this is, for any but the simplest situation, an ideal towards which we grope, rather than a standard we can reach. The "transmitter" who has the direct knowledge or experience must nearly always select from the many facets of a situation a few which he believes to be the most likely to affect the reactions of the receiver. At best the receiver will only gain knowledge about those aspects of the situation which the transmitter selects for communication within the technical, time, space, cost or mental constraints which limit the total of messages conveyed. If, for example, an accountant transmitter selects the historic cost of properties for communication in accounts, but the reaction of a receiver of the accounts would be affected also by the current realisable value of those properties, then communication is not entirely successful, at Level C, in giving the receiver the knowledge about the situation which would materially affect his reaction.[6]

Once the transmitter has selected the "abstract" of the situation which he will try to communicate, he must turn his attention to the semantic problems at Level B. The abstract needs to be coded into a message in a "language" which is capable both of being further coded for transmission along the channel of communication being used and of being reconverted into the meaning of the abstract by the receiver. The language of everyday conversation is a code of this type, and so are the more specialised symbols of accounting statements, pictures, musical notation and secret codes designed to restrict the meaning to selected receivers only. It is not only in this last instance but in all of them that the receiver can only decode the message if he and the transmitter have both had adequate tuition or experience concerning the agreed use of the code.

Journal of Accounting Research, 1 (1963), 102–107. See also Y. Ijiri, *The Foundations of Accounting Measurement*, Englewood Cliffs, N.J., 1967, 3–19.
[4] R. K. Storey, *The Search for Accounting Principles*, New York, 1964, 54.
[5] C. E. Shannon and W. Weaver, *The Mathematical Theory of Communication*, Urbana, 1964, 4.
[6] This would seem also to be a sound base from which to explore the accounting concept of materiality, but it is not the intention to pursue that topic here.

The final task of the transmitter is to pass the coded messages to the receiver. This technical or engineering level is the main concern of Shannon and Weaver,[7] especially in connection with the information capacity of telephone systems and computer systems. In accounting the problems arising at this level are usually only such technically trivial matters as ensuring accurate typing and printing and proper distribution of reports. But this Level A is the only direct point of contact between transmitter and receiver, so that what is and can be transmitted at this level sets an upper limit to the success of Levels B and C and so of the whole communication process.

The full process can be summarised symbolically as in Figure 1. Here "noise" means anything received which was not intended by the transmitter, because of error, distortion, confusion or interference. The other terms used are appropriate labels but not strictly defined terms. Since "information" is used in this type of analysis as a measure of technical performance at Level A, unrelated to the meaning of the signals transmitted, this word is not used here for the meaning communicated at higher levels.

It will be assumed henceforth that, in applying this model to the problems of accounting statements, all Level A problems have been overcome by normal administrative and secretarial skills. The "messages," the actual words and figures, that are received by the readers of accounts are those and only those which the transmitting accountant intended to send to them. But just as any shortcomings at Level A set a ceiling to the prospects of meaningful communication at higher levels, so successful semantic decoding at Level B is a prerequisite to effective communication which is the objective of the whole process.

Since this is the principal lesson for the discussion of standardised accounting to be drawn from the model, an example from another application is given to make the point clearer. Weather ships in the Atlantic observe the weather at their respective stations and report certain aspects of it at intervals to the Meteorological Office. Observers select the aspects to be reported, construct messages in the form of measurements and transmit these by radio as strings of numbers according to a prearranged sequence. If radio contact relatively free from "noise" cannot be established, there is no point in considering problems at Levels B and C. If there is some success at this Level A with the radio channel, then the meaning of each term used in the message needs to be agreed between the observers and the receivers at the Meteorological Office. The Level A process must be neutral and able to cope with all possible messages without amendment. The Level B set of agreed meanings of terms may need to be changed in the light of new thinking about effective (Level C) communication; but there must at any one time be an agreement as to current practice, and in this sense the settlement of semantic problems is prerequisite to any success at Level C.

[7] Shannon and Weaver, *The Mathematical Theory of Communication*, 6.

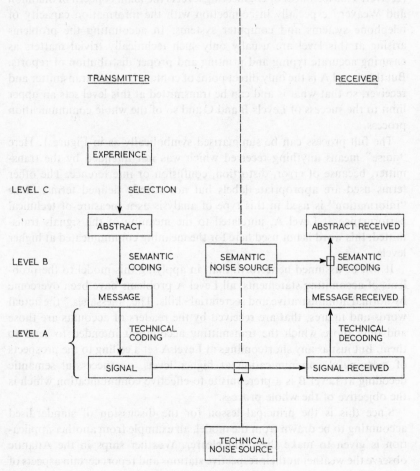

Figure 1

There may be some dispute as to which possible temperature readings are most useful – presumably for forecasting purposes. But this does not mean that an observer should be allowed to choose from maximum, minimum or average, day or night, ground or air, Fahrenheit or Centigrade readings and then to send the message "the temperature was 25 degrees." A failure to agree at the semantic level drastically reduces any possible effectiveness of communication. Almost any agreed reading would be more effective (more "informative" in the non-technical meaning of that word) than a "free-range" reading – despite the fact that the latter gave the observer so much more scope for using his professional discretion!

In this example, as in accounting practice, the meaning of all the words used in the message could be explained in the message itself. The residual problem, that this requires the receiver to understand the meaning of the words in the explanation, is no worse than in a semantic agreement in advance. But the example also illustrates the two main reasons why this solution is unsatisfactory.

One reason is that communication capacity is limited. There may be a technical limit to the signals that can be transmitted, at least within acceptable amounts of time or cost. But the restriction that is probably more important in many communication situations, and certainly where accounting is concerned, is the mental capacity of the receiver. The service rendered by an accountant transmitter is not only that of giving the reader receiver a secondhand experience of financial affairs; it is also that of reducing the complicated reality to a summary which can be grasped by a non-specialist who is outside the situation. It would defeat this object *either* to omit the Level C selection and transmit all aspects of the situation (even if this were possible) *or* to omit semantic agreements in advance and transmit selected aspects, together with lengthy explanations of every item.

Where communication is restricted either by the limited signal capacity or by the limited attention of the receiver, the challenge is to convey as much meaning as possible within these constraints. The receiver must be clear what each message means; the "semantic noise" of uncertainty or misunderstanding can prevent any clear meaning from reaching the receiver. The more "standing orders" that can be agreed in advance regarding terminology, selection and even form of messages, the more of the scarce capacity that can be used for the specific data of the particular situation. This is the reason for setting out balance sheets in a standard framework rather than according to the whim of the moment. It is also the thinking behind "management by exception," in which the limited span of attention of a decision-maker is concentrated upon the particular and the unexpected.

Advance agreement at Level B on the meaning of messages in accounting statements or other media of communication is often only possible if Level C selection decisions have also been taken in advance. The message "Depreciation £20,000" only conveys a clear meaning if quite detailed specification of the rules of practice on depreciation accounting has been notified to the receivers beforehand; if this has not been done, much scarce capacity has to be used up to explain the meaning in this specific instance. Such a practice specification can never take account of every eventuality. It will inevitably have to be supplemented with explanation on occasion; but this is acceptable provided that it is a rare and exceptional procedure.

There is another reason also why receivers need Level C selection practice to be based on a specification set in advance, why readers of accounts need "standard accounting practice" to be established. And this forms the second reason why it would not be satisfactory to have sets of accounts each accompanied by a volume of full explanation of the selection procedures and terminology used in them.

Figure 1 shows that receivers have no direct part in Level C activity. Their participation in the real situation is not part of the communication process, but is their reaction to the meaning received through that process. The effectiveness of the communication process is assessed by the degree of correspondence between the receivers' reaction to the meaning received and the way they would have reacted if they had seen the full detail for themselves and had the specialist training necessary to appreciate it. Thus the effectiveness arises with the receivers, but the selection which sets an upper limit to it is carried out entirely by the transmitters. Only by the discussion and agreement of procedures in advance can the receivers have any say in a part of the communication process of great concern to them.

The first thing that readers of accounts (and receivers of other forms of communication such as meteorologists receiving messages from weather ships) are likely to point out to transmitters in any discussion on Level C selection practice is that they receive messages about different entities from different transmitters and extract most meaning not from any messages from one source but from comparing those of several sources. If each transmitter uses his own rule book, however well explained and plausible it is, such comparison is difficult if not impossible. This point merely reinforces the Level B need for semantic clarity as an argument for standard practice.

Discussion between accountants and users of accounts prior to establishment or modification of standard practice rules also gives an opportunity for users to make clear and accountants to discover how accounts are used and what matters users want included in them. Users' needs may be found to be so diverse that no single set of accounts can meet them all. If this is the position, several sets of accounts will be needed, each addressed explicitly to a class of users whose information needs are sufficiently homogeneous and each with its own standard accounting practice.

SUMMARY OF ANALYSIS

A summary of the analysis so far may be useful before turning to professional experience in Britain, the United States and Europe:

(1) Accounts are viewed as one example of a communication process.
(2) A communication process is judged by its effectiveness at the receiving end.
(3) Level A technical problems are assumed to be trivial in accounting.
(4) The Level B semantic problem of establishing the meaning of messages can be overcome only by standardisation of nearly all practice because of the limited span of attention of readers.
(5) Comparability of messages from different sources is a quality ranked highly by receivers, and can only be achieved by standardisation of practice.
(6) Receivers can only influence what is to be considered better or worse practice in Level C selection decisions, which set an upper limit on the effectiveness of the whole process, when standard practice is being discussed before establishment or amendment, as they have no direct part in this level of the communication process.

PROFESSIONAL EXPERIENCE

For at least half of their history to date the professional accounting bodies of Britain and the United States left normal practice standards to emerge from usage without their intervention. It is in principle possible for all the criteria summarised above for effective communication in accounts to be satisfied in a natural evolution environment of this sort. This is the way in which the meaning of living languages develops. Compilers of dictionaries do not innovate or resolve disputes; they speak as they find – if there is confusion they report confusion. Yet on most occasions everyday language does effectively convey the intended meaning.

There is, however, ample evidence that complete *laissez-faire* in accounting practice produces ambiguity (semantic noise), lack of comparability and failure to adopt practices that provide readers with the knowledge they seek. Professional bodies have therefore been drawn, sometimes reluctantly, into the specification of acceptable and unacceptable practice. The stated objectives of this intervention have not usually distinguished clearly between improving the Level C selection of specific methods of reporting and the Level B clarification of the meaning of the messages on the accounts. But the emphasis in the subsequent professional activity has been closely related to the specific stimulus for the intervention, which varied in each instance.

In the United States it was first recognised that some accounting practices had contributed to the instability of the boom-and-crash period of the late 1920s. Three weaknesses were noted: (*a*) that some "bad" accounting was being practised; (*b*) that investors and other interested parties did not know what accounting methods were being used; (*c*) that interested parties did not know when accounting methods were changed (as happened frequently at this time so as to show the most favourable picture each year). Disclosure was the main remedy for all these defects in the joint proposals of the American Institute of Accountants (now the AICPA) and the New York Stock Exchange. They recommended that each company should file on public record a statement of the accounting methods it used and file amendments before putting them into effect. This proposal was quietly forgotten; maybe there was some belated appreciation of the limited capacity of reader's attention. Their other two proposals survived – that auditors should report whether the accounting methods used fell within "generally accepted accounting principles" and whether they had been consistently applied from year to year. The purpose of the first of these opinions was to give independent assurance to readers that the accounts were free of "substandard" practices – such as treating depreciation as an optional extra to be recorded only in years when the profits were high enough to bear it painlessly. But it soon raised a demand from investors and accountants to know more positively what constituted "generally accepted accounting principles."

The AICPA Committee on Accounting Procedure was set up in 1939 with instructions to investigate and publicise generally accepted accounting principles. Over the next twenty years the Committee issued fifty-one Accounting Research Bulletins and an associated committee four Terminology Bulletins. These were helpful to both readers and accountants in spelling out the limits of acceptable practice. But they suffered from three weaknesses: their status was merely advisory (the original intention to make compliance a professional ethical requirement was never put into effect); there was no priority given to reducing to one the number of recommended methods of accounting for any one specified situation; and they were piecemeal consideration of individual points with no overall coherence or underlying conceptual framework. The first two of these weaknesses hindered Level B decoding of the meaning of accounts, the second hindered Level C comparability and the last probably reduced the general Level C effectiveness of accounts.

In September 1959 the responsibilities of the Committee were transferred to a new Accounting Principles Board (APB). It was the intention that the first and third of the weaknesses of the earlier committee's work should be eliminated by (*a*) making mandatory disclosure of departures from Opinions of the new Board and from such Accounting Research Bulletins as were confirmed after review by the Board, and (*b*) following a structured work programme with Opinions issued only after consideration of the results of independent research projects, the first of which would be concerned with basic postulates and broad accounting principles.

It proved impossible to build Opinions on an agreed base of postulates and principles; in effect the Board rejected the research reports of R. T. Sprouse and M. Moonitz[8] on these topics. The Board reverted to a piece-meal approach, dealing with points of controversy as they arose. The mandatory disclosure of departure from APB Opinions was introduced in 1965. But the Board has had no commitment to approve only one method of accounting for each given situation. And so Level B decoding of actual accounts is still hindered by uncertainty in some areas as to which approved alternative has been adopted.

The United States profession has so far failed to heed the advice of Professor Boulding who sympathises with the difficult tasks of the accountant:

> He has first to reduce what is essentially a multi-dimensional reality to a one-dimensional figure; and, in the second place, he has to do this on the basis of knowledge about the future which he cannot possibly have.... Under these circumstances ... it is important that we should know what the accountant's answer means, which means that we should know what procedure he has employed. ... What the accountant tells us may not be true, but if we know what he has done, we have a fair idea of what it means.[9]

Disillusionment with the Board has grown from its willingness to approve several alternative methods, and also from the occasions when it has changed its official mind (usually under rebellious pressure and to add another alternative approved method), and from its failure to act quickly against new forms of misleading accounting. The Board is being replaced by a Financial Accounting Standards Board of seven highly-paid full-time members including non-accountants. It is not yet clear whether this change, described by Mr. Francis Wheat who was chairman of the committee which recommended it as a "bold effort to inspire public confidence," will build American accounting practice on any firmer foundation than its predecessors.

In the United States the initiative in moves towards greater uniformity has come from investors and their representatives seeking better aids to the establishment of share prices, and from members of the accounting profession seeking a clearer picture of what they must do to avoid the danger of being held in law guilty of professional negligence. At least until recently neither of these have been strong groups in "mainland" Europe. There the pressure for uniformity has come from economic planners, and its strength has been closely related to the real power of the central planners.[10] Accounts have been regarded as one type of economic statistics, which of course they

[8] M. Moonitz, *The Basic Postulates of Accounting*, AICPA Accounting Research Study No. 1, New York, 1961; R. T. Sprouse and M. Moonitz, *A Tentative Set of Broad Accounting Principles for Business Enterprises*, AICPA Accounting Research Study No. 3, New York, 1962.
[9] K. E. Boulding, "Economics and Accounting: the Uncongenial Twins," in W. T. Baxter and S. Davidson (eds.), *Studies in Accounting Theory*, London, 1962, 53–54.
[10] G. G. Mueller, "International Experience with Uniform Accounting," *Law and Contemporary Problems*, 30 (1965), 850–873. The whole of this issue is devoted to uniformity in accounting, mostly in the United States context.

are; and any statistician will insist on having agreed terms and classifications before he starts to gather data. Uniform accounting was made compulsory in Nazi Germany; by the time the law was repealed in 1946, it was attractive enough to German industrialists and accountants for much of the system to be retained and later reflected in the German Companies Act of 1965 – which is likely to be a strong influence on EEC company law. The French *plan comptable général* was approved in 1947 when planned reconstruction after the disruption of the Second World War was getting into full swing.

Those in charge of central planning, and sometimes central control also, look upon the businesses of the country as a holding company management views its subsidiaries. And they approach the uniformity question in the same way, building up what amounts to a "group accounting manual," so that consolidation and review can be made of categories which always have the same meaning.

The first step is usually the establishment of a uniform chart of accounts. For example, under the French *plan* all expense in respect of depreciation of buildings is recorded in Account 68112. Continental European preoccupation with this aspect of uniformity, which is a triviality of bookkeeping detail in Anglo-Saxon accounting eyes, alienated them from British accountants for a number of years. But really this is only a mechanism to facilitate the next step, which is the preparation of standard forms of balance sheet and profit and loss statement. These are the equivalent of the *pro forma* returns which a company usually requires its subsidiaries or branches to complete. The final step, which would also appear in most company accounting manuals, is to regulate how items are to be recorded and reflected in the accounts. The French *plan* requires stocks to be stated at the lower of cost or market, and requires cost to be calculated as weighted average historic cost; German company law requires research and development expenditure to be written off in the period in which it is incurred. In each situation only one method is approved.

These European uniform plans are highly successful at Level B of the communication model outlined above. Government planners, investors, trade-unionists, tax administrators, accountants can all study the plan and know what the terminology and classification of every set of accounts means. The plans also achieve Level C success in the matter of comparability, since all accounts use the same detailed accounting manual.

But the effectiveness of the accounts prepared in accordance with a plan of this sort depends upon the Level C selection decisions taken when the plan is being prepared or revised. Uniform accounts may have given useful data for central control in Nazi Germany and Soviet Russia. But it is doubtful if these accounts, dominated by book-keeping considerations, provide what is needed for investment decisions by central planners or private investors. This is a broad generalisation on a topic which deserves major research effort to itself. But it is based on the observation that valuation bases seem even further removed from economic opportunity values than in the English-speaking accounting tradition, and that the accounts are often presented (as in the draft EEC directive on company accounts) as a sort of annotated trial balance with no attempt to group together items which are closely related in commercial reality but not in book-keeping codes.

It seems that the British could reap the advantages of entering the field of uniformity late if they (*a*) followed the example of clarity and comparability in European plans, without getting too immersed in the details of uniform account codes; (*b*) used Anglo-American practical experience and past and continuing research to develop, with the users of accounts, a *plan* of more useful content than its European ancestors; and (*c*) heeded the warnings by Professor Baxter[11] and others of the danger of stagnation because provisions of a uniform system would command unjustified respect and discourage critical thought.

The first statements on accounting principles from the Institute of Chartered Accountants in England and Wales were issued in the midst of the Second World War. The stimulus for the introduction of the series of "Recommendations on Accounting Principles" in 1942 was the need of members of a short-staffed accounting profession for prompt advice on the accounting treatment of the effects of certain wartime legislation; from the start however the terms of reference of the series extended to all aspects of company accounts. The Recommendations were of advisory status only; most were in general terms and did not attempt to select one out of a number of plausible methods of accounting for one situation.

In the later 1960s growing dissatisfaction with the existence of so many alternative accounting methods was voiced loudly in the British financial press, and impressed upon the accounting bodies privately by representatives of investors and the Stock Exchange. It was this dissatisfaction that led to the establishment in 1970 of the Accounting Standards Steering Committee and the preparation of Statements of Standard Accounting Practice, deviations from which accountants have an obligation to disclose and justify. It has been noted that the terms of reference of the Committee are in words almost identical to those used ten years earlier in the charter of the AICPA Accounting Principles Board. But in Britain the stimulus and the intent of the Committee are actually much more strongly in the direction of approving only one method for each identified circumstance.

The three statements of Standard Accounting Practice and the exposure drafts for three further statements issued to the date of writing follow the piecemeal approach of United States practice and of previous English Recommendations. But the "one situation, one acceptable method" rule adopted in them is in notable contrast to the latter. This rule has however never been made explicit, and so there is a risk that when, as is inevitable,

[11] W. T. Baxter, "Recommendations on Accounting Theory," in W. T. Baxter and S. Davidson (eds.), *Studies in Accounting Theory*, London, 1962, 414–427.

it is attacked it will not be adhered to. The Committee, the profession and user's representatives need to be clear that standard practice should be complied with, not because it is clearly better than other possible methods, but because it has been adopted as standard for the sake of meaningful communication.

This by itself is a recipe for avoiding anarchy by causing petrifaction. The authority of standard practice statements needs to be counterbalanced by a mechanism for changing standard practice in response to changes in circumstances, research results and other indications of what constitutes more effective meaning to be communicated in accounts. The piecemeal approach will have to be abandoned at some stage at least to the extent of making an overall review to make a "standard decision" as to what classes of users of account are to be taken into consideration and what decisions they face to which communication must be relevant if it is to be effective. As noted above, it may be appropriate for standard practice to be established for each of several different sets of accounts designed for different classes of users.

If standards are to develop at all, producers of accounts must be allowed to try out non-standard practice where they consider it preferable to standard practice. But this should be done sparingly and the results should also, for the sake of comparability, be shown in accordance with standard practice. The non-standard practice should also be explained in detail; this provides a good reason for introducing it relatively rarely, in view of the limited mental capacity of receivers of information.

The pronouncements on the status of Statements of Standard Accounting Practice[12] do envisage situations in which standard practice is inappropriate, and in which non-standard methods should be used with full disclosure. The criterion of "giving a true and fair view," a notion with no explicit definition or description, is taken to be of a higher order than the dictates of standard practice. This contrasts with the mainland European type of uniform accounting under which the accounts "in the context of the provisions regarding the valuation of assets and liabilities and the layout of accounts, shall reflect as accurately as possible the company's assets, liabilities, financial position and results."[13]

The intentions with respect to revision of standards have also been made clear from the start: "From time to time new accounting standards will be

---

[12] Institute of Chartered Accountants in England and Wales, "Explanatory Foreword: Statements of Standard Accounting Practice," reproduced in *Accountancy*, February 1971, 61, paras. 6–7; and "The effect of statements of standard accounting practice on auditors' reports," (Statement on Auditing 17), reproduced in *Accountancy*, March 1971, 154, paras. 4–5.

[13] Commission of the European Communities, *Proposal for a Fourth Directive on the Annual Accounts of Limited Liability Companies*, Brussels, 1971 (Supplement to *Bulletin of the European Communities*, 12, 1971). See R. H. Parker, "A Slow Start to Company Harmonisation," *Accountancy*, June 1972, 26–29. Note also that a Study Group of the professional accountancy bodies in the ten EEC member and applicant countries has recommended that the directive should be altered to require that accounts show a true and fair view.

drawn at successive levels, and established standards will be reviewed with the object of improvement in the light of new needs and developments."[14] But new practices will not be real candidates for becoming new standards until they have been "run in" by use in actual accounts; this means that non-standard practice will have to be permitted, even encouraged, under certain conditions in the interests of pioneering in search of improvement in Level C effectiveness of communication. Such non-standard experiments destroy the semantic clarity of the accounts and their comparability; a requirement that current standard treatment be shown in addition to explanation of the experimental method is normally justified. The Steering Committee needs to give careful consideration to the problems of how it is to continue its successful beginning in building up semantic coherence in British accounts, but at the same time to encourage efforts to seek improvements in the effectiveness of their content.

SUMMARY OF PROFESSIONAL EXPERIENCE

Review of experience in various countries in the light of the general model of a communication process leads to the following tentative conclusions:

(1) The great amount of research, discussion and pronouncement by the United States profession on effective accounting practice has been an attempt to run before it had learned to walk. Higher level problems of communication have been considered, but lower level problems prerequisite to success at the effectiveness level have been repeatedly dodged.

(2) The dominant influence of economic statisticians started an emphasis in French and German accounting on uniform coding, classification and forms of reporting. This has established a firm basis of lower level success in communication – there is semantic agreement and comparability. Some of the content of this Continental practice looks primitive and unhelpful when its effectiveness for investors' decisions is looked at through Anglo-American eyes.

(3) The British have recently made a new positive approach to standardised accounting. Although more obviously influenced by the English language practice of the more mature United States profession, the Accounting Standards Steering Committee seems to have a commitment to semantic clarity closer in spirit to mainland European practice. This commitment would be less vulnerable to attack if it was made explicit. The insights of British and American research and experience are however being used in spelling out the content of what will eventually be something like a British national "group accounting manual."

(4) An attitude of dismay at the prospect of British company accounting being brought under EEC law (which this author took prior to preparing this study) is not at all appropriate. British, together with other

[14] Institute . . ., "Explanatory Foreword . . .," para. 8.

English-speaking, traditions of accounting are far in advance of the European tradition in relevance to investors and others of the content of the accounts, and must seek to influence EEC directives up towards their levels. But the Anglo-American approach has paid so much respect to the views of individual accountants that effective communication is frustrated. The more formal European framework, with Anglo-American modifications on content and with careful arrangements for revision, offers the best prospect for building accounting practice into a truly effective medium of communication.

MEASUREMENT OF DIVISIONAL PERFORMANCE IN THE LONG RUN

Michael Bromwich

THE last two decades have seen a major revolution in the practice of capital budgeting. Many firms now use investment appraisal techniques that allow in a systematic way for the timing of the cash flows expected from proposed investment projects. No similar transformation has yet occurred in the methods used by firms to monitor, evaluate and control the progress of such projects.

This short-term orientation of traditional budgetary control and return-on-investment evaluation methods makes it difficult to relate the performance of a business division in any period to the capital resources it used during the period.[1] Capital costs enter only via depreciation charges. These are normally treated as fixed costs and based on the historical cost of the division's assets. They have, therefore, no direct connection with the concepts underlying discounted-cash-flow methods of investment appraisal.[2]

The use of the usual monitoring systems may cause non-optimal behaviour in various ways. Such systems may indeed sometimes highlight what seem to be irresponsible or mistaken forecasts made in the past. Such signals may, however, become apparent only late in a project's life. By then, with the advantage of hindsight, the responsible manager may be able to produce plausible reasons for these variances. It is hard to assess such arguments unless there is a system to monitor lifetime forecasts over a project's complete span and, as the project proceeds, highlight alterations in predictions and plans. Such a system would allow a partial appraisal of forecasting ability to be made well before the completion of a project, and would go some way towards inhibiting the production of irresponsible forecasts. It should also give early warnings that plans may need to be revised.

Non-optimal behaviour may also arise where top management relies primarily on traditional measures of short-term performance to monitor the operational efficiency of its subordinates.[3] In this situation, divisional managers responsible either for making investment decisions or for suggesting worthwhile projects may opt for those giving good short-run

---

[1] For a good treatment of this topic, see D. Solomons, *Divisional Performance: Measurement and Control*, Homewood, 1965, chs. 3, 4 and 5. For a more specific treatment of the problem in the context of divisional control, see J. Dearden, "The case against R O I Control," *Harvard Business Review*, May–June 1969.

[2] J. Muriel and R. Anthony, "Misevaluation of Investment Centre Performance", *Harvard Business Review*, March–April 1965, reports American practice.

[3] For some evidence of the use of the realised return on investment and actual residual income for a period as major indicators of divisional performance, see Muriel and Anthony, *op. cit.*, and Solomons, *op. cit.*, chs. 1 and 7.

performance rather than those which would most help to achieve the enterprise's long-term financial objective.[4] Worthwhile projects may, when traditional accounting measures are applied, in their early years produce apparently poor short-term results and depress the apparent return on investment or residual income over several periods.

For similar reasons, the emphasis of traditional accounting methods on short-run performance may mean that indications of a need to take new decisions and revise plans may be lost.[5]

However, an evaluation system has been suggested recently which attempts to gauge more precisely how satisfactorily a division has used its capital assets. This has been labelled the "residual income method."[6] It involves deducting from the profit for a period an interest charge based on the value of the division's capital assets, and comparing the residue with a budgeted residual profit figure computed in the same way. The major advantage claimed for this system is that it forces divisional management to consider the cost of existing and proposed investments in decision-making, for any decision that affects the division's investment base also alters its residual income.

This method seems to represent a step towards an evaluation system based on the same theoretical foundation as discounted cash-flow models.

Indeed, Solomons claims that "the long-run counterpart of this objective ('using the excess of net earnings over the cost of capital as a measure of managerial success') is the maximisation of the discounted present value of the enterprise." Methods[7] certainly can be devised to bring the budgeted residual income for a period into correspondence with the planned increase in a division's present value over that period.[8]

The remainder of this essay discusses an approach to the measurement problem that is consistent with this idea.

The central idea on which the suggested performance evaluation system is based is the making, at the end of a period, of a revised forecast of likely future performance, based on those changes in expected cash flows,

[4] For a good selection of articles in this area see W. T. Bruns, Jr. and D. T. de Coster, *Accounting and its Behavioural Implications*, New York, 1971.

[5] To date few attempts have been made to validate by empirical research the contention that reliance on traditional appraisal technique is likely to result in actions at odds with those necessary to achieve optimal financial results, as defined by systematic planning models. The view that such situations are likely to arise is based on *a priori* reasoning. Some attempts have been made to investigate systematically the accuracy of return on investment measured by traditional accounting methods as a measure of long-term profitability: E. Solomon and J. Laya, "Measurement of Corporate Profitability: Some Systematic Errors in the Accounting Rate of Return" in A. A. Robichek (ed.), *Finanicial Research and Management Decisions*, New York, 1967; and M. Sarnat and H. Levy, "The Relationship of Rules of Thumb to the Internal Rate of Return: A Restatement and a Generalisation," *Journal of Finance*, 24 (1969), 479–489.

[6] See Solomons, *op. cit.*, especially ch. 3.

[7] Solomons, *op. cit.*, 277

[8] See, for example, J. Flower, "Measurement of Divisional Performance," *Accounting and Business Research*, No. 3 (1971), 205.

and hence in present values, that result from alterations to either the forecast environment or the level of managerial performance assumed at the beginning of the period. This revised estimate is to be made on the assumption that no managerial act has yet been planned to counteract or to exploit any of these altered expectations. For ease of presentation, it will be assumed that decisions are made only at the end of each current period.

These changes in expectations may be partitioned into at least three categories. The first encompasses revised forecasts concerning the behaviour of those uncontrollable factors in the environment to which management can respond only by altering future activity in a given way. The only response that a profit-maximising management can make to such changes is to alter its future plans to reflect their effects. An extreme example of this type of environmental change would be a new law, the provisions of which could be avoided only by quitting the enterprise's existing area of activity.

The second category incorporates those environmental changes that can be modified or exploited by managerial action, even though their occurrence is beyond the influence of management. Many instances of the second type of expectational change could be cited. It is, for example, unlikely that a firm can influence the trend of world steel prices but it may escape many of the consequences of such price changes by stockholding in the short-run and by using substitute materials in the long-run.

The third type of expectational change built into the suggested forecast is that generated by expected alterations in factors within managerial control. This category may be split into at least two subdivisions. One element of the subdivision would indicate the expected change if no action were planned to correct past inefficiencies in execution of the plan; a second would indicate, on a similar basis, the effects of incorrect original forecasts concerning factors within management's control.

It is realised that none of the above forecasts can be made with precision. However, it is likely that at least some of the advantages claimed for the proposed system are relatively insensitive to a considerable degree of inaccuracy. These ideas are merely an extension of the concepts underlying existing standard costing and budgetary control procedures. The distinction between controllable and uncontrollable variances is made in order to give management a picture of what the future will be like if the situation met in the current period is allowed to continue. The monitoring scheme based on the forecasts suggested in this essay attempts to fulfil this role over a longer time period, in a way that is consistent with the investment appraisal models likely to be in use to appraise the projects currently being monitored.[9]

[9] The suggested scheme complements other recent suggestions for improving conventional standard costing and budgetary control systems. See, for example, J. Demski, "Variance Analysis using a Constrained Linear Model," in D. Solomons (ed.), *Studies in Cost Analysis* (2nd ed.), London, 1968; and M. Bromwich, "Standard Costing for Planning and Control," *The Accountant*, April–May 1969.

The variance between the original and currently estimated present values, combined with the variance between the actual and planned cash flow covering the period between the two estimates, in so far as these variances could be assigned to uncontrollable factors, would give an idea of the uncertainty surrounding a division's activities, particularly when calculated over successive periods, so that a time series of variances was available.

Further analysis of such variances into those which the management could meet only by a change of plan and those that could be offset by appropriate action within the given plan would give a further indication of the nature of the uncertainties facing the division.

In so far as such variances were controllable and could be analysed into those due to errors in earlier planning and to those due to errors in execution of the plan, they would provide a direct indication of the need for management action to improve efficiency. The overall comparison of the actual cash flow of the period and the newly estimated end-period present value with those forecast and planned at the beginning of the period would give direct information for control related to the whole future lifetime performance of the division, and thus, subject to the range of error created by the need to re-estimate future performance, would reduce the risk of management favouring projects on the basis only of an expected good short-term performance.

Various other control procedures suggest themselves. A manager's forecasting ability might be tested by comparing the success of his predictions against those of other people. In some instances it might be possible to utilise published forecasts of particular parameters used in the manager's own forecasts. It might even be possible to compare the extent that longer-term published forecasts changed over time relative to the estimates made by the divisional manager charged with similar forecasts.

The above procedure could not be expected to give a precise picture of the estimating ability of a manager, but combined with a requirement by top management that all major changes in forecasts be fully justified and analysed with the same rigour as is normally recommended for initial proposals, it could provide an effective instrument for discouraging careless planning. Moreover, with the suggested system, the trend over time in a manager's forecasting variances would be monitored and unrealistic forecasts could be highlighted relatively early in a project's life.

Two limitations of the above scheme as a control method may be noted. The first arises because, if there is much interdependence between divisions, it may be impossible to arrive at the discounted present value of the enterprise as a whole by aggregating the present values of individual divisions.[10] This problem arises, however, with all monitoring systems.

Second, the comparisons suggested implicitly assume that the division

[10] R. S. Edwards, "The Nature and Measurement of Income," *The Accountant*, July–October 1938, reprinted in W. T. Baxter and S. Davidson (eds.) *Studies in Accounting Theory*, London, 1962.

has no alternative but to use its existing assets in approximately the way that it is planning at present. Thus, the suggested system, in common with existing evaluation methods, does not report possible performance if the division's assets were used in a way different from that planned or actually undertaken. It is not therefore a substitute for continuing exploration of alternatives.

Kaldor has argued that the economist's income concept, which implies a present value approach, involves the use of at least one subjective estimate that cannot be validated against objective data. For this reason, he argues that such an income concept cannot be used to measure the success of an enterprise over any given period.[11] Similarly, Edwards and Bell have argued that the validity of expectations concerning a future period can be ascertained only by looking at the "hard facts" once the period has passed.[12] They contend that no top management would be satisfied to evaluate the performance of a subordinate manager by comparing forecasts concerning a given event made by him at two different points in time.

These strictures apply to the scheme advocated in this article, for the procedure proposed involves just such a comparison. While the force of this criticism must be admitted, the absence of objective evaluation procedures can be regarded as a cost of introducing a control system which pays attention to the future – *i.e.* to the realities of the situation. The advocates of the net present value and internal rate of return appraisal methods are content to argue that management should be willing to invest large sums of money entirely on the basis of managerial predictions. It does not therefore seem completely unreasonable to suggest that the progress of projects accepted in this way should be monitored using the same concepts.

It may be that those who completely reject the measures discussed in this article are being too conservative. There is a little evidence that some organisations are willing to use estimates of the sort suggested in this essay in their internal planning and control systems.[13] It is wellknown that many enterprises maintain long-term plans covering the next five to ten years. Such plans are often of the "rolling type" that are updated as time passes so that they always cover a future period of constant length. This process of reviewing and extending long-term plans ideally should have as one of its stages the making of forecasts of the type recommended in this article; before revising plans, it is surely worthwhile to estimate the likely future without such revisions. Some actual planning systems go further along the

[11] N. Kaldor, *An Expenditure Tax*, London, 1955, 54–78.
[12] E. O. Edwards and P. W. Bell, *The Theory and Measurement of Business Income*, Berkeley, 1961, 38–45.
[13] For some examples of the practices of some very large American firms that were using such estimates as long ago as the 1960s, see G. A. Steiner (ed.), *Long-Range Planning*, New York, 1963.

path suggested in this essay and insist on detailed explanations of the deviations between forecasts made at different dates.[14]

Whether this and other difficulties of the proposed system are such as to make it inoperable in practice can be ascertained only by empirical experiments. Studies are also required to evaluate whether the benefits from its introduction exceed the consequent cost. Much research needs to be done before the proposed income measurement system is ready to be submitted to such practical tests. The aim of this article has been merely to suggest a conceptual framework from which a new method of measuring divisional performance might grow.

[14] See, for example, F. G. Secrest, "The Process of Long-Range Planning at Ford Motor Company," in Steiner, *op. cit.* The most sophisticated system that currently exists for monitoring changes in long-term forecasts is that which is said to be used in the American Department of Defence. This utilises many of the concepts and practices suggested in this article: see, for example, D. Novick (ed.), *Program Budgeting: Program Analysis and the Federal Budget,* Cambridge, Massachusetts, 1965, ch. 4. For a more up-to-date, and probably more realistic, survey of current practice in the American Department of Defence see J. P. Crecine, "Defence Budgeting: Organisational Adaptations to Governmental Constraints," in R. P. Byrne *et al.* (eds.), *Studies in Budgeting,* Amsterdam, 1971.

THE ROLE OF THE VALUATION MODEL IN THE ANALYSIS OF INVESTMENT DECISIONS[1]

Bryan Carsberg

INTRODUCTION

IN principle, the selection of investment projects for acceptance by an individual could be made by specifying every possible combination of available projects and estimating the pattern over time of cash available for consumption under each combination. The analysis should cover the whole of the individual's life and include borrowing opportunities as a kind of negative investment. The individual would select investments implicitly by choosing the stream of cash flows which gave him the best-liked pattern of consumption.

Such a procedure is simply stated but impracticable. Neither the required data nor the computational capacity would normally be available in a real situation. The main objective of the literature on investment decisions has been to identify conditions for appraising projects one or a few at a time so that the decisions are likely to be consistent with the overall maximisation of utility from consumption. The basic analysis is well known. If individuals and firms could borrow and lend indefinitely large amounts at a given rate of interest, that rate of interest should be used to discount the cash flows expected from a project to equivalent present values; the project should be accepted if and only if it is expected to yield a positive net present value.

The difficulties caused by the lack of perfect capital markets are widely acknowledged. It will be argued in this paper, however, that the analysis has been deficient in that it has failed to exploit modern scientific method, as applied to the analysis of business decisions. This method emphasises the importance, in decisions, of models which are subject to empirical verification. It involves the specification of an objective function, the identification of the decision variables and the development and *testing* of a model relating the values given to the decision variables with the values sought under the objective function.

Two situations, in which attempts to appraise projects independently break down, have been debated at length in the literature. The first arises under capital rationing – the situation in which projects have to compete for a limited supply of capital – or rationing of other resources. In such cases it is not sufficient to decide whether acceptance of a single project is better than rejection – an independent decision; it is also necessary to decide which combination of the available projects represents the best use

[1] I am grateful to John Arnold and Roger Mace for their generous help with this paper.

of the limited resources. A method of solution using techniques of mathematical programming has been developed.[2] Secondly, considerations of risk and uncertainty have demonstrated the limitations of independent analyses of investment projects. The risk of combinations of projects may be less than would appear from an aggregation of independent risk estimates if, for example, unfavourable results of individual projects are unlikely to arise in association. It is aggregate risk that is important to a decision-taker, and this aggregate effect is dealt with in the literature on portfolio theory.[3]

Our arguments will suggest a third reason for dealing with aggregate plans rather than individual projects in the analysis of investment decisions. It will be claimed that the "smoothness" of the pattern of cash flows and earnings over time is important in a way that is not allowed for in the traditional net present value calculations. It is aggregate pattern that is important – an erratic pattern in the cash flows from one project is important only if it is not smoothed out on aggregation. It is convenient to anticipate, at this point, the main features of the arguments of this paper. We assume that firms are interested in the well-being of their shareholders although in our analysis this will not necessarily imply maximisation of the present market value of the shares. We argue that a manager concerned with investment selection should make explicit predictions of the effect of his decisions on the market value of his firm. The acceptance of a project having a positive net present value may sometimes result in current earnings or cash flows below what they would have been had the project been rejected; and this shortfall may depress the share price assuming that managers have not published their expectations. In such a situation, there may be conflict of interest between the long-term shareholder – who would like the project to be accepted – and the shareholder who would sell at the time of the depressed share price. This conflict would have to be resolved in the specification of the firm's objectives.

The share valuation model should deal with the actual data which are available to dealers in the stock market and used as a basis for valuation. Acceptance of a project may be regarded as having two effects on a firm's value. A project may be valued for its overall contribution to wealth, a function of the cash flows and market rates of interest. It will also affect the financial results which are reported to shareholders, which help shareholders to form expectations of future results and hence set present market value – *i.e.* the results of the project constrain communications between the firm and its shareholders. It is the latter role that makes the pattern of cash flows and earnings important. The firm will (presumably) wish to avoid misleading or confusing messages to shareholders – messages

[2] H. M. Weingartner, *Mathematical Programming and the Analysis of Capital Budgeting Problems*, Englewood Cliffs, 1963.
[3] H. Markowitz, "Portfolio Selection," *Journal of Finance*, 7 (1952), 77–91; W. F. Sharpe, "Capital Asset Prices: a Theory of Market Equilibrium under Conditions of Risk," *Journal of Finance*, 19 (1964), 425–442.

which affect the share price in a way that is not justified by informed expectations; this is most easily done if it has a stable pattern of cash flows and earnings in aggregate. A firm could partly avoid the use of past results as a means of communicating expectations if it gave explicit numerical forecasts of future results.[4] Managers have, however, firmly resisted this practice and we assume such a solution to be politically infeasible at the present time.

Our analysis will make use of certain simplifying assumptions in order that the main points of the argument may be exposed without unnecessary complexity. We shall restrict ourselves to considering single-valued estimates of the outcomes of projects accepted although we shall not assume certainty of those outcomes; and we shall ignore the incidence of taxation and the possible advantages of raising long-term, fixed interest capital in some of the situations examined. None of these simplifications is critical to the main point of the analysis.

TRADITIONAL CAPITAL BUDGETING THEORY

It is helpful to begin our analysis with a short review of the theory that underlies the use of net present value calculations – here called traditional theory. The basic behavioural model is related to the decision processes of an individual.[5]

An individual decision-maker is faced with a number of investment opportunities which he can rank according to estimates of their rate of return and a number of borrowing opportunities which he can rank according to estimates of their rate of cost. Each possible combination of investment and borrowing opportunities may be associated with an esti- mate of the amount of cash available for consumption at different times.

It is assumed that the individual behaves in a way which implies the assignment of a consistent value – utility – to each amount available for consumption. The ratio of marginal utilities from the present contempla- tion of consumption at two points in time is defined as the marginal rate of time preference – it reflects the impatience for consumption. The optimal set of decisions is the one involving acceptance of investments with the highest rate of return and borrowing with the lowest rate of cost so that, at the margin, the rate of return on investment is equal to the rate of cost of borrowing and the rate of time preference. This is simply the condition that ensures that no change in plan would improve the aggregate utility from consumption.

The marginal rate of time preference represents a cut-off rate which can

[4] H. C. Edey, "Accounting Principles and Business Reality," *Accountancy*, 74 (1963), 998–1002 and 1083–1088.
[5] This exposition follows the development in I. Fisher, *The Rate of Interest*, New York, 1907, and I. Fisher, *The Theory of Interest*, New York, 1930. More recently, tradi- tional theory has been developed in J. Hirshleifer, "On the Theory of Optimal Investment Decisions," *Journal of Political Economy*, 46 (1958), 329–352.

be used in the assessment of investment and borrowing opportunities, either to confirm the original decisions or to make decisions for new opportunities, representing small changes from the original plan, not considered when the original plan was formulated. It follows from the definitions of the behavioural model of traditional theory that the present value of a cash receipt discounted at the marginal rate of time preference represents the present amount of consumption valued equally with the consumption actually available from the receipt at the time it arises. Present consumption may be used as a common measuring rod to assess the value of all future consumption arising from different plans. The present value of all cash flows associated with a plan, defined as the wealth of the decision-maker, is a measure of the satisfaction from the consumption that will follow the adoption of the plan. Hence, wealth maximisation is simply the wish to obtain the stream of consumption which yields maximum satisfaction and the acceptance of an investment project having a positive net present value is the acceptance of a project which will increase the value of consumption.

The model which yields these relationships, holds strictly only when certain restrictive conditions are assumed. It is necessary that investment and borrowing projects should be divisible both in the length of time over which they are undertaken and in the amount invested (without effect on the rate of return or cost); it is necessary that projects and consumption opportunities should be reasonably approximated by monotonic and continuous mathematical functions. If these assumptions do not hold strictly, the conditions for optimality may still hold as an approximation.

The traditional model as reviewed here does not have empirical content – it deals with subjective expectations which are not directly observable. It is rather a means to rationalise and give structure to decision processess which individuals may be assumed to undertake implicitly.

We next consider the extension of the traditional model to decisions in the firm. We could simply note that if the firm is interested in maximising the welfare of its shareholders – their utility from consumption – it should accept any investment projects which have a positive net present value when the shareholder's marginal rate of time preference is used as a discount rate. The reasoning is the same as that applied to the individual decisions. It is helpful to develop this statement further, however.

Investment in the ordinary shares of a firm is one of the investment projects included in the optimal plan of its shareholders. Continued holding of the shares involves a cash sacrifice equal to their current market value, V_o, and offers cash receipts in the form of expected future dividends, d_j at time j. This leads to the well-known traditional valuation model for the whole firm:

$$(1) \quad V_0 = \sum_{j=0}^{\infty} \frac{d_j}{(1+i)^j}$$

Where i is the shareholders' marginal rate of time preference, assumed constant over time. The equation of the market value and the discounted value of dividends implies that holding the shares yields a zero net present value. It would be inconsistent to assume a negative net present value because the holding of shares would not then be worthwhile for individual shareholders. Equally it would be inconsistent to assume a positive net present value; in that case, the shareholder would wish to buy more shares, since he would thereby increase the present value of his consumption (we assume that there is not one shareholder holding all the shares already). A zero net present value is the only consistent possibility.

The market value of the shares, as given by expression (1), represents the wealth of the shareholders locked up in the firm, the present value of the satisfaction they will derive from consumption expected to be generated by their holdings. The firm that wishes to maximise shareholders' satisfaction will wish to maximise its value.

Suppose a firm is considering the acceptance of an investment project which will yield a cash flow of a_j at time j (a_0 being negative and representing the outlay). If the dividend stream is adjusted by changes in cash receipts and payments the new value according to the traditional model will be:

$$(2) \quad V_0 = \sum_{j=0}^{\infty} \frac{d_j + a_j}{(1+i)^j}$$

The project will be accepted if it increases the firm's value, *i.e.* if

$$(3) \quad V_0' - V_0 > 0$$

so that

$$(4) \quad \sum_{j=0}^{\infty} \frac{d_j + a_j}{(1+i)^j} - \sum_{j=0}^{\infty} \frac{d_j}{(1+i)^j} > 0$$

and

$$(5) \quad \sum_{j=0}^{\infty} \frac{a_j}{(1+i)^j} > 0$$

The project will be accepted if it has a positive net present value when the marginal rate of time preference is used as a discount rate.

Traditional theory accordingly envisages that a firm will appraise projects by estimating shareholders' marginal rate of time preference, and using it to discount estimated cash flows. If there were a perfect capital market the estimation of the discount rate would be easy – it would simply be the market rate of interest at which everyone could borrow and lend indefinitely large amounts. In reality the estimation is much harder. It can be made by estimating shareholders' dividend expectations and finding the interest rate which equates them to the current market value. Such an estimate is highly speculative in view of the poverty of evidence concerning shareholders' expectations; nevertheless it is generally assumed by writers who support traditional theory that the procedure outlined is the best available at the present time.

It is important to understand the implicit assumptions of traditional theory about the behaviour of the market value of a firm following acceptance of an investment. Consider a simple illustration. Suppose that a firm is formed especially to undertake a single investment. It requires an outlay of £2,000 and will yield cash flows, equal to dividends, of: £200 at t_1; £286 at t_2; £464 at t_3; £0 at t_4 and t_5; and £200 at t_6 and annually for the indefinite future.[6] Shareholders' marginal rate of time preference is assumed to be estimated with confidence at 8 per cent. per annum. The present value of receipts from the project is £2,500.

Table 1: Market value and rates of return over time (£)

	Market value at t_j	Return, year ended t_j $\dfrac{V_j + d_j}{V_{j-1}} - 1$
V_0	$200(1{\cdot}08)^{-1} + 286(1{\cdot}08)^{-2} + 464(1{\cdot}08)^{-3} + 200(1{\cdot}08)^{-6} + \ldots = 2,500$	
V_1	$286(1{\cdot}08)^{-1} + 464(1{\cdot}08)^{-2} + 200(1{\cdot}08)^{-5} + \ldots = 2,500$	$\dfrac{2,500 + 200}{2,500} - 1 = 0{\cdot}08$
V_2	$464(1{\cdot}08)^{-1} + 200(1{\cdot}08)^{-4} + \ldots = 2,414$	$\dfrac{2,414 + 286}{2,500} - 1 = 0{\cdot}08$
V_3	$200(1{\cdot}08)^{-3} + \ldots = 2,143$	$\dfrac{2,143 + 486}{2,414} - 1 = 0{\cdot}08$
V_4	$200(1{\cdot}08)^{-2} + \ldots = 2,314$	$\dfrac{2,314 + 0}{2,143} - 1 = 0{\cdot}08$
V_5	$200(1{\cdot}08)^{-1} + \ldots = 2,500$	$\dfrac{2,500 + 0}{2,314} - 1 = 0{\cdot}08$

The pattern of market values over time, as predicted by traditional theory, is given in Table 1. If all shareholders have a marginal rate of time preference equal to 8 per cent. per annum all will agree that the venture is worthwhile. The first shareholders will secure a "windfall" gain – they will contribute £2,000 to secure a market value of £2,500, a gain of £500, the net present value of the project. Over all subsequent periods, assuming the original estimates to be correct, they will receive a rate of return equal to 8 per cent. per annum, the marginal rate of time preference – a satisfactory result; similarly, new shareholders, buying shares after the start of the operation, will receive a return of 8 per cent. per annum. If the project had been a new part of the undertaking of an established firm, the analysis would yield similar conclusions. The gain of £500 (or its equivalent in present value terms) would come when the project was first envisaged by the market and subsequently returns would equal the marginal rate of time preference.

Thus, on a strict interpretation of traditional theory, all shareholders, regardless of their holding period, earn a minimum rate of return equal to their marginal rate of time preference, and those who hold shares when new ventures are envisaged get "windfalls" equal to the net present values of the new projects. No one receives an unsatisfactory rate of return.

In practice, however, we could not assume that a firm would attain the market values given in Table 1 following the acceptance of the project described. It might do so if the firm were to publish its cash-flow expecta-

[6] We assume that accounting profits are equal to cash flows so that there is no legal restriction on the proposed dividends.

tions; the hypothesis cannot be studied because firms do not publish detailed projections of that kind. It might do so if the market had some means of making good forecasts. The reporting of the results year by year in conventional accounting form would, however, not represent a good basis for forecasts in the early years of the project. Actual market values will match the theoretical values described above only by chance. Before we can assume that all shareholders will receive a satisfactory return, following acceptance of an investment project with a positive net present value, we must consider further the process by which actual market values are set, including the means by which the stock market receives and interprets information on future prospects.

EMPIRICAL VALUATION MODELS

It is by no means easy to summarise the results of the research undertaken on the influence of different variables on share prices. No concensus has yet emerged on what is the most satisfactory valuation model.

In an ideal situation, managers of a company would prepare long-term budgets incorporating the estimated financial results of new investment projects which they proposed to accept; the budgets would be published for shareholders and would presumably be related to the market price via a valuation model such as that implied by traditional theory. In practice, it seems unlikely that the market price will respond directly to changes in directors' expectations because they are not published in quantitative form. The possibility cannot be ruled out completely. It might hold because of leakage of information about directors' expectations or because shareholders or their advisors were able to predict directors' expectations from other information. The question has not been investigated empirically, presumably because of the difficulty in obtaining systematic information about a firm's budgets (indeed long-term budgets may not exist in explicit form). In this paper, it is assumed that one cannot rely on the existence of a consistent relationship between market price and directors' expectations.

Since directors' budgets are not available to guide shareholders' investment decisions, let us consider what information is available. The information may be assumed to fall under three headings:

(1) Previous financial results published by the firm. The more important components include dividends paid by the company (interpreted in conjunction with information about changes in the issued share capital)[7]; broad details of investments undertaken in the past, in so far as they have resulted in the acquisition of assets recorded in balance sheets; the surplus of accounting profits over dividends paid; and, implicitly at least, sources and uses of funds statements.

(2) Additional information about the firm's plans given in statements made

[7] F. Modigliani and M. Miller, "Dividend Policy, Growth and the Valuation of Shares," *Journal of Business*, 34 (1961), 411–433.

by its officers, *e.g.* by the chairman in his annual statement, or implied from various actions of the firm.[8] This information is normally of a general and imprecise nature, one which does not lend itself to conversion into quantitative predictions.

(3) General views about likely economic trends. These would include estimates of prospects of economic growth and of cyclical fluctuations; they would also include views on the prospects for relative growth in the demand for the products of different industries.

The importance of accounting information to shareholders has been studied empirically.[9] One study has shown that an abnormally high proportion of the volume of transactions in a firm's shares and of the changes in their market price is concentrated in the period around the publication of the annual earnings result. This may be interpreted as evidence that shareholders are changing their expectations at such times and, provided that directors can forecast their forthcoming accounting results more effectively than shareholders, reinforces our assumption that market prices are not closely related to directors' expectations.

Empirical investigations of the variables that influence share prices have generally concentrated on accounting and other readily quantifiable information; the impact of qualitative information has, in effect, been assumed to be random. The investigations have followed two main lines of approach. One has been to develop a model of shareholders' dividend expectations and use these expectations in the traditional valuation model. The other has been to relate directly, in simple linear models, share prices and the variables which feature most prominently in conventional financial analysis.

The best-known example of the first approach is Gordon's growth model.[10] The simplest form of this model involves the assumption that dividends will grow at the constant rate g, so that future annual dividends will be:

$$d_1; \; d_1(1+g); \; d_1(1+g)^2; \ldots; d_1(1+g)^n; \ldots$$

If we substitute these dividend estimates in the traditional valuation model we obtain:

$$(6) \quad V_0 = \frac{d_1}{(i-g)} = \frac{d_0(1+g)}{(i-g)}$$

Gordon developed a model under which a firm reinvests a constant proportion of its earnings, b, to earn a constant average rate of return, r, and

[8] E. F. Fama, L. Fisher, H. C. Jensen and R. Roll, *The Adjustment of Stock Prices to New Information*, The Center for Mathematical Studies in Business and Economics, University of Chicago, 1967.

[9] W. H. Beaver, "The Information Content of Annual Earnings Announcements," in University of Chicago, *Empirical Research in Accounting: Selected Studies 1968*, 67–92.

[10] M. J. Gordon, *The Investment, Financing and Valuation of the Corporation*, Homewood, 1962.

showed that dividends (distributed earnings) would then increase at the constant rate rb.[11] Hence, substituting in equation (6) and rearranging, we have:

$$(7) \quad \frac{d_0\,(1+rb)}{V_0} = i-rb.$$

Gordon assumed that the parameters r and b would be estimated from accounting information. Shareholders might, however, behave consistently with a growth model and yet estimate the rate of growth in some other way – *e.g.* simply by extrapolating past growth rates in dividends over some period.

The model given in expression (7) and several similar ones have been tested empirically. [12] A rough summary of the conclusions, sufficient for our purpose, is that the models have some power in predicting the behaviour of market prices; current dividends alone explain a considerable proportion of variations in price (*i.e.* for shares in the same industry, assumed subject to similar risks, current dividend yields do not vary greatly). Firms with high retained earnings, however, seem to have lower value than would be expected on the basis of the growth assumptions of equation (6).

These conclusions have given rise to much controversy concerning the effect of dividend distribution policy on share values; the details of the debate are beyond the scope of this paper.[13] We may note, however, that the conclusions of the empirical studies are hard to interpret because they involve the use of accounting calculations of earnings. The economic significance of accounting calculations may be distorted by the particular choice of accounting conventions used by the firm and the nature of such distortion is not normally apparent to the shareholder. For example, depreciation and cost of goods sold are normally calculated on a historical cost basis in the computation of earnings; in consequence, in times of inflation, the existence of retained earnings does not guarantee that funds are available to increase real levels of investment – they may be needed simply to maintain the current level of investment in real terms. The position will differ from firm to firm.

[11] Gordon's model employed continuous discounting and investment functions, but the results are similar to those derived from the simpler formulation given in this paper.

[12] M. H. Miller and F. Modigliani, "Some Estimates of the Cost of Capital to the Electricity Supply Industry, 1954–1957," *American Economic Review*, 56 (1966), 333–390; M. J. Gordon, *The Investment, Financing and Valuation . . .*; E. F. Brigham and M. J. Gordon, "Leverage Dividend Policy and the Cost of Capital," *Journal of Finance*, 23 (1968), 85–104.

[13] D. Durand, *Bank Stock Prices and the Bank Capital Problem*, New York, National Bureau of Economic Research, 1957; F. Modigliani and M. H. Miller, "The Cost of Capital, Corporation Finance and the Theory of Investment," *American Economic Review*, 48 (1958), 261–297; D. Durand, "The Cost of Capital, Corporation Finance and the Theory of Investment: Comment," *American Economic Review*, 49 (1959), 639–655; F. Modigliani and M. Miller, "The Cost of Capital, Corporation Finance and the Theory of Investment: Reply," *American Economic Review*, 49 (1959), 655–669; "Variability in Earnings – Price Ratios of Corporate Equities," *American Economic Review*, 51 (1961), 81–94; I. Friend and S. Puckett, "Dividends and Stock Prices," *American Economic Review*, 54 (1964), 656–682.

The alternative approach to the explanation of movements in share prices makes no explicit use of the traditional valuation model or of dividend expectations. It involves the development of valuation models which use the common ratios of financial analysis, price-earnings ratios, dividend yields and so on,[14] and perhaps acknowledges that "Wall Street has never paid much attention to theoretical thinking".[15] The models investigated empirically involve variations of equations such as.

$$(8) \quad V_0 = b_1 d_0 + b_2 (Y_0 - d_0).$$

where Y_0 represents last reported earnings and b_1, b_2 are valuation coefficients.

Again a short summary of the empirical results is sufficient for our purposes. There is general agreement that dividends are a significant determinant of market price. Retained earnings also appear to have some influence on market price, though its nature is not well established. The estimate of the valuation coefficient of retained earnings (b_2 in equation (8)) varies greatly from sample to sample, even for the results of a given set of firms over different years. The contribution of £1 of retained earnings to value appears generally to be lower than that of £1 of dividends, contrary to theoretical expectations, though the interpretation of this conclusion is subject to the same difficulties as described in relation to the Gordon growth model. Other variables have been investigated in valuation models, for example measures of asset structure, but in general there has been a failure to establish significant relationships.

We have already noted that current accounting practice is lacking in uniformity. Various conventions may be used in the calculation of earnings, and a given set of business transactions may be reflected in various reported earnings numbers, according to which conventions are used. It is pertinent to our study to know whether investors are "fooled" by the accounting conventions used or whether a given set of transactions will lead to a given market share price, regardless of what conventions are used in calculating earnings.

It is difficult to investigate this question because of the lack of adequate information about the nature and effect of accounting conventions used by particular firms in practice. Studies have been undertaken, however, using both actual empirical price and earnings data for cases where the accounting conventions were known and classroom valuation exercises based on data obtained by simulation.[16] The results have not been clear cut. The

[14] G. R. Fisher, "Some Factors Influencing Share Prices," *Economic Journal*, 71 (1961), 121–141.

[15] B. Graham, D. L. Dodd, S. Cottle and C. Tatham, *Security Analysis*, New York, 1962, 408.

[16] T. R. Dyckman, "The Effects of Alternative Accounting Techniques on Certain Management Decisions," *Journal of Accounting Research*, 2 (1964), 91–107; T. R. Dyckman, "On the Effect of Earnings Trend, Size and Inventory Valuation Procedures in Evaluating a Business Firm," *Research in Accounting Measurement*, Minesha, 1966; R. E. Jensen, "An Experimental Design for Study of Effects of

balance of evidence suggests that investors make some adjustment for the effect of different accounting conventions and do not simply accept a reported earnings number without regard for how it was calculated. The adjustment is probably only partial, however; there seems to be some residual difference in the equity value of a company which depends on which accounting conventions are used.

The above discussion has provided a short review of some of the statistical studies undertaken into the factors which affect the market value of a firm's shares. The intention has been only to identify some broad conclusions which are relevant for this paper; accordingly detailed results and the experimental difficulties have not been discussed. Our review emphasises that share prices depend in part on quantitative information communicated to shareholders, particularly, it seems, on current dividends and retained earnings, taking some account of the accounting conventions used. The precise influence of these variables is uncertain.

It will be convenient to illustrate the rest of the argument of this paper with reference to some particular valuation model. We shall assume the applicability of the Gordon growth model

$$(6) \quad V = \frac{d_0 (1+g)}{i-g}$$

and we shall further assume that shareholders estimate g as the actual rate of growth in dividend over the last year, $\frac{d_0 - d_{-1}}{d_{-1}}$. We thus endow our shareholders with unrealistically short memories, but the assumption simplifies the calculations without altering the principles at issue. Similarly, we shall argue, the assumption of some other valuation model within the range of those studied in the empirical literature, would yield similar conclusions, and in some cases conclusions of a more extreme kind.

THE APPLICATION OF EMPIRICAL VALUATION MODELS TO INVESTMENT DECISIONS

We now illustrate the importance of the pattern over time of cash flows from a project.

Consider a firm, which we will call Fabricius, with expected operating earnings in cash from present activities of £10,000 per annum in perpetuity. According to present plans 60 per cent. of cash earnings will be paid out as dividend each year and the remainder will be retained for reinvestment. Each year, worthwhile investment opportunities will be available to absorb the retained earnings. Each one will yield a cash flow in perpetuity of

Accounting Variations in Decision Making," *Journal of Accounting Research*, 4 (1966), 224–238; J. L. O'Donnell, "Relationships between Reported Earnings and Stock Prices in the Electricity Supply Industry," *Accounting Review*, 40 (1965), 135–143.

10 per cent. per annum of the amount invested (by dealing in perpetuities, we avoid the problem of how to provide for depreciation). We assume that there is no taxation or inflation and that shareholders have a marginal rate of time preference of 8 per cent. per annum over the indefinite future.

The situation described is summarised in Table 2. It is an idealised "steady-state" situation. Each year, dividends grow by 4 per cent. – the rate of retention of earnings times the rate of return on investment (0.40) (0.10); market values similarly grow at 4 per cent. per annum. Shareholders earn a return equal to their marginal rate of time preference regardless of their holding period. (Rearranging equation (7), we have $i = d_0 \dfrac{(1+rb)}{V_0} + rb$; the return for year 3, for example, is $\dfrac{6,490}{162,500} + 0.04 = 0.08$.)

Let us suppose that the steady state planned by the directors of Fabricius is disturbed at time 2 when the original investment proposals can no longer be implemented. £4,160 is to be invested at this time; but only £2,160 can be invested in accordance with the original plan, *i.e.* to yield a return of £216 per annum to perpetuity. The remaining £2,000 can be invested only in the project described above in Table 1, *i.e.* to yield £200 at time 3, £286 at time 4, £464 at time 5, nothing at times 6 and 7 and £200 per annum at time 8 and subsequently. It was shown in Table 1 that this project would have the same present value (£2,500 gross) as the receipt of £200 per annum in perpetuity envisaged in the original plan and also that under traditional theory each shareholder would be assumed to receive a satisfactory return following acceptance of the project regardless of the period over which he held his shares.

Table 2: Summary of cash flows and market values–original plan

Time	1	2	3	4	5	6	7	8	9
Cash flows from investments:									
Previously	10,000	10,000	10,000	10,000	10,000	10,000	10,000	10,000	10,000
time 1	(4,000)	400	400	400	400	400	400	400	400
2		(4,160)	416	416	416	416	416	416	416
3			(4,326)	433	433	433	433	433	433
4				(4,499)	450	450	450	450	450
5					(4,679)	468	468	468	468
6						(4,867)	487	487	487
7							(5,061)	506	506
8								(5,264)	526
9									(5,474)
Dividends	6,000	6,240	6,490	6,750	7,020	7,300	7,593	7,896	8,212
Value, ex. div.	156,000	162,500	168,700	175,500	182,500	189,800	197,400	205,300	213,500

If shareholders were given full information about the substitute project and they believed it, no shareholders would fail to realise their required minimum rate of return even though the pattern of cash flows and market values over time would differ from the original "steady-state" plan.

However, if we adopt the more realistic assumption that shareholders rely on annual historical accounts to learn what they can about a firm's investment plans, the picture is altered. Table 3 describes the revised cash flows which would be expected by the directors if the substitute investment were accepted at time 2 and other investment plans were unchanged. This table also gives estimates of the market values which would prevail at each time using the Gordon growth valuation model, $V_j = d_j (1+g)/(i-g)$, and assuming that growth rates are estimated as equal to the growth in dividend over the previous year.

Under the revised plan, market values show an extraordinary volatility. The extent of the fluctuations is, perhaps, improbably large because of our simplifying assumption that growth rates are estimated from the change in dividend over one year rather than some longer period. However, if the dividend plan described in Table 3 were followed in practice, it is likely that the market value of shares would diverge from the predictions of traditional theory in the direction indicated. The illustration serves to make the point that it may be unreasonable, in practice, to assume that the acceptance of an investment project with a positive net present value will benefit all shareholders at the time of acceptance. Shareholders who hold their shares up to time 9 would presumably agree that the project was worthwhile (with the benefit of hindsight), for they would have received a return equal to their marginal rates of time preference overall. Some of those who sell earlier will realise very large gains – *e.g.* those who sell at time 8. Others, *e.g.* those who sell at time 6, will fail to earn their required return by a large margin. Such shareholders might well fare better if the new investment (of £2,000 at time 2) were rejected. Thus there may be a conflict of interest between short-term and long-term shareholders or, more generally, between shareholders who will hold their shares for different periods.

Table 3: Summary of cash flows and market values–revised plan

Time	1	2	3	4	5	6	7	8	9
Cash flows from investment:									
Previously	10,000	10,000	10,000	10,000	10,000	10,000	10,000	10,000	10,000
time 1	(4,000)	400	400	400	400	400	400	400	400
2a		(2,160)	216	216	216	216	216	216	216
2b		(2,000)	200	286	464	0	0	200	200
3			(4,326)	433	433	433	433	433	433
4				(4,499)	450	450	450	450	450
5					(4,679)	468	468	468	468
6						(4,867)	487	487	487
7							(5,061)	506	506
8								(5,264)	526
9									(5,474)
Dividends	6,000	6,240	6,490	6,836	7,284	7,100	7,393	7,896	8,212
Growth		6,240	6,490	6,836	7,284	7,100	7,393	7,896	8,212
rate	6,000	6,240	6,490	6,836	7,284	7,100	7,393	7,896	
Per cent.		4·0	4·0	5·3	6·5	(2·5)	4·1	6·8	4·0
Value ex. div.	156,000	162,500	168,700	266,700	517,200	65,900	197,300	702,800	213,500

The directors of Fabricius may well decide that the plan described in Table 3 is unacceptable. Their decision will depend on what view they take of their objectives. It does seem that the maximisation of market value at the time an investment decision is taken is not a satisfactory objective, once the assumptions of the traditional valuation model are abandoned; for such market value may not reflect informed cash-flow expectations.

It seems impossible to sustain an argument that there is a particular set of objectives which a firm should adopt because it is "correct." Faced with the conflict exposed above, a firm may decide that it should attempt to secure some specified minimum rate of return for all shareholders, regardless of their holding period, possibly a return lower than the estimated marginal rate of time preference; this would imply a need to be concerned with the pattern of share prices over time. On the other hand, a firm might decide to concentrate solely on the interests of long-term shareholders. Furthermore, it might decide to consider the interests of prospective future shareholders; it might decide to try to avoid the loss in prospect for a shareholder who buys at time 5 and sells at time 6 (Table 3) if only to preserve the capacity of the firm to raise new capital. We shall assume for purposes of illustration, that the directors have decided to seek to maximise the present value of cash flows subject to the constraint that they must earn a minimum return of 8 per cent. per annum for all shareholders, regardless of when they sell their shares.

Faced with the pattern of share prices predicted in Table 3, the directors would not immediately decide to reject the project under consideration. They would first consider whether the pattern of results could be improved by adopting any combination of the additional borrowing and lending – or investment – opportunities available.

If a firm is able to borrow and lend sufficiently large amounts at a rate of interest equal to shareholders' marginal rate of time preference, it will always be able to obtain a satisfactory pattern of cash flows and hence satisfactory market prices from the acceptance of a project with a positive net present value. This follows from the well-known result that the cash flows from an investment, adapted by borrowing and lending at the marginal rate of time preference to give a desired pattern of consumption, will have the same net present value as the original cash flows. In the case of Fabricius, as shown in Table 4, it is simply necessary to lend £86 at time 4 and £264 at time 5 and realise £200 at times 6 and 7 to restore the growth path originally planned.

Table 4: Amendment of cash-flow pattern by lending at 8 per cent. per annum

Time	3	4	5	6	7	8
Cash flow from project	200	286	464	0	0	200
Lending brought forward	0	0	86	356·9	185·4	0
Interest on lending at 8 per cent per annum	0	0	6·9	28·5	14·6	0
New lending (lending repaid)	0	86	264	(200)	(200)	0
Lending carried forward	0	86	356·9	185·4	0	0
Revised cash flow	200	200	200	200	200	200

However, a firm may be unable to alter the pattern of its cash flows by investing or lending at a rate equal to shareholders' marginal rate of time preference. Suppose that the only lending opportunities available to Fabricius offer a return of 2 per cent. per annum. One set of cash flows that might be secured is described in Table 5. The rates of return offered to shareholders now come much closer to those in the original plan than those of the plan described in Table 3. Shareholders who sell at time 7, however, will fail to realise their marginal rates of time preference. They will find that the market value is only £173,800 compared to £197,400 in the original plan, the minimum required to secure a rate of return of 8 per cent. per annum. (Table 2).

Table 5: Amendment of cash-flow pattern by lending at 2 per cent per annum

Time	1	2	3	4	5	6	7	8	9
Cash flow from projects as per Table 3	6,000	6,240	6,490	6,836	7,284	7,100	7,393	7,896	8,212
Lending brought forward	0	0	0	0	86	351·7	158·7	0	0
Interest on lending at 2 per cent per annum	0	0	0	0	1·7	7·0	3·2	0	0
New lending (lending repaid)	0	0	0	86	264	(200)	(161·9)	0	0
Lending carried forward	0	0	0	86	351·7	158·7	0	0	0
Revised cash flow	6,000	6,240	6,490	6,750	7,020	7,300	7,555	7,896	8,212
Growth rate per cent		4·0	4·0	4·0	4·0	4·0	3·5	4·5	4·0
Value *ex. div.*	156,000	162,200	168,700	175,500	182,500	189,800	173,800	235,800	213,500

In the situation assumed, the objective of providing a return of 8 per cent. per annum for all shareholders, regardless of their holding period, cannot quite be met, as can be seen by calculating the effect of borrowing at time 7 in order to raise the dividend and restore the former market value. The original plan, described in Table 2, met the objective with no margin to spare; the revised plans given in Tables 3 and 4 had the same overall present value as the original; but the amendments described in Table 5 improved the pattern of cash flows at the cost of a reduction in present value, and hence necessarily yield a lower return.

Faced with this situation, the managers may reasonably decide to accept the project as amended in Table 5. On the other hand, the adjustments required to secure a satisfactory pattern of cash flows may, in some cases, have so large a negative net present value that all the benefits of the original project are eroded. The wish to secure a satisfactory pattern of cash flow might then lead to a decision to reject the original project, *i.e.* to reject a project having a positive net present value. In both types of case, we have an illustration of the conflict of interest between long-term and short-term shareholders.[17] The securing of a satisfactory pattern of cash flows, in order to protect the returns to short-term shareholders, leads to a reduction in the net present value of cash flows for long-term shareholders.

[17] *cf.* A. J. Merrett and A. Sykes, *The Finance and Analysis of Capital Projects*, London, 1963, 457–459; J. Dean, *Capital Budgeting*, New York, 1951, 39–48.

The context in which the importance of cash-flow patterns has been examined, the appraisal of the single "rogue" investment project supplemented by borrowing and lending, is artificially simple. In practice, there will be many projects, each having distinctive cash-flow patterns. The argument of this paper, relating to the effect of cash-flow patterns on share prices, should be applied to aggregate cash flow – not the pattern of individual project cash flows, *per se*. The need for smoothing in aggregate cash flow may simply reflect the irregularities in particular individual projects; it is also possible, however, that the aggregate problem is less because some of the individual project irregularities are offsetting.

In principle, the aggregate decision problem may be conveniently expressed in mathematical programming form:
Maximise

$$F = \sum_{k=0}^{n} \frac{d_k}{(1+i)^k} + \sum_{j=0}^{n} \sum_{h=1}^{m} \frac{x_{hj}\, t_{hj}}{(1+i)^n}$$

Subject to:

(1) $\quad d_k + f_k \qquad\qquad \leqslant \sum_{j=0}^{k} \sum_{h=1}^{m} a_{hjk}\, x_{hj}$

(2) $\quad V_{k-1}(1+r) - d_k \quad \leqslant V_k$
$$\qquad d_k,\, x_{hj} \geqslant 0$$

where

d_k is the dividend at time k;

x_{hj} is the number of times project h available at time j is accepted (for some projects, which can only be wholly accepted or rejected, the constraints $x_{hj} \leqslant 1$, x_{hj}=integer will be required);

t_{hj} is the value, at a horizon date n, of cash flows arising after time n of project hj;

a_{hjk} is the cash flow of project hj, arising at time k, receipts being defined as positive and outlays as negative;

f_k is the amount of fixed costs, *i.e.* costs independent of what projects are accepted, at time k;

V_k is the market value of the firm at time k, *ex. div.*, defined in terms of whatever valuation model is selected as giving the best empirical predictions;

i is the shareholders' marginal rate of time preference;

r is the minimum rate of return required to be earned each year in the interests of short-term shareholders;

and

m is the number of projects available for acceptance at each time j.

The formulation given is a simple model, for a firm which has no debt capital and which restricts new equity finance to internally generated cash flows. A discussion of extensions and the general problems of such formulations is beyond the scope of this paper.[18] The basic ingredients of the model are an objective function, requiring the maximisation of the present value of shareholders' cash flows, subject to the constraints that cash receipts and payments at each time k must balance (Constraints type 1) and that short-term shareholders must have a minimum rate of return r (Constraint type 2). There would be one constraint of type 1 and one constraint of type 2 for each time period up to the horizon time n. An optimal solution to the model can be guaranteed only if the market value, V_k, can be represented as some linear function of the variables; in other cases, a simulation method may be needed. The inclusion of type 2 constraints may, for the reasons described in this paper, lead to the acceptance of some projects with negative net present values (obtained by discounting at the opportunity cost of capital, conventionally defined) and to the rejection of some projects with positive net present values.

In illustrating the importance of cash-flow patterns, we assumed the applicability of a version of the Gordon growth valuation model. We noted above that some writers have preferred to investigate firm's market values using other valuation models, notably models representing market values as a linear function of current dividends and retained earnings. We preferred the Gordon model because it is capable of direct reconciliation with a model of dividend expectations and therefore appears to be more soundly based theoretically.

It can be shown, however, that the analysis of the importance of cash-flow patterns given in this paper may be applied in conjunction with other valuation models to yield similar conclusions. Limitations of space prevent the description of the full analysis in this paper. The main point, however, is that wherever market prices reflect expectations arrived at from a study of past results and those results are not related to informed expectations by some model with stable coefficients, market prices may fail to reflect informed expectations; shareholders may then sell their shares at prices which are "too low" or indeed "too high," judged by comparison with the present value of informed cash-flow expectations.

We have already referred to the fact that different accounting conventions may be applied to a given set of transactions to yield various different earnings numbers. In our illustration above, we used a form of valuation model which abstracted from explicit use of accounting earnings. Accounting earnings may normally influence a firm's market value, however. They have an explicit role in models which include retained earning as a parameter; and, in models such as the Gordon growth model, they may have some role in the estimation of the growth rate. In such cases, there are at least two variables which influence a firm's market value – shareholders'

[18] For a detailed study, see, H. M. Weingartner, *Mathematical Programming and the Analysis of Capital Budgeting Problems*, Englewood Cliffs, 1963.

cash flows and earnings. There is some empirical evidence, noted above, that share prices may be influenced by the choice of what accounting conventions are used in computing earnings, apparently because this choice determines what earnings numbers are given to the market. Different methods of depreciation or stock valuation, for example, may affect the pattern of earnings reported over time and hence the pattern of share prices over time, for a given pattern of cash flows.

Where there is a choice, permitted by law, it is tempting to argue that the accounting conventions should be chosen in a way which makes it possible for short-term shareholders to receive the target minimum rate of return with as little adjustment to the cash flows by borrowing and lending as possible. This would imply that accounting conventions should be chosen for the predictive quality of the resulting earnings numbers. However, the implications of this proposal require further analysis before it can be claimed as a viable method of practice.

CONCLUSION

The idea that the prediction of actual share prices is somehow relevant to investment decisions in the firm is not new – though it has been the subject of little formal analysis in the literature. Some writers accept the traditional valuation model without comment or recognise that the traditional model raises some conceptual difficulties but assume, with little discussion, that it remains the best approach available in the circumstances.

Other writers develop the discussion of the difficulties further. They note that the model does represent a prediction of an actual value that should prevail in the market and that it is, as such, testable. Durand has written ". . . we can measure the costs of capital about as accurately as we can measure the value of common stock and any of us who think that stock appraisal is a form of crystal gazing should prepare to include research on the cost of capital in the same category."[19] Porterfield acknowledges that the traditional model is unlikely to be valid, given the uncertain conditions of the real world. However, he regarded his task as the development of a normative framework which describes how people should behave in ideal conditions.[20]

It may be argued that the actual behaviour of business firms involves an approximation of that required by the methods of analysis proposed in this paper. That behaviour is presumably frequently intuitive – not guided by explicit analysis. Practical concern to secure steady trends in dividend and earnings growth may reasonably be explained in terms of a desire to secure

[19] D. Durand, *Cost of Debt and Equity Funds for Business Trends and Problems of Measurement*, New York, National Brueau of Economic Research, 1952.
[20] J. T. S. Porterfield, *Investment Decisions and Capital Costs*, Englewood Cliffs, 1965, 18 and 68.

a steady trend in market prices of shares and avoid losses for shareholders holding for different periods.[21]

Merret and Sykes presumably have similar considerations in mind when they suggest that directors should consider increasing dividends when a major project is in its gestation period – and hence not contributing to reported earnings or cash flows – in order to emphasise their confidence in future results. They do not make explicit their assumptions about the valuation model, however.[22]

It is in the writings of Gordon that the importance of the valuation model has received most emphasis.[23] He argues the desirability of formulating a valuation model in terms of observable parameters, of validating the model by careful empirical testing and incorporating the model directly in the analysis of investment decisions. His analysis is not directly applicable in a firm, however, because he expresses returns from investment opportunities as a simple function of the amount invested rather than providing for the estimation of the results of several discrete projects in a form in which they would arise in practice. He also expresses the firm's objective as the maximisation of the *present* (empirically predicted) market price and ignores the pattern of market prices over time. This seems to be a deficiency in his analysis because the flows of information in the market have the effect of diminishing the significance of a market value at a single point in time as an estimate of the value of future expectations.

Gordon does acknowledge that some difficulties may arise because of shareholders' ignorance of management's expectations. He suggests that "setting (retained earnings) on the basis of the corporation's superior knowledge will result in a lower price"; but he adds "consideration of long-run price maximisation opens up a Pandora's box, and this is something that we had better not undertake here."[24]

The argument of this paper is that a firm should seek to maximise the present value of future cash flows, at the estimated marginal rate of time preference of shareholders, subject to the constraint that the pattern of share prices over time should offer a specified minimum return to short-term shareholders. These share prices should be estimated by a valuation model which has stood the test of empirical investigation. A good deal of research into empirical valuation models is needed before this approach can be applied with confidence in practice. A switch of emphasis in capital budgeting studies, to give prominence to the role of the valuation model, seems to be desirable for the impetus that it would give such research.

[21] J. Lintner, "Distributions of Incomes of Corporations among Dividends, Retained Earnings and Taxes," *American Economic Review*, 46 (1956), 97–113; E. M. Lerner and A. Rappaport, "Limit DCF in Capital Budgeting," *Harvard Business Review*, September–October, 1968.
[22] A. J. Merrett and A. Sykes, *op. cit.*, 459.
[23] M. J. Gordon, *The Investment, Financing . . ., passim.*
[24] M. J. Gordon, *op. cit.*, 216–217.

ANCIENT GREEK AND ROMAN
MARITIME LOANS

G. E. M. de Ste. Croix

1. INTRODUCTION

THIS essay deals with the loans made in Greek and Roman antiquity upon security of a ship or its cargo or both, for a specified voyage or voyages, at a high rate of interest, on the terms that if the ship or the goods did not arrive safely the borrower (provided he had not been at fault) was to be released from all liability for repayment even of the capital sum borrowed. This practice is referred to nowadays under many different names. When consulting indexes to books in French on ancient history one can expect to find the subject under "*prêts maritimes,*" in German under "*Seedarlehen,*" in Italian under "*prestito marittimo*"; in English one is in doubt whether to look first under "maritime loans", "nautical loans," "sea-loans" – or even "bottomry" or "respondentia," the terms used in English in modern times for transactions corresponding very closely with the ancient (or mediaeval) maritime loan. (The security given under a bottomry bond is, strictly, upon a ship, in respondentia upon a cargo; but "bottomry" is often used loosely to cover both types of transaction.) Although the modern bottomry loan, unlike the ancient and mediaeval sea-loan, may have arisen particularly as a means by which money could be raised to cover the cost of repairs to a ship in a foreign port, I propose on occasion to use the expressions "bottomry" and "respondentia" for the ancient maritime loan, since all these transactions are in principle similar, above all in that they recognise the fundamental principle that the loan is repayable only if the voyage ends safely, and therefore contain an element of insurance. The subject of maritime loans in the Greek and Roman world has often been discussed, but seldom to much purpose in English.[1]

[1] In English, G. M. Calhoun, "Risk in Sea Loans in Ancient Athens," *Jnl. of Econ. and Business Hist.*, 2 (1930), 561–584, is the best introduction to the material for the fourth century B.C. but goes no further. Walter Ashburner, *The Rhodian Sea-Law*, Oxford, 1909, ccix–ccxxi gives a useful survey. H. Michell, *The Economics of Ancient Greece*, 2nd ed., Cambridge, 1957, 274, 345–350 is weak and inaccurate. The fullest treatments are by Jean Rougé, *Recherches sur l'organisation du commerce maritime en Médit. sous l'emp. romain*, Paris, 1966, 345–360, cf. 397–413, etc.; Fritz Pringsheim, *Der Kauf mit fremden Geld* (= *Romanistiche Beiträge zur Rechtsgesch.*, I, Leipzig, 1916), 4–27, 143–147; and E. Cuq, in Daremberg-Saglio, *Dict. des antiquités grecques et romaines*, IV. i (1904), 13–17, *s.v. nauticum foenus.* Three works dealing in detail with the Greek evidence are U.E. Paoli, *Studi di diritto attico*, Florence, 1930, 9–137 ("Il prestito marittimo nel diritto antico"); August Böckh, *Die Staatshaushaltung der Athener*, I, 3rd ed., 166–175 (ed. Max Fränkel, Berlin, 1886; *cf.* pp. 182–192 of the Eng. trans. of the 2nd German edition, by Anthony Lamb, *The Public Economy of the Athenians*, London, 1857); and W. Schwahn, in Pauly-Wissowa, *Real-encyclopädie der classischen*

The ancient maritime loan (the standard expressions for which are in Greek *nautika, nautikos tokos,* and in Latin *pecunia traiecticia, fenus* [*foenus*] *nauticum*) may be seen as a precursor of marine insurance, indeed the nearest thing to insurance that the ancient world ever knew.[2] It is true that if one regards the payment of a premium in advance as an essential element in insurance, then ancient maritime loans must be kept quite distinct. But at least they served the same useful social purpose as insurance: *spreading the risk.* This was all the more important in antiquity for two reasons. First, the traders of the Greek and Roman world were usually quite humble men,[3] who would rarely have enough capital to buy a large cargo in the first place; and if they had, would be reluctant to risk it all on a single venture. Although some of them might become rich, they would then be likely to retire from commerce and buy land, thereby giving themselves, or at any rate their children, a chance of becoming members of the upper class. And secondly, the risks of commerce were very great. In antiquity virtually all long-distance trade was always conducted by sea, land transport being inefficient and exceedingly expensive. Even a merchant who could afford to send a large cargo to sea might hesitate to do so at his own risk. Piracy was often a serious threat in the Mediterranean,[4] and the risk to a ship of being sunk or damaged by storm or being swept on to rocks by adverse winds or currents was ever present.[5] In Classical poetry the sea is never romanticised, never regarded as a friend and ally: at its best it is a treacherous neutral, at its worst a merciless enemy. "To meet disaster among the waves of the sea," Hesiod had said, "is dreadful." Good and prosperous men "do not voyage in ships, but the grain-giving earth bears them fruit. If poverty and despair drive you to trade, then wait for the fifty days after the summer solstice, before you take your steering-oar down from where you have hung it up for the winter, above the smoke of your fire; spring sailing is dangerous. When you launch your ship, don't take all

---

Altertumswissenschaft, XVI. ii (1935), 2034–2048; this last can be supplemented by Klingmüller's art. on *fenus* in *ibid.* VI. ii (1909), 2187–2205, which deals with Roman *fenus nauticum* in cols. 2200–2205. See also, on the Roman *fenus nauticum,* Paul Huvelin, *Études d'hist. du droit commercial rom.,* Paris, 1929, 196–218. On interest rates, etc. there is useful information in Gustav Billeter, *Gesch. des Zinsfusses im griechisch–römischen Altertum bis auf Justinian,* Leipzig, 1898, 30–41, 242–254. For modern English bottomry and respondentia (now obsolete), see *Halsbury's Laws of England,* 3rd ed., 1, London (1952), 53–55; 35 (1961), 136–137, 433–434.

[2] The arrangement described in Ps.-Arist., *Oecon.* II. ii 34b, 1352ᵇ33–53ᵃ4 (Antimenes of Rhodes), which is often referred to as the earliest example of insurance, is not so in reality: Antimenes ran no risk whatever.

[3] For the Greek world this will not be disputed. For the Roman world see esp. A. H. M. Jones, "The Econ. Life of the Towns of the Roman Emp.," *Recueils de la Soc. Jean Bodin,* 7, 1955, 161 *et seq.; The Later Roman Emp. 284–602,* Oxford, 1964, 855 *et seq.,* esp. 866–872. Cic., *De Offic.* I.151, while depreciating traders, condescends to accord grudging approval to the successful, large-scale trader who, "sated – or rather satisfied – with his profits, retires from the harbour to the fields."

[4] See H. A. Ormerod, *Piracy in the Ancient World,* Liverpool/London, 1924, and the texts assembled by E. Ziebarth, *Beiträge zur Gesch. des Seeraubs u. Seehandels im alten Griechenland,* Hamburg, 1929, 100–117.

[5] The general conditions of navigation are outlined in Part I of the admirable comprehensive work by Rougé, *op. cit.* (in n. 1 above).

your property aboard: leave most of it behind, lest you lose all you have[6]."

That was the outlook of the archaic age, at about the beginning of the seventh century B.C. By the fifth century, improvements in shipbuilding and the art of navigation[7] had extended the sailing season[8] and greatly increased the volume of maritime commerce, which had also been stimulated by the colonising movement of the eighth and seventh centuries and the general opening-up of horizons which had resulted. The poverty of most traders, however, was still a very serious handicap. The important social function of the maritime loan was to *spread the considerable risks of commerce* over the much larger and richer landowning class, allow it to provide the initial capital the merchant needed to buy his cargo, and in effect to insure him (in return for a high rate of interest) against the risks of sea-trading. Because of the element of insurance, many a merchant may have borrowed the money with which to buy his initial cargo even if he did not actually need to do so. It is a mistake to put too much reliance on a much-quoted statement in the Demosthenic oration *Against Phormio* (Ps.-Dem. 34.51), to the effect that "the resources of those who do business come not from those who borrow but from those who lend; and no ship or shipowner or passenger can put to sea if the lenders do not play their part" – and so of course the Athenian courts must protect the moneylenders! Like other statements made *ex parte* by litigants, such a generalisation must be treated with scepticism; but I do think it is very likely that many if not most merchants would actually prefer to insure themselves by means of a maritime loan, provided they could see enough profit ahead to justify incurring a debt at a high rate of interest.

2. THE FIFTH AND FOURTH CENTURIES B.C.

The first certain evidence for the existence of ancient maritime loans including the element of insurance[9] comes not from the fourth century B.C., as is often stated,[10] but from the late fifth: a speech of the orator Lysias, delivered before an Athenian court about the year 400, refers to nautical

[6] Hesiod, *Works and Days*, 225–237, 618–694, etc.
[7] The most useful works are Rougé, *op. cit.* (in n. 1 above); and Lionel Casson, *Ships and Seamanship in the Ancient World*, Princeton, 1971.
[8] The evidence is conflicting. Most useful for the "official view" of the Roman government is a constitution of A.D. 380 (*Cod. Theod.* XIII. ix. 3.3; *cf. Cod. Just.* XI. vi. 3.3), ordering the *navicularii* (responsible for administering and financing state supplies) to accept cargoes from April 1 to October 1, and to be liable to continue sailing right up to October 15. Vegetius (*Epit. rei milit.* 4.39), writing perhaps nearly a century earlier, says that the safe sailing season ("*secura navigatio*") was only from May 27 to September 14 (*cf. Act. Apost.*, 27. 9), and that the seas were closed ("*maria clauduntur*") from November 11 to March 10; that sailing was dangerous ("*periculose maria temptantur*") between March 10 and May 15, and risky ("*incerta navigatio*") between September 14 and November 11. But Pliny the Elder, writing in the first century, speaks of the seas as being opened to voyagers on February 8 (*nh* 2.122), and he rightly denies that they were ever completely closed to navigation: first pirates, he says, and later, avarice, drove men to risk death on the winter seas (*nh* 2.125). And see Casson, *op. cit.*, 270–273.
[9] For possible Mesopotamian antecedents, see Appendix below.
[10] Even *e.g.* by F. M. Heichelheim, in *The Oxford Classical Dict.*, 2nd ed., 1970, 177.

loans made by a wealthy Athenian citizen, Diodotus, who had been killed
in battle at Ephesus in 409 (Lys. 32.6–7). The figure given is $7\frac{2}{3}$ talents, a
very large sum indeed, amounting to nearly half the total property of this
man,[11] who was really rich by the very modest standards of the day. The
sum will certainly have been made up of a whole number of different
loans, for all our other evidence suggests that a bottomry bond for as
much as one talent would be exceptionally large.[12] We have no way of
deciding how long a development the maritime loan had had before this
time. Certainly by then it must have been a very familiar institution, for
Lysias can refer to Diodotus' loans quite casually, as *nautika ekdedomena*,
the expression *nautika* being evidently already the standard technical term
for maritime loans. The nature of the evidence for Greek economic history
is such that we should have no right to expect evidence of bottomry transactions before the age of forensic oratory begins, in the late fifth century,
even if they were invented much earlier. But I would hazard the guess (it
can be no more) that these loans may perhaps have developed first about
the second quarter of the fifth century, in connection with the Athenian
corn trade, which was conducted entirely by sea and must have grown
steadily in volume during the course of the century – by the middle of the
fifth century it must have been the most important single item of Greek
trade, involving the import of perhaps a million and a half bushels a year
or even more.[13]

Between the 370s and the 320s there are several interesting references to
nautical loans, mainly in the forensic speeches in the Demosthenic corpus
attacking alleged defaulters in such transactions. Three such speeches are
of particular interest to us. They were all delivered in those special "mercantile suits," *dikai emporikai*,[14] which from about the middle of the fourth
century were governed by special rules: in particular, they were within the
small category of *dikai emmēnoi*, suits which had to be heard within one
month.[15] In all these cases there was a written contract, a *syngraphē*.

In the 35th oration in the Demosthenic corpus, *Against Lacritus*,[16]

[11] See the useful analysis in J. K. Davies, *Athenian Propertied Families 600–300 B.C.*,
Oxford, 1971, 152–153.

[12] The other figures (some of which may be fictitious or exaggerated) for maritime loans
in the fourth century all come from the Demosthenic corpus: (a) 4,500 dr., in 34.6;
(b) 4,000 dr., in 52.20; (c) 3,000 dr., in 56.6, and also in 35.8, 10; (d) 100 Cyzicene
staters, or not more than 2,800 dr. (cf. 34.23), in 35.36; (e) 2,000 dr., in 34.6, 23;
(f) 1,100 dr., in 35.23; (g) 1,000 dr., in 34.6; (h) 800 dr., in 50.17. The sum of 7,000 dr.
in 27.11 probably represents the total of more than one loan, and the 1,500 dr. in
50.17 and 3,000 + 1,000 dr. in 33.6 were probably not bottomry loans (see below).

[13] See my *Origins of the Peloponnesian War*, London, 1972, 46–49, cf. 217–218, 265–266.

[14] See L. Gernet, "Sur les actions commerciales en droit athénien," *Revue des études
grecques*, 51 (1938), 1 *et seq.*, repr. in Gernet's *Droit et société dans la Grèce anc.*,
Paris, 1955, 173–200; A. R. W. Harrison, *The Law of Athens*, [II] *Procedure*, Oxford,
1971, 16, 64, 86, 109–115, 121–123, 188; J. H. Lipsius, *Das Attische Recht u. Rechts-
verfahren*, II. ii, Leipzig, 1912, 631–634.

[15] There is a puzzle about the order of the months in Ps.-Dem. 33.23: I agree with Paoli,
Gernet, Harrison and others that the text ought to read "from Munychion to Boed-
romion" (the summer months): see Gernet's book (cited in n. 14), 184, n. 3.

[16] There is a useful annotated edition by F. A. Paley and J. E. Sandys, *Select Private
Orations of Demosthenes*, I, 3rd ed., Cambridge, 1898, 52–97.

delivered in or about the 340s, we are actually given a complete respondentia contract (paras. 10–13), occupying a whole page of Greek text. I will give a shortened paraphrase, with a few verbal quotations.

The document begins by stating that Androcles an Athenian and Nausicrates a Carystian had lent to two merchants of Phaselis, Artemon (the deceased brother of Lacritus) and Apollodorus, 3,000 silver drachmae, "from Athens to Mende or Scione [towns on the westernmost of the three peninsulas south-east of the modern Salonika] and thence to Bosphorus [the Bosphoran or Pontic kingdom, centred at Panticapaeum in the Kertch peninsula at the eastern end of the Crimea] or, if they prefer, along the left-hand coast [of the Black Sea] as far as the Borysthenes [the Dnieper], and back again to Athens." The rate of interest was to be 22½ per cent. ("225 per 1,000"), to be increased to 30 per cent if the borrowers sailed back out of the Black Sea "after [the rising of] Arcturus," about September 19 – shortly before the autumn equinox, when stormy weather might be expected to begin. The security was to be 3,000 casks of Mendaean wine, to be conveyed "from Mende or Scione in the *eikosoros* owned by Hyblesius." (An *eikosoros* is, literally, a twenty-oared ship; but this would have been primarily a sailing-vessel, like all Greek merchantmen.)[17] There is then a declaration by the borrowers that they have not already charged the goods with payment of a debt to anyone else and will not do so in the future. They undertake "to bring back to Athens in the same ship all the goods they take on board from the Pontus [the Black Sea]. If the goods are brought safely to Athens, the borrowers will pay to the lenders the money due under this contract within twenty days after their arrival, in full except for such jettison as those sailing in the ship may have made by common agreement and anything they may pay to enemies [see below]; but no other deduction is to be allowed." The borrowers must hand over the entire security on arrival at Athens until they have paid their debt: "if they fail to pay within the stipulated time, the lenders, jointly or severally, may pledge or sell the security for whatever it will fetch; and if there is any deficiency the lenders may levy the amount by execution against Artemon and Apollodorus and against all their property, on land and sea, wherever it may be, just as if a judgement had been obtained against them and they had failed to satisfy it." (There is no specific penalty clause, which must often have appeared in such contracts.)[18] There follows a clause which is not entirely clear, but which seems to say that if the borrowers do not enter the Black Sea [presumably because of adverse winds] they are to remain in the Hellespont (the Dardanelles) "for ten days after [the rising of] the Dog Star" (in late July when bad weather could be expected), before returning to Athens, "disembarking their cargo in some place where the Athenians have no right of reprisal" – and where ships trading from Athens should therefore be in no danger of seizure. The document then states that if the ship meets with some irretrievable disaster and anything is saved, whatever is recovered is to be the joint property of the lenders; and there is a final provision to the effect that "in regard to these matters nothing is to have greater validity than this contract." Three witnesses are named, also the person (an Athenian citizen) with whom the document was to be deposited.

[17] See my *op. cit.* (in n. 13 above), 394 n. 6; Casson, *op. cit.* (in n. 7 above), 169 and n. 5.
[18] *e.g.* Ps.-Dem. 34.26, 33; 56.20, 27, 38, 44–45.

The amount of the loan, 3,000 drachmae or half a talent, was a very usual one, as far as one can judge from the limited evidence available; and the rates of interest were probably also not unusual for these maritime loans.[19] (There was no legal limit on the rate of interest which could be charged at Athens: Lys. 10.18.) I must emphasise here that the two rates of interest are not to be taken, as they would be today, to refer to percentages per annum, but are for the actual period of the loan, the duration of the voyage, however short it might be. If the whole affair went off quickly, in a few weeks, the borrowers would be paying interest at a rate which we should consider – thinking, as we do, always in terms of an *annual* rate – to be far above 100 per cent.[20]

I need not go in detail into the things which then happened, or are said by the speaker of Ps.-Dem. 35 to have happened. Apollodorus (one of the original borrowers) obtained another loan of 1,100 drachmae from a man of Halicarnassus named Aratus, doubtless at respondentia, which Aratus testified he would never have made had he known the goods were already hypothecated (paras. 22–23); and the shipowner Hyblesius is also said to have borrowed an unnamed sum at bottomry from Antipater of Citium in Cyprus, upon security of the ship and the freight it was earning (paras. 32–33). The plaintiff Androcles alleged that the borrowers shipped no more than 450 casks of wine instead of 3,000, and this was confirmed by the evidence of the helmsman of the ship and of the supercargo acting for the lenders (paras. 19–20, 34). The borrowers are also accused of taking practically no return cargo on board, and finally of claiming that the ship had been wrecked on the Crimean coast (paras. 28–32). The interesting provision about deductions for jettison or payments to enemies will be discussed in Part 4 below.

More entertaining, if less instructive, is a speech composed by Demosthenes himself for his relative Demon and delivered in another mercantile suit in an Athenian court about the same time as the one against Lacritus: this is Dem. 32, *Against Zenothemis*.[21] Demon had lent money at respondentia (the amount and rate of interest are not stated) to Protus, a corn-merchant, who was going to buy corn in Sicily and bring it to Athens. Protus sailed to Syracuse and back in a ship belonging to Hegestratus. We have only Demon's story, which (like any other ancient forensic speech) may contain any amount of fiction; but we have no way of reconstructing the other side's case, and I am going to assume, for convenience, that Demon's account is true. There was another merchant travelling on

---

[19] For capital sums advanced, see n. 12 above. Our other examples of interest-rates are Dem. 34.23 (30 per cent for a similar double journey); Xen., *De Vect*. 3.9 ("almost 20 per cent, just like *nautikon*"). The $12\frac{1}{2}$ per cent in Ps.-Dem. 50.17 is a special case: see below.

[20] The Greeks and Romans usually calculated their interest by the month ("1 per cent interest" in an ordinary Greek or Roman transaction would mean 1 per cent per month unless the contrary was stated). *Cf*. Part 3 below.

[21] Although the speech has been rejected as a rhetorical exercise by some, I see no reason at all to distrust its genuineness.

Hegestratus' ship, namely the wicked Zenothemis, Demon's opponent in the action. While in the port of Syracuse, Hegestratus and Zenothemis concocted a most ingenious swindle. Each of them separately borrowed money on the cargo of corn which really belonged to Protus, and which they themselves therefore had no right in at all. Having got their money, Hegestratus and Zenothemis sent it off to Massalia (Marseilles), their home town, and embarked for Athens. They waited until they were two or three days out from land, and then, in the dead of night, they tried to scuttle the ship, having prepared the ship's boat for their getaway. While Zenothemis remained on deck with the other passangers, Hegestratus went down into the hold and began to cut a hole in the bottom of the ship. He bungled the job, however, making so much noise that before he had finished the passengers heard him and came down to investigate. Hegestratus was caught in the act, and to escape the righteous indignation of the passengers he had callously planned to drown he tried to escape into the boat which he and Zenothemis had got ready; but in the darkness he missed it and was drowned. Zenothemis, whose complicity was not yet suspected, tried to induce the other passengers and the crew to abandon ship and take to the boat, on the ground that the ship was already beginning to sink; but Demon's supercargo, who was travelling with Protus' corn (the precaution was apparently quite usual then, as in more modern times), promised the sailors a large reward if they succeeded in bringing the ship safely into harbour – as they eventually did, coming into port at Cephallenia. From there Zenothemis tried to take the ship back to Sicily, but the case came before the courts and an order was made for the completion of the journey to Athens. After this the story becomes very complicated. Zenothemis pretended that *he* had lent money at respondentia to the deceased Hegestratus, on security of the corn which really belonged to Protus but which he represented as the property of Hegestratus; and Demon was obliged to take possession of Protus' corn by force, to save it from Zenothemis, thereby exposing himself to a legal action by Zenothemis. To make matters worse, Protus, a vital witness, went over to the other side and gave evidence for Zenothemis. Demon says that this was because the price of corn at Athens had fallen after the ship had arrived there (para. 25; *cf.* 56.9), so that Protus could see no profit for himself and he decided to settle for a bribe from Zenothemis. The speech breaks off suddenly.

Quite apart from any weaknesses we may believe ourselves able to detect in Demon's case, we must not conclude from this speech and the others I am describing here that commercial morality was at an exceptionally low level in fourth-century Greece. As it happens, all the speeches we possess dealing at length with maritime loans were written for lenders, so naturally we tend to form a rosy picture of them and to see the merchants and shipowners who do the borrowing as crooks. But litigants could boast of having traded and lent money for many years at Athens, without ever having had to come before the courts (see Ps.-Dem. 34.1); and the very fact that bottomry and respondentia contracts were evidently so common is itself a testimony to the general reliability of the merchants operating from Athens – for once the money had been handed over and the ship had sailed away, what was to prevent a dishonest merchant or shipowner from sailing off to a distant port and never returning at all? In a disunited world consisting of very many independent states, the lender in such a transaction had no certainly effective remedy against a fraudulent borrower. We must not assume that the sharp practices and frauds revealed (or asserted) by these speeches were frequent: it is the exceptional case which comes before the courts, at any time.

It is worth recalling that the reception of bottomry loans with fraudulent intent was once common enough in England to require statutory intervention. Part of an Act of Parliament passed in 1670 (22 & 23 Car. II, c. xi, s.12) reads as follows:[22]

> Whereas it often happeneth that Masters and Mariners of Ships having ensured or taken upon Bottomary [*sic*] greater Sums of Money than the Value of their Adventure, do wilfully cast away, burn or otherwise destroy the Ships under their Charge, to the Merchants and Owners great Loss; (2) for the Prevention thereof for the future, Be it enacted . . . That if any Captain, Master, Mariner, or other Officer belonging to any Ship shall wilfully cast away, burn, or otherwise destroy the Ship unto which he belongeth, or procure the same to be done, he shall suffer Death as a Felon.

The third and last of the bottomry speeches I am discussing in some detail is the one *Against Dionysodorus*, Ps.-Dem. 56.[23] The action in which this speech was delivered arose out of a bottomry contract in which Darius and Pamphilus, both metics (resident aliens) at Athens, lent Dionysodorus and his partner Parmeniscus 3,000 drachmae on security of their ship for a voyage to Egypt and back to Athens,[24] carrying corn. The rate of interest is not stated. The bottomry contract had been deposited with a banker – probably quite a usual precaution (para. 15; *cf*. 34.6). Now this speech, delivered in 323 B.C. or a year or two earlier, has a particularly interesting background: the time of serious grain shortage all over the eastern Mediterranean in 330 and the years following, which was aggravated by the activities of Cleomenes of Naucratis,[25] whom Alexander the Great had put in an administrative position in Egypt in 331 and who soon

---

[22] Later Statutes contain similar provisions, though without specific reference to bottomry: 1701, 1 Ann., c. ix, s. 4; 1717, 4 Geo. I, c. xii, s. 3 (with a reference to insurance); 1724, 11 Geo. I, c. 29, ss. 5–7.

[23] There is a useful annotated edition by Paley and Sandys, *op. cit.* (in n. 16 above), I, 3rd ed., 246–284.

[24] The technical term used here (para. 6) and elsewhere for the double voyage is *amphoteroplous*; a single voyage is *heteroplous*; but see Paoli, *op. cit.* (in n. 1 above), 25–29 (esp. 25 n. 2), 64–68.

[25] The main sources are paras. 7–8 of this speech and Ps.-Arist., *Oecon.* II.ii.33a, 1352ª16–23 (*cf*. 33e, 1352ᵇ14–20): see B. A. van Groningen, *Aristote. Le second livre de l'Économique*, Leiden, 1933, 183–185, 190–192. All available information about Cleomenes is given by H. Berve, *Das Alexanderreich*, II, Munich, 1926, 210–211, no. 431.

became satrap of that province, remaining in that position until he was executed by the first Ptolemy after Alexander's death, in 323/322. Cleomenes apparently established a personal monopoly of the export of corn from Egypt, making a gigantic profit for himself – it was the most famous and successful monopoly we ever hear of before the Hellenistic period that begins with the death of Alexander. Darius, the speaker in our case, accuses Dionysodorus and Parmeniscus of being the creatures of Cleomenes and of acting in collusion with him (para. 7): of course this may be quite false. After receiving the 3,000 drachmae, Parmeniscus sailed off to Egypt, while Dionysodorus remained behind at Athens, where famine prices prevailed. But before long a corn-fleet arrived from Sicily[26] and the price of corn at Athens fell sharply (para. 9). Dionysodorus decided to warn Parmeniscus not to bring his cargo back to Athens, as he was bound to do under the bottomry contract – and indeed, quite independently, under an Athenian law forbidding anyone living at Athens[27] to carry corn anywhere else than to Athens. So Dionysodorus sent a messenger to Rhodes, "knowing for certain that the ship [of Parmeniscus] would have to put in at Rhodes" on its way back.[28]

Parmeniscus discharged his cargo at Rhodes, where he evidently got a better price than he would have done at Athens, and he used the time he had saved to make an additional journey to Egypt and back. For a second year, the speaker complains (para. 16, *cf.* 30), he went on trading between Egypt and Rhodes, leaving the lenders to whistle for their money. Darius is much concerned lest the court should think that he and his partner have been parties to the breach of another stringent Athenian law, forbidding anyone living at Athens to lend money on a ship carrying corn (or certain other goods) to any other place (para. 5–6, 13–14);[29] and they are seeking to enforce a penalty clause in the bottomry bond, according to which the borrowers have to pay double if they fail to fulfil their part of the bargain strictly (para. 20, 27, 38, 44–45) – apparently another standard clause (see above and n. 18).

I need not spend much time on the other maritime loans which we hear of in the fourth-century sources. One that requires more than a passing mention is referred to in the speech *Against Phormio*, Ps.-Dem. 34, dating from about the mid-320s.[30] The unnamed speaker and his partner, an Athenian metic, had lent 2,000 drachmae at 30 per cent. (para. 6, 23) to

---

[26] On this passage and the Sicilian–Athenian corn trade in general, see my *op. cit.* (in n. 13 above), 217–218.

[27] The best form of this law is that in Ps.-Dem. 34.37; *cf.* 35.50 and Lyc. *c. Leocr.* 27. Ps.-Dem. 58.8–13 may record a prosecution under this law.

[28] The reasons for this are well explained by L. Casson, "The Isis and her Voyage," *Trans. Amer. Philol. Assoc.*, 81 (1950), 43–56. I would add that there is an account of a winter voyage from Alexandria to Athens in the mid-fourth century C.E., interrupted by a storm from which the ship eventually found refuge at Rhodes, in Greg. Naz., *Orat.* 18.31 (Migne, *Patrol. Graeca* xxxv. 1024–1025); *De vita sua* 124–211 (*Ibid.* xxxvii. 1038–1044; *cf.* xxxv. 166–167).

[29] The best form of the law is that in Ps.-Dem. 35.51, *cf.* 50.

[30] There is a useful annotated edition in Paley and Sandys, *op. cit.* (in n. 16 above), I, 3rd ed., 1–51.

Phormio, a merchant who was probably also a metic,[31] for a voyage to the Pontic kingdom in the Crimea and back, upon security of a cargo to the value of 4,000 drachmae which Phormio undertook to put on board. (It seems to have been a regular practice to demand security to the value of twice the amount of the loan.)[32] The speaker claims that Phormio, being unable to sell his goods in the Crimea (the Pontic dynast Paerisades being at war with the native Scythians, para. 8), failed to re-embark for the return journey to Athens, on which the ship was wrecked. The speech, although for various reasons one of the most important documents we have for Athenian economic history, is rather a mess, so that the facts of the case are very obscure, and as usual we cannot tell how much truth there is in the speaker's allegations. But, unless he is lying wholesale, it looks as if Phormio first claimed the benefit of the clause excusing him from repayment if the ship did not return safely to Athens (paras. 33–35: the plea was obviously absurd if, as the speaker alleges, Phormio had never placed a return cargo on board), but later changed his ground and declared that he had repaid the money to the shipowner Lampis in the Crimea (paras. 5, 9, 11–15, 22 *et seq.*). The plaintiff also alleges that Phormio had borrowed an additional 4,500 drachmae from Theodore, a Phoenician, and another 1,000 drachmae from Lampis the shipowner (paras. 6–7), doubtless in each case at respondentia on security of the outgoing cargo, which according to the speaker was of far less value than demanded by the conditions of Phormio's various contracts of loan.[33]

One text, Ps.-Dem. 50.17, dealing with the autumn of the year 361,[34] records two transactions one of which at least was a bottomry loan. Apollodorus, the elder son of Pasion the banker (now deceased), found it necessary, while acting as trierarch (the captain of a warship), to borrow money to pay his crew. He had already mortgaged some land before leaving Athens (para. 13), and when at Sestus in the Hellespont he borrowed twice more. One loan, from his fellow-citizen Archedemus, is merely said to be of 1,500 drachmae "at interest" (*epitokon* – if this is the right reading), and there is no good reason to regard it as a bottomry loan: we are not told what the security was, and for such a small loan to a very rich man no security may have been thought necessary. We might have been tempted to think that the other loan, on security of Apollodorus' trireme, was not a genuine bottomry transaction either, since there is no other evidence to suggest that such loans were secured on any except merchant ships. In this case, however, the second loan, of only 800 (or 700) drach-

---

[31] Not the man, originally a slave of Pasion, who rose to become a wealthy Athenian citizen – incidentally the only man we hear of in Classical Athens who is known (see Ps.-Dem. 45.64) to have owned more than one ship. See on him Davies, *op. cit.* (in n. 11 above), 431–432, 435–437.

[32] *Cf.* Ps-Dem. 34.7; 35.18, with 8 and 10.

[33] See above, and n. 32. I believe that the text at the beginning of para. 7 may be faulty, and (with Reiske) that the speaker perhaps referred to "150" and not "115" minae (15,000, not 11,500 dr.); *cf.* Paley and Sandys, *ad loc.*

[34] See para. 4, with 12, 14, 19–20.

mae, made by Nicippus the shipowner, is expressly said to have been "at maritime interest, 12½ per cent" (*nautikon . . . epogdoön*), repayment to be conditional upon the safe return of the ship to Athens. (The ship was to go on convoy duty to the Bosphorus and back eventually to Athens.) This, therefore, must certainly be treated as a bottomry loan, even though the ship was a trireme and the rate of interest was far lower than for any other maritime loan we know about at this period. No doubt it was thought that when Athens had complete command of the sea an Athenian trireme ran less risk of loss than a merchantman.

The remaining examples of maritime loans from fourth-century Athens can be dealt with briefly. In Ps.-Dem. 52.20 we hear of a loan of 4,000 drachmae made during the 370s,[35] for a voyage probably to the Phoenician town of Ake (Acre),[36] to two Athenian citizens, Megacleides and Thrasyllus, by Lycon of Heraclea, a customer of Pasion's bank (para. 3), who shortly afterwards was attacked and fatally wounded by pirates (paras. 5, 10). In the litigation which he undertook against his fraudulent guardians in 363, Demosthenes listed the assets which, he claimed, had formed part of his father's estate at his death in 376/375,[37] and among these is one item of 7,000 drachmae for which Demosthenes uses the technical expression, *nautika . . . ekdosis*,[38] and which must therefore represent either a single bottomry loan or a series of such loans, made either to the individual who is named, Xuthus, or through his services as an intermediary.[39] In a speech of Isocrates relating to the 390s the speaker claims to have lent a large sum of money on a merchant ship (17.42): this was presumably a bottomry loan. Xenophon (*De Vect.* 3.9) speaks of a high rate of interest as "almost 20 per cent. just like that on a nautical loan" (*hōsper nautikon*), clearly bottomry. Hypereides in 322 accuses Demosthenes of having converted to his own use the money furnished by the Persian king, intended to help Thebes: he says that Demosthenes dispensed this money to his own advantage in maritime commerce and loans,[40] as well as buying a house. Current gossip also reported that Zeno, the founder of Stoicism and a Cypriote, had a large fortune when he came to Greece in the late fourth century, of "more than 1,000 talents," invested in maritime loans (Diog. Laert. 7.13).

[35] Pasion died in 370/369 (Ps.-Dem. 46.13), Lycon several years earlier (Ps.-Dem. 52.3–5, with 5–7, 8–15, etc.).
[36] The MSS. read "to Thrace," but I accept the reading suggested by Henri de Valois (on the strength of an entry in Harpocration) and printed in *e.g.* the Oxford text.
[37] For this date, and the preceding one, see Davies, *op. cit.* (in n. 11 above), 123 *et seq.*
[38] Dem. 27.11; *cf.* 29.35–36.
[39] *Cf.* on this R. Bogaert, "Banquiers, courtiers et prêts maritimes à Athènes et à Alexandrie," in *Chron. d'Égypte*, 40 (1965), 140–156, at pp. 141–144, esp. 141 n. 4. I agree with him (against many other scholars) that there is no reason to see Xuthus as a banker, and that we have no good evidence (see below, on Ps.-Dem. 33.5–8) of a banker making a maritime loan, although the contracts for such loans were evidently often deposited with a banker for safe custody, as in Ps.-Dem. 34.6, and surely 56.15.
[40] Hyper. V (*c. Dem.*), col. 17. Among several restorations, the best seems to me that of G. Colin (in the Budé edition, 1946): [ἐξ ὧν ναυ]τικοῖς ἐργαζη χ[ρήμα]σιν καὶ ἐκδόσεις δί[δως]. The accusation is mentioned also in Plut., *Comp. Dem. et Cic.* 3.6.

I think it is quite possible that a small fragment of the orator Isaeus, from a speech *Against Calliphon*,[41] has to do with a bottomry loan, since it refers to interest at 33⅓ per cent. And Ps.-Dem. 33.6 presumably refers to a bottomry bond for 4,000 drachmae previously given by Apaturius on security of his ship – although, as I shall explain in a moment, I believe that the loan subsequently made to Apaturius by the speaker, which is always treated as bottomry, was really something quite different.

Those are the only passages I know from the fifth–fourth centuries which certainly or probably refer to transactions in the nature of bottomry or respondentia. At least three other texts are sometimes quoted, but in my opinion there is not even a probability that they refer to bottomry transactions, although of course one or two may do so. First we may take the thirty-third oration in the Demosthenic corpus, *Against Apaturius*, another of the *dikai emporikai* mentioned earlier, and cited in the preceding paragraph. The speech first reveals that the shipowner Apaturius of Byzantium, who had sailed to Athens, had defaulted on a debt of 4,000 drachmae, the payment of which to his creditors was secured on his ship, now in the Peiraeus (paras. 5–6). As we saw in the last paragraph, that transaction is likely to have involved a bottomry bond. To enable Apaturius to satisfy his creditors and save his ship from seizure, the speaker procured a loan of 3,000 drachmae to Apaturius from the banker Heracleides (who shortly afterwards became insolvent, para. 9), for which he stood surety, and himself made a further loan to him of 1,000 drachmae. For all this Apaturius gave security by a form of charge which we often meet with in connection with Athenian landed property: a sale (of the ship and of some slaves) with an option of redemption on payment of the debt in full (paras. 6–8). This is commonly taken to have been a bottomry bond; but this seems to me impossible, for the ship was not about to sail out on a voyage (see paras. 9–11), and the form of transaction, a sale with option of redemption (*ōnē* or *prasis epi lysei*, para. 8), is unknown, as far as I am aware, in bottomry transactions. Nor is there any compelling reason to suppose that a passage in Aristotle's *Rhetoric* (III.10, 1411ᵃ 15–18) is referring to bottomry when it quotes a speech by Moerocles about a man who "played the rogue at 33⅓ per cent, he himself only at 10 per cent," for there was nothing intrinsically disgraceful about the making of maritime loans, the high rate of interest being justified by the exceptional risk, and it is hard to see what opportunities a *lender* in such cases can have had for "playing the rogue," a role which could much more easily be filled by a defaulting *borrower*. And finally, the merchant captain who arrives from Byzantium, in a play by Diphilus,[42] is surely speaking of a profit of "10 or 12 per cent" which he has made out of his own trading activity, rather than of a maritime loan, as supposed by Böckh and others.[43]

[41] Isae., fr., 79 Sauppe, *ap.* Harp., *s.v. epitritais*, etc.
[42] Diphilus, fr. 43.18–22, *ap.* Athen. VII. 292b.
[43] Böckh, *top. ci.* (in n. 1 above), I, 3rd ed., 170–171.

3. THE HELLENISTIC AND ROMAN PERIODS

No one will wish to deny that maritime loans continued throughout the Hellenistic period (roughly the last three centuries B.C. in the eastern Mediterranean world), although as it happens there is very little evidence. The very fact that a law giving relief to debtors, passed at Ephesus in 85 B.C.,[44] can speak casually of "lenders of money by way of maritime loans," at the head of a long list of different forms of debt, is sufficient to show that these transactions remained very familiar. By the mid-second century B.C. at the latest they were being employed by Romans, for a much-discussed passage in Plutarch's *Life* of that quintessentially Roman figure, Cato the Elder (who died in 146 B.C.),[45] speaks of Cato – a man who could say in public that moneylending was dishonourable, and that the usurer was worse than the thief[46] – as taking a cautious share in the granting of maritime loans, through his freedman Quintio, who went on the voyages as supercargo.

Only a single Hellenistic papyrus has so far been discovered which could possibly be taken to record a maritime loan: a fragmentary Berlin papyrus, probably of the first half of the second century B.C., published with an excellent commentary by Wilcken in 1925.[47] This records a loan granted by a certain Archippus to a group of five sea-traders for a voyage to Somaliland and back, undoubtedly in connection with the spice-trade, which was a royal monopoly of the Ptolemies (as Wilcken explains in the last paragraph of his article). The five borrowers include a Spartan and a man from Massalia; the ethnics of the other three have not survived. The transaction seems to have been arranged through an intermediary, Gnaeus (a name of Roman or Italian origin), perhaps a kind of broker. Five guarantors were provided: a man from Thessalonica (Salonika), another from Elea in south Italy, a third from Massalia called Cintus (probably a known Celtic name rather than a derivation of "Quintus"), a fourth who was a Carthaginian, with the completely Greek name "Demetrius, son of Apollonius" (an interesting indication of Hellenistic influence at Carthage), and finally another Cintus whose ethnic has perished. The five borrowers and their five guarantors, none of them men of local origin, are a fascinating collection – "eine recht internationale Gesellschaft," as Wilcken put it. All except the Carthaginian were apparently serving in some military capacity under the Ptolemies. This document, in so far as it is preserved, is very different in some important respects from the earlier ones from Athens which we have noticed above: it has none of the standard technical terms

---

[44] *SIG.* 3rd ed., 742, lines 50–51.
[45] Plut., *Cato Maj.* 21.6–7. Interpretation is not simple. See Rougé, *op. cit.* (in n. 1 above), 355, 357–358, 426–428.
[46] See Cato, *De agri cult., Praef.* 1, 3. For his opinion of merchants, see *Praef.* 2.
[47] U. Wilcken, "Punt-Fahrten in der Ptolemäerzeit," in *Ztschr. für ägyptische Sprache,* 60 (1925), 86–102; the text (p. 90), which is *P. Berl.* 5883 and 5853, has been reprinted in *SB* III (1926), 7169, and by Ziebarth, *op. cit.* (in n. 4 above), 126–127 (no. 24), cf. 54–55. For recent bibliography see Bogaert, *op. cit.* (in n. 39 above), 147 n. 1.

used in connection with nautical loans (*nautika*, etc.); and it is even doubtful, both whether ship or goods were given as security in addition to the
backing of the five guarantors, and whether the clause I have been treating
as an essential one in maritime loans, namely that the ship or the goods are
at the risk of the lenders, was actually present in this case – although the
latter may have appeared, *e.g.* in the lacuna in lines 13–14.[48] Wilcken even
believed that the loan was free of interest; but this need not be right, and in
any event some form of profit-sharing may have been substituted for
interest, as Wilcken supposed. The document as a whole raises problems
too complicated to discuss here, and I will only say that in my opinion the
best explanation has been produced by Bogaert, in an article published in
1965[49] which takes account of the peculiarities of the economic system of
Ptolemaic Egypt. I should add that the absence of other papyri recording
bottomry transactions is not as surprising as it may sound, when we remember that virtually all our papyri come from Upper Egypt and the Fayum,
whereas the great majority of maritime loans would have been entered into
at Alexandria.

Only one papyrus referring to a maritime loan survives from the Roman
period: this is a Vienna papyrus, dated in the reign of the Emperor
Antoninus Pius (A.D. 138–61), first published in full by Lionel Casson in
1956.[50] This is not the document embodying the bottomry contract itself
but merely a statement by the person through whose bank the money was
made available by the lenders to the borrowers that the balance of the loan
is now at their disposal. If the document has been correctly restored in all
essentials, as seems very probable, it refers specifically to a maritime loan
(*daneion nautikon*) and the transaction is doubtless bottomry: certainly the
ship with its equipment and the freight earned by its latest cargo are
hypothecated to the lenders. In this case, all four borrowers come from
Ascalon in Palestine.

There are scattered references to maritime loans in the sources for the
Roman Principate and Later Empire (covering the first few centuries of the
Christian era), as when Philostratus makes Apollonius of Tyana deride
"the evil-omened tribe of merchants and shipowners" who sail around
from one market to another, paying "unholy rates of interest" (*anosioi
tokoi*) and not scrupling to sink and abandon their ships when they see no
profit for themselves in a voyage: they are evidently conceived as having
incurred maritime loans which they will be able to repudiate if the ship is
lost (*Vita Apollon.* 4.32). Even the Fathers of the Church speak of maritime
loans now and again as something that would be familiar to their audience.[51]

---

[48] *Cf.* Bogaert, *op. cit.*, 150–151, esp. 150 n. 2.
[49] *Op. cit.*, 148–154.
[50] *P. Gr. Vindob.* 19792 (an inventory number). See L. Casson, "New Light on Maritime
Loans," *Symbolae Raphaeli Taubenschlag dedicatae = Eos* 48 (1956), 89–93 (text
and Eng. trans., pp. 90–91); reprinted as *SB* VI (1963), 9571; *cf.* Rougé, *op. cit.* (in
n. 1 above), 348–349 (with text, n. 4); Bogaert, *op. cit.*, 154–156.
[51] *e.g.* Gregory of Nyssa, *Contra usurarios* 29–30, in Migne, *Patrol. Graeca* XLVI. 441
(*nautikon daneisma*).

Above all, the legal sources have some very interesting passages: there are titles, *De nautico fenore* (*faenore*), both in Justinian's *Digest* (XXII. ii) and in his *Codex* (IV. xxxiii), and there is one particularly valuable Novel of Justinian (CVI, of 540) which we shall look at presently. Another text in the *Digest* (XLV. i. 122.1) probably refers to a maritime loan in our sense, for a journey from Beirut to Brindisi and back, if only a hypothetical one.[52]

An outstanding feature of maritime loans in the Roman world is that they were regularly excluded from the laws passed again and again by the Roman government with the aim of limiting the rate of interest on loans. We saw earlier that no legal limit on the rate of interest for ordinary loans existed at Athens; but any Greek city might legislate on the subject, especially when a debt crisis developed; and in Egypt the Ptolemies, in the early third century B.C., prescribed a maximum rate of 24 per cent. per annum, by a royal decree which long remained valid. The situation at Rome is very obscure.[53] Attempts were made at various times, from the early Republic onwards, to place general or special limits upon interest rates, but seldom, it appears, with much effect. In the Roman empire the situation varied greatly between different areas, [54]but it is probably true to say that, broadly speaking, *usurae legitimae* at 12 per cent. per annum (1 per cent. per month) constituted a theoretical maximum. Maritime loans, however, were a special case: what was probably always the rule governing them is best expressed in the legal compilation dating from about A.D. 300 which is known as the *Sententiae* of Paulus (II. xiv. 3): "Money lent on maritime loans can bear interest at any rate because it is at the risk of the lender as long as the voyage lasts." The technical term used in this passage for these transactions is the most common one: *traiecticia pecunia*, which normally (though not quite invariably)[55] means a maritime loan at the risk of the creditor.

In 528 the Emperor Justinian made a general ruling on interest rates: apart from certain exalted personages (*illustres*, etc)., who were limited to 4 per cent., the maximum rates (per annum) that could be charged in future were to be 12 per cent. for maritime loans (*traiecticii contractus*), 8 per cent. for business loans, and 6 per cent. for others (*Cod. Just*. IV. xxxii. 26.2). The edict admits that earlier laws had allowed higher rates than 12 per cent.

---

[52] I am not as worried as some are by the fact that *fenus nauticum* and *mutuum*, two different kinds of loan, are combined in the opening sentence ("mutuam pecuniam nauticam"), for this happens elsewhere, *e.g.* in *Dig*. XXII.ii.6 ("faenerator pecuniam usuris maritimis mutuam dando . . .") and *Cod. Just*. IV. xxxiii.5 ("traiecticiae quidem pecuniae quae periculo creditoris mutuo datur"). The fact that the loss of the ship ("submersa nave") is material and could even be considered as a possible ground for release of the debtor from liability surely means that the transaction is basically *fenus nauticum*. But the text in its present state is unsatisfactory, and the emendation suggested by Mommsen in his standard edition, although an improvement, is far from certain.

[53] See *e.g.* Klingmüller, *op. cit.* (in n. 1 above), esp. 2196–2205; Billeter, *op. cit.* (in n. 1 above), esp. 169 *et seq.*, 269 *et seq.*; and, for an account much more easily intelligible by the "general reader," J. A. Crook, *Law and Life of Rome*, London, 1967, 211–213.

[54] See *e.g. Dig*. XIII. iv. 3; XVII. i. 10.3; XXII. i.1.pr.; XXVI. vii. 7.10; XXX.39.1; XXXIII.i. 21.pr.

[55] See *Cod. Just*. IV. xxxiii. 5; *Dig*. XXII. ii. 4.pr.

for maritime loans but is insistent that this is henceforth to be the maximum. And I think it is quite possible that the interest on these loans here, for once, is conceived as 12 per cent. *per annum*, in our sense, and not for the duration of the voyage, whatever it might be (nearly always less than a year). I am of course using modern terminology to express the Latin rates: the edict in fact speaks of *illustres* as being limited to "the third part of a hundredth," which (as everyone would know) would mean one-third of 1 per cent. *per month*; business loans could go up to "two-thirds of a hundredth" (per month, again), and other loans up to "half a hundredth" (per month) – and so when maritime loans are limited to "a hundredth," it may well mean 1 per cent. *per month*, or what we should call 12 per cent. Twelve years later, after receiving a petition from two men who made a practice of lending at bottomry, the emperor ordered a conference of shippers to take place, with the Praetorian Prefect in the chair, to ascertain what the traditional practice was and declare it on oath. The decision was that practice varied widely: sometimes interest was charged at $12\frac{1}{2}$ per cent. ("the eighth part"), not for any fixed period but as a flat rate for the whole duration of the voyage, not being more than a year; and sometimes the rate was 10 per cent. and in addition the lender was entitled to demand that the borrower carry one *modius* of wheat or barley for each gold piece (*solidus*) of the loan, free of charge and of duty. Justinian accepted this and made it the law (*Nov. Just.* CVI); but a few months later, in 541 (*Nov. Just.* CX), he repealed this enactment and returned to the rule laid down in 528. (Justinian was rather given to such sudden changes of mind. In another law issued in 541, *Nov. Just.* CXI, he begins with a preamble explaining that "what medicine does for diseases, laws do in business matters: the effect may be the opposite of what is intended, and experience may prove what was thought efficacious to be useless.") It looks as if the main effect of reimposing the 12 per cent. maximum may have been to deter lending of this kind.[56]

It must always have been understood, of course, as in the earlier period, that if a borrower broke the terms of his contract, for instance by not keeping to the specified voyage (*cf. Cod. Just.* IV xxxiii. 4), he would not escape liability for repayment.

[56] See Jones, *Later Roman Emp.* (n. 3 above), II, 869. It is convenient to mention here a few more possible (but not certain) late examples of maritime loans. For Synesius, *Epist.* 129 (*c.* A.D. 400), see Rougé, *op. cit.* (in n. 1 above), 352–353; but I very much doubt if this was a maritime loan. Two other possible examples are Agnellus Ravennas, *Liber Pontif. Eccl. Rav.* 18, *De S. Neone* 30 (= *MGH, Res Lang. et Ital., saec.* VI–IX, pp. 293–95), relating to the mid-fifth century; and Greg. I Magn., *Epist.*, IX, 108 (of 599), suggested by Jones, *op. cit.*, III, 291 n. 108, as a possible attempt to evade Justinian's law. Of course the risk in the transport of state supplies had by degrees been largely taken over by the government: see Rougé, *op. cit.*, 359.

4. JETTISON, AND THE "LEX RHODIA"

One other question remains to be dealt with: jettison, and the much-discussed *Lex Rhodia de iactu*.[57] It will be remembered that the respondentia contract in the Lacritus case provided for repayment in full by the borrowers, in the event of safe arrival at Athens, "except for such jettison as those sailing in the ship may have made by common agreement, and anything they may pay to enemies" (Ps.-Dem. 35.11). The wording of the first part of the exception is curiously laconic: it does not specify whether, on repayment of the loan, the borrowers are to be allowed to deduct a proportion equal to the proportion borne by the value of the jettisoned goods to the total value of the goods carried, or whether the amount repayable is simply to be reduced by the value of the jettisoned goods, or whether some other principle is to be applied. Perhaps the first of these alternatives is the most likely; but in any event the use of such a brief expression as "except for jettison" (*plēn ekbolēs*), without any further explanation, shows that generally recognised rules of commercial practice in regard to jettison had already developed.[58]

By at least the third or early second century B.C. there had been a remarkable development of the law of jettison, introducing what has become known in modern times as "general average": the principle that if the goods of several merchants are being carried in one ship, and in time of danger the goods belonging to one or some of the merchants only are jettisoned, then all the merchants concerned have to bear the loss proportionately. We do not know when this principle was first recognised: it may conceivably have been as early as the fourth century B.C., and it can hardly have been later than the third or early second, when Rhodes was the leading maritime power in the eastern Mediterranean,[59] for the Roman lawyers, who also recognised the principle of general average, refer to it under the heading of "the Rhodian law of jettison," *lex Rhodia de iactu*. The title in the *Digest* (XIV. ii) referring to jettison is headed "De lege Rhodia de iactu," and the first section of the title states, "It is provided by the *lex Rhodia* that if merchandise is jettisoned to lighten the ship, the loss incurred for the benefit of all must be relieved by the contribution of all." A little further on (2. pr.) we hear that "It is eminently just that the loss should be shared by those who, because the goods of others have been sacrificed, have secured the safety of their own property." How far the Roman law of jettison was simply taken over from Greek commercial practice, and how

[57] There is a particularly sensible treatment of this difficult subject (otherwise largely a preserve of Roman lawyers) by Rougé, *op. cit.* (in n. 1 above), 397–413. For further bibliography, see Crook, *op. cit.* (in n. 53 above), 325–326 n. 92; A. Berger, *Encyclopedic Dict. of Roman Law* (= *Trans. Amer. Philos. Soc.*, n.s. 43.2, Philadelphia, 1953), 558–559, *s.v.* "Lex Rhodia de iactu."

[58] Aristotle, in the *Nicomachean Ethics* (III.1, 1110^{a}9), can use jettison as a commonplace example in a discussion of voluntary and involuntary actions.

[59] Polyb. 4.47.1 (a passage often mistranslated), relating to *c.* 220 B.C., shows that the Rhodians were then the acknowledged champions (*prostatai*) of those who sailed the sea.

far it is (as some scholars have argued) a parallel development, is a much-disputed question we need not consider here,[60] for the Greek and Roman law of jettison is in itself completely independent of their law relating to maritime loans: the two were related only in so far as jettisoned cargo happened to be security for a maritime loan at respondentia. Certainly, the name "lex Rhodia" for the law (or some of the law) relating to jettison and general average long continued in use, for we find it in a curious Byzantine compilation of the eighth century calling itself *The Rhodian Sea-Law*,[61] which also contains some confused regulations on the subject of maritime loans.

5. THE MIDDLE AGES

Maritime loans continued in existence well into the Byzantine period and are dealt with in the *Basilica* (LIII v), the codification of Byzantine law ordered by the Emperor Basil I (867–886) and completed and issued towards the end of the ninth century by his son Leo VI ("the Wise," 886–912). In the West they also continued to exist, and we find them flourishing particularly in the twelfth and thirteenth centuries in the great commercial city of Genoa, where the notarial records contain a remarkably large number and variety of contracts of maritime loan.[62] For a long time this kind of transaction seems to have been regarded as exempt from the Church's prohibition of usury,[63] but the much-discussed decretal *Naviganti* of Pope Gregory IX (1227–1243)[64] declared the sea-loan usurious. How much practical effect the ecclesiastical prohibition had is disputed; but certainly the maritime loan now gave way to other methods of financing trade,[65] such as the *cambium maritimum*, which concealed the lender's profit by providing for repayment in a different currency, the *commenda* and the *societas maris*, which were forms of partnership, and of course, from the second quarter of the fourteenth century onwards, the contract of marine insurance. By about the end of the fourteenth century a prudent merchant like Francesco Datini of Prato was insuring every cargo.[66] The later revival

[60] See the works cited in n. 57 above.
[61] Edited with a long Introduction and Eng. trans. by Ashburner: see n. 1 above; *cf.* the further bibliography in Rougé, *op. cit.* (in n. 1 above), 407 n. 5.
[62] See *e.g.* Calvin W. Hoover, "The Sea Loan in Genoa in the Twelfth Century," *Qly. Jnl. of Economics*, 40 (1925–26), 495–529.
[63] For which see, briefly, G. Le Bras, in *Camb. Econ. Hist. of Europe*, III (1963), 564–570; and in detail J. T. Noonan, *The Scholastic Anal. of Usury*, Camb., Mass., 1957.
[64] *Corpus Iuris Canonici*, II, 2nd ed., ed. E. Friedberg, Leipzig, 1881, col. 816, Decretal V.xix.19. See Noonan, *op. cit.*, 137–138, 139–143, cf. 50; also T. P. McLaughlin, "The Teaching of the Canonists on Usury (XII, XIII and XIV Centuries)", *Mediaeval Stud.*, 1 (1939), at pp. 103–105, 147.
[65] There is a good brief sketch of the various methods of financing trade in the thirteenth century by R. de Roover, in *Camb. Econ. Hist. of Europe*, III (1963), 49–59; *cf.* R. S. Lopez, in *ibid.*, II (1952), 267, 323. For the growth of marine insurance, see R. de Roover, in *ibid.*, III, 99–100; F. Edler de Roover, "Early Examples of Marine Insurance," in *Jnl. of Econ. Hist.*, 5 (1945), 172–200.
[66] See Iris Origo, *The Merchant of Prato*, rev. Penguin [Peregrine] ed., 1963, 138–139.

of bottomry and its decay in modern times are beyond the scope of this essay.[67]

APPENDIX

I do not myself believe that there is as yet any clear evidence earlier than that which I have cited from fifth- and fourth-century Greece for the existence in the western world or the Near East of maritime loans in the sense in which I have been using that expression: loans which the borrower did not have to repay unless the ship or the goods arrived safely at the agreed destination. A. L. Oppenheim, in his article, "The Seafaring Merchants of Ur," *Jnl. of the American Oriental Soc.*, 74 (1954), 6–17, seems to be suggesting (at p. 10) that certain Old Babylonian cuneiform texts were intended to have an effect similar to that of a Greek bottomry contract and that the loan was repayable only if the ship arrived safely, for he takes certain Akkadian phrases in some eight texts of the Old Babylonian period to contain an expression equivalent to the "*sana eunte nave*" of mediaeval contracts of maritime loan, which certainly expressed the principle that the loan was repayable only if the voyage ended safely. But surely the phrases which Oppenheim takes as the equivalent of *sana eunte nave* were intended to have merely temporal and not (as in the mediaeval and the ancient contracts) conditional force: the loan is to be repaid "on the successful completion of the journey." (The actual word "ship" seems not to be used here, although in certain cases a reference to one might perhaps be inferred.) The contracts concerned are all very short, and the many contingencies they do not mention, such as (if I am right) the sinking of the ship, would be covered by the general law of the period. Certainly the *Code of Hammurabi*, para. 103, provides that enemy action is to release the borrower from all liability; but para. 102, dealing with a loan *ana tadmiqtum* (an expression the meaning of which is disputed), says that the borrower who "suffers a loss" must nevertheless restore the full amount advanced. For a commentary on paras. 101–103 of the *Code*, see G. R. Driver and J. C. Miles, *The Babylonian Laws* [I]. *Legal Commentary*, Oxford, 1952, 190–194, esp. 192 n. 2, which seems to me to put the matter very well. The "Hammurabi Code" is available in English in various translations: see esp. *ibid.*, II, 1955, *Text and Translation*; and J. B. Pritchard, *Ancient Near Eastern Texts Relating to the Old Testament*, 3rd ed., Princeton, 1969, 163 *et seq.* The question can be left open. But trade by land and by river-boat played a much more important part in the economy of most Mesopotamian towns than trade by sea; and I would require more definite evidence before accepting the existence of bottomry loans in the Old Babylonian period, especially as there seems to be no later evidence of any such institution in the Mesopotamian world.

[67] I am delighted to have this opportunity of paying a grateful tribute to Professor Baxter, who was mainly responsible for stimulating my interest in ancient accounting and commercial practices when I was an Assistant Lecturer in Ancient Economic History at the London School of Economics in 1950–1953.

of boundary and ideology in modern times are beyond the scope of this essay.

RATIO ANALYSIS AND THE PREDICTION OF COMPANY FAILURE

Susan Dev

THIS essay[1] is a survey of the use of ratio analysis in assessing the short- and longer-term solvency prospects of companies, with special reference to (a) its early use (from about 1870) as discussed in the literature in the United States of America[2] and (b) empirical work on the ratio characteristics of what can broadly be classified as failed companies.[3]

THE ORIGINS OF THE USE OF RATIO ANALYSIS IN ASSESSING SOLVENCY

In the 1870s short-term unsecured loans were granted by United States bankers to enable their creditworthy customers to take advantage of the large cash discounts being offered by wholesalers as a consequence of the economic problems arising out of the Civil War.[4] The intention was that the loans should be repaid out of the proceeds of sale of the goods concerned. In support of applications, potential borrowers were required to supply current statements of their assets and liabilities and such other information as the banker required "as a means of enabling the banker to pass intelligently upon loan applications,"[5] the object being that "credit extended to the merchant must be predicated upon his solvency."[6] With the growth of the credit system, by the 1890s requests for financial statements in the United States became "an accepted custom."[7] It was the view of Cannon, a pioneer of financial statement analysis, that "an itemised statement (provided it is correct) is to a banker what a map is to a traveller

[1] The author gratefully acknowledges the helpful comments and suggestions of Professor H. C. Edey and of Professor James O. Horrigan of the University of New Hampshire.
[2] A detailed history is given in Sister Isadore Brown, *The Historical Development of the use of Ratios in Financial Statement Analysis to 1933*, Ph.D. dissertation, Catholic University of America, 1955. See also James O. Horrigan, "A Short History of Financial Ratio Analysis," *The Accounting Review*, 43 (1968), 284–294.
[3] Throughout this essay "failure" and "solvency" will be used as antonyms, failure being used in a loose sense to mean the inability of a company to pay its obligations as they fall due. The particular events taken to constitute failure vary in the empirical studies cited later.
[4] An account of the changes in the bank credit arrangements after the Civil War is given in C. A. Phillips, *Bank Credit*, New York, 1926, 123–60 and also in R. A. Foulke, *Practical Financial Statement Analysis*, New York, 1968, 12–21.
[5] Phillips, *op. cit.*, 161.
[6] James G. Cannon, "Uniform Statement Blanks and Credit Department Methods," *Bankers' Magazine*, New York, 59 (1899), 577.
[7] James G. Cannon, "Bank Credits," *Bankers' Magazine*, New York, 70 (1905), 587.

– it points out and makes clear things and conditions that would otherwise be obscure and mysterious."[8]

Initially, analysis of financial statements was based on casual inspection of the various assets and liabilities. In the 1890s some American companies began to use the terms "current assets" and "current liabilities" in their balance sheets[9] and, during this decade, it became customary amongst bankers to compute the ratio of current assets to current liabilities, after taking into account the proposed loan and its use, in order to assess credit-worth. In 1905, Cannon wrote that the "rules of the credit science" of the time were:

Rule No. 1   Quick assets only are a basis for loans.

Rule No. 2   Fixed assets, only considered as giving an unknown support to the quick assets.

Rule No. 3   The debt limit of the borrower has been exceeded when his liabilities exceed fifty per cent. of his quick assets.[10]

The rationale of the 2:1 current ratio was that companies were looked at more from a liquidation angle than as going concerns and it was considered that "current liabilities must be met out of quick assets."[11] On liquidation, liabilities would have to be met in full but "there is bound to be a shrinkage of assets, in that some accounts will be slow and bad and some merchandise out of season and antiquated."[12] Consequently, an allowance had to be made for shrinkage and 50 per cent. was "generally regarded as sufficient."[13]

After a while, the current ratio was criticised as the sole quantitative criterion of solvency and it was also recognised that the 2:1 minimum standard was not appropriate for all businesses. Some of the criticisms were summarised later by one writer as follows:

> Since, therefore, general business conditions, the nature of the business itself, the character of the management, the age of the business, and even its geographical location may vitally affect the current ratio, it becomes highly important to discover other relations which will throw further light on this ratio, and particularly to examine the *quality* and not merely the *quantity* of the current ratio.[14]

[8] James G. Cannon, "Losses by Bad Debts," *Bankers' Magazine*, New York, 51, (1895), 199.

[9] Foulke, *op. cit.*, 181.

[10] Cannon, "Bank Credits," *op. cit*, 588. In this and the following quotation, quick assets are what would now be described as current assets.

[11] Phillips, *op. cit.*, 162. It appears that this requirement was probably due to extreme caution, *e.g.* it was argued that "the current asset value is generally a rough index of the liquidating value" in Benjamin Graham and David L. Dodd, *Security Analysis*, New York, 1934, 495.

[12] Alexander Wall, "Study of Credit Barometrics," *Federal Reserve Bulletin*, 5 (1919), 229.

[13] Phillips, *op. cit.*, 197.

[14] E. E. Lincoln, *Applied Business Finance*, New York, 1926, 341.

It was also recognised that use of it alone could lead to "window dressing" on the part of some potential borrowers[15] for, if a certain minimum ratio were required, they would somehow ensure that their balance sheets displayed the desired relationship even if other sections of it showed the business to be decidedly unhealthy. The importance of cash flow rather than a static measure was explicitly recognised by a later author who wrote:

> The real question is how fast will money come in from the current assets as compared with what is needed to meet the current liabilities. This is the true current ratio, but it is difficult to express in the balance sheet.[16]

Despite the criticisms and the development of new ratios, the current ratio came to be the most widely used ratio in assessing solvency and, according to a recent edition of Foulke's book on financial statement analysis,

> for many years this "two for one" current ratio was the alpha and omega of balance sheet analysis; even today the businessmen are legion who believe this single ratio to be the one infallible guide to balance sheet interpretation.[17]

That businessmen are apparently still misled may well be partly the fault of textbook writers for the 2:1 ratio is still commonly referred to.[18] Although some authors express doubt whether the 2:1 value is always appropriate, the mere quoting of it no doubt causes it to stick in some readers' minds.

Arising from dissatisfaction with the current ratio, other ratios were developed. As early as 1905, for example, Cannon used ten ratios in a study of business borrowers.[19] An important contributor to the literature was Wall who was described as "the leading exponent of the pure ratio analysis."[20] In 1919 he attempted to "analyze the current ratio, the capitalization plans, and the vitality of the business."[21] His thesis was that it was important to examine relative changes in the components of the working capital ratio in interpreting the ratio over time. He logically developed six

---

[15] *e.g.* see Paul J. FitzPatrick, *Symptoms of Industrial Failures*, Washington, 1931, 23 and Harry G. Guthmann, *The Analysis of Financial Statements*, New York, 1925, 154–155.

[16] H. R. Hatfield, *et al.*, *Accounting Principles and Practices*, Boston, 1940, 356.

[17] Foulke *op. cit.*, 178.

[18] *e.g.* see B. Graham *et al.*, *Security Analysis*, New York, 1962, 219 and A. J. Merrett and Allen Sykes, *The Finance and Analysis of Capital Projects*, London, 1963, 109.

[19] See Brown, *op. cit.*, 65–66. The ratios were: current assets/total assets, fixed assets/ total assets, liabilities/total assets, net worth/total assets, liabilities/current assets, sales/current assets, sales/total assets, working capital/total capital, sales/working capital and sales/total capital. The complete study is apparently in the *Bulletin of the National Association of Credit Men*, 6 (1906), 21–29. A summarised version is given in the *Bankers' Magazine*, New York, 70 (1905), 589–590.

[20] FitzPatrick, *op. cit.*, 21.

[21] Wall, *op. cit.*, 231.

ratios to supplement "the hard-boiled two-for-one theory."[22] An example of his reasoning follows:

> If we find that the percentage of the receivables to the merchandise is increasing we may be certain that there is a larger percentage of profit included in the current assets, and logically we should expect to see an increase in the current ratio itself. If this is not the case, it makes it possible for us to inquire from the customer how this change or pro-portion has been affected, and why the current ratio has not risen.[23]

He applied the seven ratios to data taken from 981 financial statements and produced useful evidence to show that average ratios varied in size according to industry and geographical location.

In their belief that a number of ratios were important in assessing solvency, Wall later formulated, with Duning, an index of credit strength.[24] This was a weighted index of the ratios that they considered relevant in assessing creditworth. The weights were assigned arbitrarily and the analyst could alter them "so as to express his individual feeling of relative impor-tance."[25] As might be expected, their novel approach met with criticism.[26] However, it may be viewed as an important contribution, being a naïve attempt to formulate what statisticians would now call a multivariate linear discriminant function. As will be seen later, multiple discriminant analysis does not appear to have been used in the empirical work on the ratio characteristics of failed companies until the 1960s.

Wall's work seems to have provided an impetus to other American writers[27] for, in the 1920s, there were many publications on various aspects of ratio analysis in credit evaluation,[28] and his work was often referred to. However, logical reasoning for the introduction of new ratios and published empirical evidence of their practical relevance in assessing solvency were generally lacking.[29]

---

[22] *ibid*, 232. The ratios were: debtors/stock, net worth/fixed assets, sales/debtors, sales/stock, sales/net worth and total liabilities/net worth. A notable exception to the list is the "quick" or "acid test" ratio. It was certainly in use shortly afterwards, and the minimum standard of 1 : 1 had developed. See H. R. Hatfield, *Accounting*, New York, 1927, 457.

[23] *ibid*, 230.

[24] Alexander Wall and R. W. Duning, *Ratio Analysis of Financial Statements*, New York, 1928, ch. 10.

[25] *ibid*, 158.

[26] One critic described Wall as the "incurably optimistic theorist futilely and absurdly chasing the ratio absolute." See Myron M. Strain, *Industrial Balance Sheets*, New York, 1929, 169–170.

[27] The use of, and literature on, ratio analysis in Britain seems to have lagged behind. In 1949, Bray and Sheasby wrote: "In this country the use of accounting ratios is still somewhat of a novelty." See F. S. Bray and F. H. Sheasby, *Design of Accounts*, London, 1949, 15. See also Frank H. Jones, *Guide to Company Balance Sheets*, London. Ratios were not included in his chapter on the analysis of published accounts in the 1948 edition but they were introduced in the 1951 edition.

[28] At this time there was also considerable growth in the literature on ratio analysis for managerial purposes. A comparison of Henry C. Magee, "Department Store Accounts," *Journal of Accountancy*, 19 (1915), 268–291 and J. Edward Masters, "Fin-ancial Statements as a Basis of Credit," *ibid*, 334–343 indicates that the managerial use of ratios was the further developed.

[29] The usefulness of ratio analysis was not without its critics, *e.g.* see Stephen Gilman,

From this time, many more ratios were developed for use in short- and longer-term credit evaluation[30] and some writers appear to have added more just for proliferation's sake.[31] Bliss was a notable exception to this approach as he attempted to provide a logical framework within which he developed a ratio model of the firm.[32] His view was that

> financial statements, including balance sheets and income statements, are in reality expressions of fundamental business relationships more than anything else. In fact, all financial and operating statistics should be read with a view to determining the fundamental relationships. . . . [Ratios] should be thought of as indicators of the status of fundamental relationships within the business. They are barometers of the relationships and business conditions within the organization.[33]

Although writers with practical experience advocated the ratios that they found useful in credit evaluation, they did not provide evidence to show that their ratios were, in fact, good discriminators. For example, Wall and Duning stated that

> on the average the current ratio and the worth-to-debt ratio[34] have equal analytical values. So many instances have been noticed in which the worth-to-debt ratio has raised the first suspicion of weakness that it often seems the preference for importance should be given to the worth-to-debt ratio if given to either.[35]

Also, Foulke gave maxims for each ratio that he put forward and wrote that each was based on "extensive experience in the analysis of financial statements."[36] For example, "the examination of thousands of balance sheets yearly in all lines of industrial and commercial activity has led to the conclusion that rarely, if ever, should the aggregate of funded liabilities exceed the net working capital."[37]

The use of arbitrary standards by American bankers in credit evaluation was not confined to the requirement of a 2:1 current ratio for

> in addition to the current ratio, some bankers . . . suggest that the net worth should be at least twice as great as the working capital, and

---

Analysing Financial Statements, New York, 1925, 111–112. Also, its limitations were recognised, *e.g.* see W. A. Paton, "Limitations of Financial and Operating Ratios," *Accounting Review*, 3 (1928), 252–260 and FitzPatrick, *op. cit.*, 30–34.

[30] *e.g.* see Lincoln, *op. cit.*, ch. 14 for an explanation and illustration of over forty ratios for use in credit evaluation.

[31] *e.g.* see Strain, *op. cit.*, 56: "Many ratios are suggested that have no earthly relevance, either between the items compared or to the purported object of making the comparison."

[32] James H. Bliss, *Financial and Operating Ratios in Management*, New York, 1923.

[33] *ibid.*, 35 and 37.

[34] *i.e.* share capital plus reserves/total liabilities.

[35] Wall and Duning, *op. cit.*, 155.

[36] *op. cit.*, 386. This, and the following quotation were very similar in the first edition published in 1945. Foulke was an opponent of the view that a theory of ratio analysis could be developed from *a priori* reasoning. See R. A. Foulke, "Financial Ratios Become of Age," *Journal of Accountancy*, 64 (1937), 203–213.

[37] Foulke, *Practical Financial Statement Analysis*, 275. "Funded" and "long-term" liabilities are synonymous.

that the net sales may be expected to be three or four times as great
as the working capital. Another suggestion is that the net worth
should always be much higher than the bank loan – from two to four
times as large. Others would limit the loan to 25 per cent. or 30 per
cent. of the net quick assets.[38]

From the early 1920s there was considerable growth in the publication
of industry average ratios.[39] It appears from the literature that these
were considered to be useful to credit evaluators. Average ratios may be
useful standards for assessing the performance or position of a company.
However, to predict whether a company that is doing worse than average is
likely to fail, a knowledge of the ratio characteristics of failed companies
might well be helpful.

EMPIRICAL WORK ON THE RATIO CHARACTERISTICS OF FAILED COMPANIES

The heavy incidence of business failures in the depression years of the 1930s
was most probably a reason for the interest shown by some American
researchers in examining the ratios of failed companies for, in the 1930s,
the results of at least five studies were published. By today's standards,
the statistical methods used would, no doubt, be criticised. However, they
provided useful published evidence of which ratios appeared to be important; and, in some cases, ratios were shown to indicate weakness several
years in advance of failure. The ratios found to be most relevant in these
five and some later studies, all of which will be described, are ticked or
ranked in Table 1 under the researchers' names.

Two of the early studies were by FitzPatrick, who was "desirous of
discovering what ratios were significant, and which may be useful hereafter, when analysing the financial statements of industrial enterprises."[40]
His first study[41] was an examination of twenty then nationally known
companies that failed during the 1920s. He calculated thirteen ratios for
each company for several years before failure and, from an examination of
the ratio trends for two years beforehand, he ranked four as being the best
indicators of impending failure. In his second study[42] he compared each
company's ratios with those of a comparable successful company. He
found the ratios of the successful companies to be much better for three
years before failure and singled out three as being much better discriminators than the current and quick ratios which "are running a poor second."[43]

[38] Lincoln, *op. cit.*, 402.
[39] *e.g.* the Harvard Business School and the credit agency, Robert Morris Associates,
both started to collect annual ratio data in 1923. The Bureau of Business Research,
University of Illinois published a number of bulletins in the 1920s and 1930s giving
average ratios for several public utilities.
[40] FitzPatrick, *op. cit.*, viii.
[41] *ibid.*
[42] Paul J. FitzPatrick, *A Comparison of the Ratios of Successful Industrial Enterprises
with those of Failed Companies*, Washington, 1932.
[43] *ibid*, 21.

Smith studied twenty-nine companies that failed from the early 1920s.[44] He found that at least fourteen of the ratio relationships tested revealed symptoms of failure, some for ten years prior to failure and others for up to three or four. The ratios ticked under his name in Table 1 are those "whose trends resulted in an uninterrupted indication or symptom of weakness for the majority of companies in at least the last eight years before failure."[45] With Winakor, he extended his study[46] to cover 183 failures between 1923 and 1931 and, in general, the overall findings were similar. However, they discovered substantial variations in the ratios when the data were analysed according to industry and firm size. A serious criticism of these studies is that, unlike FitzPatrick's, a control group with which to compare the results was not used.

Ramser and Foster[47] examined ratios calculated from the single set of accounts that each of 173 companies submitted to support their applications for permission to sell securities in Illinois between 1919 and 1925. By the end of 1927 about 30 per cent. of the companies had failed, and they found that for these, together with the companies that had not paid regular dividends since permission for sale was granted, a number of ratios differed from those of the more successful companies. As they did not indicate which ratios they considered to be the best discriminators, what they termed the "13 most significant ratios"[48] have been ticked in Table 1.

In 1942 Merwin published the results of a study[49] in the same vein as FitzPatrick's and Smith and Winakor's. He analysed a large number of ratios calculated from the accounts of 581 "continuing" and "discontinuing"[50] small companies in five manufacturing industries. By comparing industry mean ratios, he found that three were very sensitive portents of discontinuance up to four or five years before the event. He also found that the length of the prediction period varied between industries.

There seems to have been a twenty-four-year gap before the next American study on the ratio characteristics of failed companies appeared. In the meantime, a number of American studies that were primarily concerned with other economic matters were published. They all included some work on companies that had got into financial difficulties and, in

---

[44] Raymond F. Smith, *A Test Analysis of Unsuccessful Industrial Companies*, Bureau of Business Research, University of Illinois, Bulletin No. 31, 1930.

[45] *ibid*, 52.

[46] Raymond F. Smith and Arthur H. Winakor, *Changes in the Financial Structure of Unsuccessful Corporations*, Bureau of Business Research, University of Illinois, Bulletin No. 51, 1935.

[47] J. R. Ramser and Louis O. Foster, *A Demonstration of Ratio Analysis*, Bureau of Business Research, University of Illinois, Bulletin No. 40, 1931.

[48] *ibid*, 14.

[49] Charles L. Merwin, *Financing Small Corporations in Five Manufacturing Industries, 1926–36*, New York, 1942, ch. 4.

[50] "Discontinuing" companies were those that ceased filing federal tax returns. "This does not mean that all these companies were failures in the legal or even in the economic sense; some may have discontinued business voluntarily, and others may have changed to a sole proprietorship or partnership form of organization." *Ibid.*, 18.

Table 1: Ratios shown to be good discriminators between failed and non-failed companies in univariate studies

Ratio[a]	FitzPatrick 1931	1932	Smith 1930	Smith and Winakor 1935	Ramser and Foster 1931	Merwin 1942	Tamari 1964	Beaver 1966 and 1968
Current asset and liability ratios								
Current	4th					✓	✓	
Quick or "acid test"								
Stock/current assets								
Capital structure ratios								
Net worth/total liabilities		3rd	✓		✓	✓		
Net worth/total assets			✓		✓			
Total liabilities/total assets		2nd						3rd
Net worth/fixed assets			✓		✓			
Reserves/total assets					✓			
Asset structure ratios								
Fixed assets/total assets					✓			
Current assets/fixed assets		Best			✓			
Working capital/total assets				Best	✓			
Net profit ratios								
Net profit/net worth					✓			
Net profit/total assets					✓		✓	2nd
Net profit/sales					✓			
Sales ratios								
Sales/stock								
Sales/total assets								
Sales/net worth								
Cash-flow ratios								
Cash flow/total debt						Best		Best
Other data								
No. of ratios tested	13		24	21	33	Many	10	30
No. of failed companies studied	20		29	183	51[b]	200	28	79
Years in which failures occurred	1920-29		1923-28[b]	1923-31	1920-27	1926-36	1958-60	1954-64
Country studied	U.S.A.		U.S.A.	U.S.A.	U.S.A.	U.S.A.	Israel	U.S.A.

[a] To facilitate comparison with the original studies, equivalent ratios have been bracketed together rather than given a single description.

[b] This is an approximation as the exact information was not given in the study.

each case, a few ratios were calculated to discover whether characteristics of these companies were different from those that did not get into difficulties. Hickman[51], for example, carried out an extensive study of corporate bond issues made between 1900 and 1943. He tested two ratios said to be the most widely used by security analysts in assessing the risk of loan default, these being the after tax cover for fixed charges (*e.g.* loan interest and rents) and the ratio of net profit available for dividends/sales. He found that both ratios, calculated from accounting data prior to offering, were good predictors of eventual interest default. Another example is the work by Saulnier and others[52] who examined 5,700 business loans granted by the Reconstruction Finance Corporation that were overdue at the end of 1951. They tabulated the trends in sales, net profit, net worth and the current ratio for three years before the loans were granted for all borrowers. They also computed the current and net worth/total debt ratios for one year beforehand. Their study was hampered by lack of information on some companies, but their figures suggested that the trends of the current ratio and net worth of the overdue borrowers were less favourable for three years prior to their loan applications and that the current ratio itself was a good indicator of default a year beforehand.

In 1964 an Israeli study by Tamari[53] was published. He compared ten ratios calculated from the accounts of twenty-eight industrial companies that failed[54] between 1958 and 1960 with those from all Israeli industries. He found that the financial ratios of the failed companies were worse than the all-industry ratios in the year prior to failure and that most had been deteriorating for up to five years beforehand.[55] The three ratios he singled out as showing the most marked adverse trends are ticked under his name in Table 1. Tamari observed that a large proportion of successful companies had at least one weak ratio, some had two and only a few had three. From this he concluded that "the analyst cannot rely on one ratio alone in measuring the degree of risk.[56]" He then constructed a risk index similar to Wall and Duning's and found that, after assigning weights in a fairly simple manner, his index was successful in discriminating between companies that subsequently failed within the period studied and those that did not. The ratios included in his index are shown in Table 2 alongside those

[51] W. B. Hickman, *Corporate Bond Quality and Investor Experience*, Princeton, 1958, see especially 394–431.

[52] R. J. Saulnier *et al.*, *Federal Lending and Loan Insurance*, Princeton, 1958, see especially 451–482.

[53] M. Tamari, "Financial Ratios as a Means of Forecasting Bankruptcy," *Bank of Israel Bulletin*, 21 (1964), 15–45. This was the only non-American study found from a search of the literature.

[54] These were "16 industrial companies which had been declared bankrupt and 12 industrial companies which had been given consolidation loans or granted a moratorium on their debts for a considerable period and were virtually bankrupt," *Ibid*, 18.

[55] It is interesting to note that Israeli bankers were apparently not in the habit of examining the accounts of borrowers, and potential borrowers. If they had, some loans might well not have been made and action on others to avoid failure might have been taken for 17 of the 28 failed companies made losses for at least four of th ʿfive years prior to failure.

[56] *ibid.*, 22.

of later multivariate studies to be described, all of which used more sophisticated statistical techniques than he did.

In the 1960s interest grew amongst American academics, notably from Chicago, in the use of accounting data for predicting various events of concern to decision-makers. [57]Arising out of his particular interest in the predictive ability of ratios, Beaver carried out a study of failed companies.[58] He compared the ratios of 79 companies that failed between 1954 and 1964 with those of the same number of similar, but non-failed, companies using univariate analysis. On the lines of the earlier studies, he initially compared mean values of ratios and found that the means of all six ratios that he selected for detailed study were less satisfactory for the failed companies for five years before failure than for the non-failed companies. His study differed from the earlier ones in that he tested cash flow ratios and, in the later part, he used more sophisticated statistical techniques. Eventually, he found that the apparently previously untested cash flow/total debt ratio[59] was the best predictor of failure.

In the early literature, "non-liquid asset" ratios (*e.g.* those involving profits, fixed assets or long-term debt) were considered to be relevant only in judging longer-term solvency whereas "liquid" ratios (*i.e.* involving components of working capital) were used in short-term evaluation.[60] As Beaver had found three non-liquid ratios – namely cash flow/total debt, net profit/total assets and total liabilities/total assets – to be the best predictors, even for the year before failure, he extended his study[61] by adding a further eight liquid ratios to his tests. He still found that his three non-liquid ratios were the best predictors of solvency in the short-term.

Some work is being done on Finnish companies by Jägerhorn[62] who is testing ten ratios calculated from the accounts of 108 pairs of failed and non-failed companies using methods similar to Beaver's. His preliminary, unpublished, test results indicate that the working capital/total assets ratio is the best predictor, for as much as four years in advance of failure.

All the empirical studies considered so far, except part of Tamari's,

---

[57] For example, see references cited in William H. Beaver *et al.*, "Predictive Ability as a Criterion for the Evaluation of Accounting Data," *Accounting Review*, 43 (1968), 675. There was also interest in the effect that the use of alternative accounting conventions had on ratios, *e.g.* see George C. Holdren, "Lifo and Ratio Analysis," *Accounting Review*, 39 (1964), 70–85 and A. Tom Nelson, "Capitalising Leases – The Effect on Financial Ratios," *Journal of Accountancy*, 116 (1968), 49–58.

[58] William H. Beaver, "Financial Ratios as Predictors of Failure," *Empirical Research in Accounting: Selected Studies, 1966*, Supplement to *Journal of Accounting Research*, 4 (1966), 71–111. He defined failure as a company defaulting on interest payments on its debt, overdrawing its bank account or declaring bankruptcy.

[59] Cash flow was defined as net profit after taxation with depreciation, depletion and amortisation charges added back.

[60] *e.g.* see Foulke, *op. cit.*, 72 and 516 and also B. B. Howard and M. Upton, *Introduction to Business Finance*, New York, 1953, 131–143.

[61] William H. Beaver, "Alternative Accounting Measures as Predictors of Failure," *Accounting Review*, 43 (1968), 113–122.

[62] I am grateful to Professor Jägerhorn of the Swedish School of Economics, Helsingfors, Finland, for kindly supplying the information on his study.

Table 2: Ratios shown to be good discriminators between failed and non-failed companies in multivariate studies

Author and year of publication Ratio	Tamari 1964	Altman 1968	Edminster 1972	Blum —
Current asset and liability ratios				
Current	√			
Quick ratio: firm/industry average			√	
Net quick assets/stock				√
Trend breaks[a] of net quick assets/stock				√
Capital structure ratios				
Net worth/total liabilities	√			
Reserves/total assets		√		
Current liabilities/net worth			√	
Market value of equity[b]/total liabilities		√		
Asset structure ratios				
Working capital/total assets		√		√
Net profit ratios				
Profit before interest and tax/total assets		√		
Profit trend				
Rate of return on equity[b]				√
Sales and cost of sales ratios				
Stock/sales			√	
Sales/total assets		√		
Net worth/sales			√	
Working capital/sales			√	
Sales/debtors	√			
Value of production[c]/stock	√			
Value of production[c]/working capital	√			
Cash-flow ratios				
Cash flow/current liabilities			√	
Cash flow/total debt		√		
Other data				
No. of ratios tested	10	22	19	12
No. of failed companies studied	28	33	21	115
Years in which failures occurred	1958–60	1946–65	1958–65	1954–68
Country studied	Israel	U.S.A.	U.S.A.	U.S.A.

[a] A trend break is defined as any performance by a variable less favourable in one year than in the preceding year.

[b] These are the only ratios referred to in this essay that are not calculated wholly from accounting data.

[c] Value of production = sales + change in stocks of finished goods and work-in-progress.

treated ratios individually. Like Tamari, Altman[63] expressed his concern that a univariate approach could lead to faulty interpretation. He explained that what was needed was a technique such as multiple discriminant analysis that can take into account all the ratio characteristics at one time.[64] He used this technique on data relating to 33 companies that failed[65] between 1946 and 1965 and an equal number of non-failed concerns. The components of the function that best discriminated between the failed and non-failed companies are given in Table 2 under his name. It is interesting to note that Altman's function did not include the ratios that he found to be the best predictors when considering the ratios individually.[66] Also, Beaver's best predictor was not included in the set of ratios tested because Altman was unable to obtain depreciation figures for all the companies which were needed to compute cash flows. However, exclusion of the cash flow/total debt ratio did not worry him as he found that his results were superior to those of Beaver. He concluded that

> the discriminant-ratio model proved to be extremely accurate in pre-
> dicting bankruptcy correctly in 94 per cent. of the initial sample with
> 95 per cent. of all firms in the bankrupt and non-bankrupt groups
> assigned to their actual group classification . . . bankruptcy can be
> accurately predicted up to two years prior to actual failure with the
> accuracy diminishing rapidly after the second year.[67]

Altman later used the same technique on the financial ratios of railroad companies[68] and came up with a function that contained different variables from his earlier study which concerned manufacturers. He applied the function to the data of Penn Central Transportation Company, after it had failed in 1970, and found that it had been a likely candidate for failure one-and-a-half years before failure actually occurred. This appears to have been the only published attempt to apply ratios shown to be good dis-criminators in an earlier study to fresh data, albeit after the company was known to have failed.

Edminster used multiple discriminant analysis "to select a set of ratios and analytical methods which best discriminate between loss and non-loss borrowers and guarantee recipients from the Small Business Administra-tion."[69] He examined the ratios of 42 borrowers, a sample concerning an

[63] Edward I. Altman, "Financial Ratios, Discriminant Analysis and the Prediction of Corporate Bankruptcy," *Journal of Finance*, 23 (1968), 589–609.
[64] Without the use of a computer it would seem hardly worthwhile carrying out a study of this type due to the vast number of calculations required to derive the best function.
[65] The failed companies were those that "are legally bankrupt and either placed in receivership or have been granted the right to reorganise under the provisions of the National Bankruptcy Act," Altman, *op. cit.*, 589.
[66] I am grateful to Dr. Marc Blum, whose work is referred to later, for pointing out that this is not surprising. One reason he gives is that part of the efficacy of a multivariate analysis, and in particular discriminant analysis, is taking advantage of information supplied by variables which correlate very poorly on a univariate basis with the dependent variable.
[67] *ibid.*, 609.
[68] Edward I. Altman, *Corporate Bankruptcy in America*, Lexington, 1971, ch. 7.
[69] Robert O. Edminster, "An Empirical Test of Financial Ratio Analysis," *Journal of Financial and Quantitative Analysis*, 7 (1972), 1477–1493.

equal number of loss and non-loss cases. His tests showed that no single variable predicted as well as a small group of variables and, as in Altman's main study, variables which were not significant predictors alone added discriminatory quality to a function containing selected other variables. He found that at least three consecutive financial statements were needed to get a good prediction of small business failure whereas, for larger companies, both Beaver and Altman got good predictions with one for each company.

A recent study referred to in the literature but, as yet, unpublished is by Blum[70], who constructed a ratio model based on accounting and share price data. He argued that "a model that can be useful in the prediction of business failure must have a theoretical foundation . . . without such a foundation, the model may not be fundamentally related to the event which is to be predicted, business failure"[71] and he pointed out that Altman's main study did not use a theoretical approach. Blum examined the ratios of 115 failed[72] industrial companies and those of a paired sample of 115 similar, but non-failed, companies, using multiple discriminant analysis and found that

> The Failing Company model predicts failed companies to fail and non-failed companies not to fail with an accuracy of approximately 93% to 95% at the first year before failure. Predictive accuracy is approximately 80% at the second year before failure and is 70% at the third, fourth and fifth years before failure. Discrimination between failed and non-failed companies is not found to be statistically significant at the sixth year before failure.[73]

His results compared favourably with Altman's and he remarked that differences were probably due to defects in Altman's methodology. The ratios ticked in Table 2 are those that, according to Edminster's interpretation[74] generally performed best over all the time periods for which Blum's function was estimated.

Blum also compared his Failing Company model with Beaver's best ratio, cash flow/total debt, and found that

> the models seem to be about equally effective overall, although the Failing Company model is better at the first year before failure. This conclusion is surprising. It was expected that a multivariate model would be much more accurate than a univariate approach.[75]

[70] Marc P. Blum, *The Failing Company Doctrine*, Ph.D. dissertation, Columbia University, 1969, referred to in Edminster, *ibid.*, 1478. I am most grateful to Dr. Blum for sending me a portion of this thesis and for his valuable comments on the latter part of an earlier draft of this essay.
[71] Blum, *ibid.*, 73–74.
[72] Of the failed companies, 90 per cent. had filed bankruptcy petitions and the other 10 per cent. had entered into private arrangements with creditors.
[73] *ibid.*, 128
[74] Edminster, *op. cit.*, 1478.
[75] Blum, *op. cit.*, 178.

CONCLUDING REMARKS

A review of the empirical work has indicated that a number of researchers have found ratios to be good predictors of failure on the basis of studies carried out *after* the event. The tables show that some ratios have performed well in more than one study, but, even in the recent work where more sophisticated statistical techniques have been used, there is no unanimity on which ratios are the best indicators of impending failure. It would seem that this must present problems to credit analysts wishing to make good use of the findings in practice. Variations in the application of statistical techniques and in the interpretation of results,[76] and differences in the size of companies examined and in the economic environment of the various studies may well be some of the contributing factors.

It appears that much more research is required.[77] For example, it would seem to be a useful exercise to test whether the ratios advocated by various researchers are good predictors of failure when applied to data other than that used in their selection. It might well be that a set of ratios can be applied reliably only to situations very similar to those from which they were selected (*e.g.* Edminster's ratios might be found to be the most reliable only for the prediction of small business failure.) On the other hand, it might be found that different economic events surrounding failure at different times and in different places resulted in none of the sets of ratios performing well when applied to new data. Furthermore, lack of uniformity in the application of accounting principles and other accounting problems, such as the failure to account for the changing value of money, might also be disturbing factors.

[76] See Craig G. Johnson, "Ratio Analysis and the Prediction of Firm Failure," *Journal of Finance*, 25 (1970), 1166–1168 for his criticism of the recent studies. He concluded that "the practical value of ratio analysis to the failure issue is still an open question." Altman's reply follows on 1169–1172.

[77] A call for further research on the predictive ability of ratios has been made by Beaver, "Financial Ratios as Predictors of Failure," 100 and James O. Horrigan, "Some Empirical Bases of Ratio Analysis," *Accounting Review*, 40 (1965), 558–568.

DEPRIVAL VALUE AND
FINANCIAL ACCOUNTING

Harold Edey

1

A major weakness of financial accounting is the absence of a clear relationship to management policy and plans.[1] Despite many efforts through the years to improve and adapt it, in essence it remains a mixed collection of rules of thumb, still strongly influenced by the nineteenth-century legal problems that it was originally designed to meet. The position of management is becoming increasingly like that of the captain of a ship who plans his voyages on an up-to-date Admiralty chart, steers his ship using the same chart and the navigational aids made available by modern technology, and is then required to report his progress to his owners by plotting it on a sixteenth-century map. It is, therefore, a major merit of the deprival value approach to asset valuation and profit calculation, introduced by Professor W. T. Baxter in his recent book on depreciation,[2] that its application in financial accounting could help to relate the latter more closely to information that is directly relevant for management action and therefore, presumably, of direct interest to those interested in the results of management.

In its simplest form, deprival value is a method of valuing an individual asset whose expected series of financial contributions, positive or negative, can be estimated reasonably closely and independently of other assets of the same concern. In Section 2, I shall demonstrate the idea of deprival value as I understand it, on the basis of this simplifying assumption, following Baxter. In Section 3, I shall consider the effects of removing the simplifying assumption in order to cover the more general case where the operation of an asset and the financial results of this operation may be strongly interconnected with the operation and results of other assets. In Section 4, I shall discuss how the deprival value concept might be used to improve the basis of financial accounting.

[1] I shall use the term "financial accounting" in this paper as a generic term for the preparation and presentation of formal annual accounts such as are required by the British Companies Acts 1948 to 1967, the enactments setting up the various state industries in Britain, the rules relating to publication of accounts of the Securities and Exchange Commission, and so on. "External accounting" (as opposed to "internal" management accounting) might be a better term, but "financial accounting" is so well established as a term that it seems best to stick to it.

[2] W. T. Baxter, *Depreciation*, London, 1971.

2

An asset can be regarded as a store of services. The financial effects of such services can be expressed as a set of expected future cash receipts and payments – a "cash flow."[3] The "receipts" may be actual cash realisations or may be savings of cash payments which, but for the asset, would have been made. Similarly, the "payments" are either actual cash outgoings or sacrifices of cash receipts caused by the asset. Typical receipts are the net revenues from the asset's services and the net sales proceeds when it is finally disposed of. Typical payments are the initial purchase price of the asset and payments for its operation, repair and maintenance. Receipts and payments may also be imputed if cost-benefit analysis calls for this.

Consider first the case of an asset that is not capable of replacement such that if it is lost or destroyed the service it provides must cease.

From the management point of view (and this must be presumed to reflect the point of view of those whom the management is there to serve, whether shareholders, government department, or some other group) the commercial value of the asset to the concern – the maximum amount that it would be worth their while to pay in order to acquire it in its present condition – cannot be greater than whatever present value is attributed to the best cash flow that its use or sale is expected to contribute to the concern (including in this, where necessary, the amount imputed to any non-financial benefits).[4] Any excess of past outlay over this present value is an expense or loss incurred or suffered by the management, to be written off.

Nor can the asset be worth less to the management than this amount, for if the concern were for some reason deprived of it – *e.g.* by a fire – it would be this present value and no less which, by definition, would just compensate for the loss: hence the term *deprival value*.

Good management calls for continuing knowledge of this value, that is, for periodic assessment of expected cash flows and their present values, in order to judge the current best use of the asset and the optimal date of its final disposal. So, perhaps less obviously, does the preparation and audit of financial accounts, even under the present rules, for no asset should, without note or comment, stand in the balance sheet at less than the value

[3] For purposes of exposition I shall ignore the fact that management are normally concerned not only with an "expected" outcome (in the probability sense) but also with the dispersion of possible outcomes about the expected quantity or set of quantities. This abstraction does not affect the central point under discussion here.

[4] The calculation of a present value requires, if discounting is to be used, the selection of an "appropriate" rate or rates of discount. The problems that arise in choosing such a rate or rates are outside the scope of this paper. It is evident, however, that any management must have some scheme for relating the financial benefits expected from an asset to its purchase price, or to its sales value, when they decide to buy, sell, or retain, the asset, and this implies some kind of assessment of the present value of the expected cash flow. The net cash proceeds of immediate sale of the asset can be regarded as a special case of a "one item" cash flow with a discounting factor of unity.

of the amount that it is expected eventually to bring in to the concern.[5] Where the possibility of replacement is excluded, deprival value, as defined above will, under present thinking, be a present value arrived at by discounting or by some other process. As Baxter points out, depreciation by reference to successive values calculated in this way at the end of each year will, in general, not be constant year by year. The net receipts created by an asset will vary from year to year with the incidence of cash outlays on running and upkeep, as well as with any variation in annual gross revenue earned. With constant revenue it is not depreciation, but the sum of depreciation, running cost, repairs and maintenance, and the adopted target return on investment (obtained by applying the selected discount rate to the written down value) that will – if all goes according to plan – be constant.[6]

If all does not go according to plan, the deprival value computed in the light of actual conditions will throw up a variance in the sum of these items as compared with the planned and budgeted deprival value: this is what one expects of management accounts.

Up to now it has been assumed that the asset is not capable of replacement. Suppose now that if it were lost or destroyed it could be replaced. This is the more likely situation. The present value of the best cash flow obtainable from use or sale of the asset will evidently remain an upper limit to value. The cost of replacement in case of hypothetical loss does, however, introduce an alternative upper limit, which may be lower than the one set by present value. If the asset were lost or destroyed, the financial loss would be limited to the outlay on replacement, that is, the outlay needed to put the owner back in his original position. (The "cost of replacement" here is assumed to include the amount of any loss of revenue and outlays caused by delay, where immediate replacement is not possible.) This upper limit set by replacement cost has clear economic and management significance. It is the maximum insurable loss. It is also the maximum amount any sensible purchaser with the same knowledge is likely to pay for the asset. Under competitive conditions the present value of the cash flow contributed by the asset is unlikely for long to exceed its replacement cost, for should it appear likely to do so, it will, by definition, be profitable for competitors to bring into use similar assets, the competition from which will drive down the contribution from the original asset until it reaches something approximating to a normal competitive return on investment (*i.e.* on replacement cost, allowance being made, as shown by Baxter, for any difference in cash contribution due to different age and physical characteristics of the hypothetical replacing asset.) In such

---

[5] ". . . it is obvious that capital lost must not appear in the accounts as still existing intact; the accounts must show the truth . . ." *per* Lindley L. J. in *Verner* v. *General Investment Trust Ltd.* [1894] 2 Ch. 239.

[6] The annuity method of depreciation is a special case of this where annual net cash receipts are assumed constant: in this case it is the sum of depreciation and target return on investment that is constant.

conditions it can be assumed that a management would wish to relate its pricing policy to the amount of a competitive return on the replacement cost of the assets concerned as a guide in judging the risk of over-pricing and losing sales or inviting more competition.

Calculation of the cost of hypothetical replacement can thus be regarded as part of the process of estimating the future cash flow and present value of the asset: in the end it is these, and these alone, that determine the usefulness of the asset, and therefore its financial worth, in the management's eyes.

Deprival value can therefore be defined more generally as the lower of: (*a*) the highest present value expected to be earned by use or sale of the asset, and (*b*) the current replacement cost of the asset, including in this replacement cost an addition for any loss that would be caused by delay in replacement and for other incidental outlays, and also an allowance for any amount by which the services of the replacing asset were expected to earn a higher (or lower) contribution because its age and physical characteristics differed from those of the original asset.

It may be objected that if competition were restricted, the net revenue contribution of an asset could remain above the normal competitive level and hence maintain its value to the concern above the replacement cost. However, this situation would imply that an additional asset had been introduced into the calculation, namely the property right, licence, reputation or other factor which enabled the competition to be excluded. The valuation would now relate to two assets instead of one, and replacement would have to be considered in relation to both together: replacement cost would have to include the cost of replacing the asset that gave the protection from competition. The introduction of a significant restriction on competition thus makes inapplicable the simple case of the single independent asset on which discussion has so far rested. The problem raised does not exclude the use of the deprival value approach, but it requires extension of the argument to cover a more general use. This is dealt with in Section 3.

3

On the simplifying assumption provisionally made in Section 2 (namely that an asset's contribution can be clearly distinguished from those of other assets of the concern) the deprival value concept provides a conceptually clear basis for the determination of asset value. Value determined in this way is necessarily based on estimate and opinion; but this is common to all value assessments except those based on some purely arbitrary rule that excludes all consideration of the future of the asset in question.[7]

---

[7] *e.g.* the written-down value of an asset for capital allowance purposes under corporation tax; but *not* the conventional balance sheet value, which requires at least consideration of the asset's future contribution, though this is normally only used in determining whether the asset should be written down.

Moreover, it can be argued with some force that the information and estimates used in arriving at the deprival value are in any case needed by an efficient management for planning and decisions, and can therefore be assumed to be available when the financial accounts are drafted and audited.

The next step is to consider the more complicated and general case of a complex of assets whose financial effects are closely interconnected. The cash flow contribution of a single taxi to a concern that owns a fleet of taxis which are hired out to drivers can be determined after the event without serious theoretical or practical difficulty.[8] The assessment of the expected future cash flow in such a case involves an estimation problem but not a conceptual one. What, on the other hand, is the cash-flow contribution of a railway bridge on a main railway line? If, for the moment, it is assumed that the bridge cannot be replaced (*e.g.* because of an earthquake) so that the line has to close, it can be said that its deprival value is measured by the whole net cash flow earned by the section of the line that it occupies less the net disposal value of the remaining railway assets, since this is the loss that the bridge's destruction would cause (the rest of the railway being assumed unharmed and intact). But this could be said of every bridge, tunnel, cutting, etc. on the line. Evidently cash-flow contributions, and their discounted values, calculated in this way for each asset in turn cannot be aggregated to give a meaningful total. This is an old economic conundrum.

A similar conceptual problem is likely to arise in many real-life situations when replacement cost of hypothetical replacement comes to be estimated. Replacement cost may have little significance if it is defined strictly in terms of a specific physical asset. It is true that, where exact replacement is possible, its cost (allowing for cost of delay) always provides an upper limit to value to the owner; but the limit may be so high as to be useless as a guide. It would probably seldom be sensible to replace an asset in exactly the same form. Sometimes this is obvious: one would not normally consider replacing a railway locomotive built in 1890 by another with the same physical specification. Nor can this point be met except in very simple cases (such as that of the taxis above) merely by stating the problem as that of costing the replacement of the asset's services. The difficulty arises because changes in consumer tastes or in technology since the asset was acquired may call for changes in a whole complex of jointly-operating asset services.

The output of an electricity generating undertaking, supplied at a given time by the services of a coal-fired plant, linked with similar plants by a network of interconnected transmission lines, may at a later time be more cheaply provided, say, by a single nuclear station supported by one or more

[8] It is assumed that the taxis cannot be identified as belonging to the same fleet for this could cause financial interaction between them, *e.g.* because the fleet acquired a reputation for reliability and comfort, so that the whole fleet earned more than taxis would if operated independently.

gas turbine generators, without a large-scale interconnected grid. How in such a case can the "services" of the original coal-fired station be defined in order to calculate the cost of their replacement, taken by themselves without the services of the rest of the network? It must not be forgotten that one of the aims of calculating replacement cost is to estimate the likely price that will be set upon output by a competitor coming into the industry; or, in a state industry, to estimate the current cost of the best method of supply, in order to test current pricing policy. The cost of replacing individual old machines in their existing form may have little relevance in this context.

In principle it would be possible to compute "replacement cost" of an existino asset in a complex situation of this kind by making two separate estimates: one of the present value of all the future costs of the whole complex with the station in question, and the second of the present value of all the future costs of the whole complex if the station alone, but no other part, had been destroyed and then replaced, including the outlay on replacement.[9] The difference between the two would be the "replacement cost" of the station. The replacement of one station would not allow the complete reconstruction of the system as a whole on the best basis available at the time of hypothetical replacement, but the new station would almost certainly be somewhat different in its technological characteristics from the old one, and would represent the best that could be done, given the rest of the existing system.

If all assets were to be valued separately on this basis, the sum of the "replacement costs" so obtained could in general be expected to exceed significantly the hypothetical replacement cost of the system as a whole. It follows that, apart from special cases (like the taxis) a replacement cost estimate based on taking individual assets one by one is not likely to be a useful figure in relation to such matters as the valuation of the concern as a whole or the assessment of the current most economical way available to a newly created concern of producing the enterprise's product or products – a question closely related to valuation.[10]

This does not invalidate the deprival value approach. It does indicate, however, that its proper use for valuation requires that the dual test of expected cash contribution and replacement cost be applied to the concern

---

[9] The costs here would be expressed as the flow of cash outlays in running, maintenance and future replacement into the indefinite future, receipts on disposition of assets being credited. The second flow would also include the immediate hypothetical outlay on the new station. If revenues were affected by the change, this too would have to be allowed for.

[10] This does not imply that the deprival value of an individual asset has no significance when that asset is a member of a closely co-operating set of complementary assets. It will be relevant in testing whether it is worthwhile actually replacing an individual asset. For this purpose the type of calculation described above is necessary – that is, the calculation of the two sets of cash flows into the indefinite future for the whole group of assets, with the old asset and with the replacing one. To test whether replacement is worthwhile the disposal value of the old asset must then be brought into comparison with the difference in present values of the two flows: if it is significantly more than the deprival value in present use the asset should be replaced.

as a whole. The replacement cost so calculated for the concern as a whole gives an overriding maximum value, reflecting the cost to a hypothetical competitor of creating a similar organisation. This implies that the calculation should include an allowance for the cost of creating a working organisation – that is, for the creating of the intangible element commonly called "goodwill" as well as for the physical assets. This would include an allowance for return on investment forgone during the working up period.

The present value of the best expected cash-flow returns that can be earned for the owners of the concern may however be less than this replacement cost. It is then that present value which sets the overriding maximum. As in the case of individual assets, the net liquidation value, as a one-item cash flow, sets a lower limit.

The estimation of these values is difficult and the result is normally likely to be subject to a high degree of uncertainty. This, however, is due to the nature of the world, and it is no good complaining about it or arguing that the result is not "objective." It cannot legitimately be argued that making such estimates would place an undue burden on management: it is the job of management to form opinions on such matters as part of the normal process of running the concern and assessing its continuing economic efficiency.

It would also appear – and it is doubtful if this is fully appreciated – to be a duty of auditors to express an adverse opinion if, in their view, the balance sheet value of the net assets as a whole is in excess of their business value defined in this way.[11] It is difficult to see how such an opinion can be reasonably formed without evidence that the management have directed their mind to the above questions; in general this would seem to imply that there should be documentary evidence available to auditors in the form of planning studies and at least outline budgets.

The application of deprival value in the way suggested above amounts in effect to linking the valuation of the concern to its long-run planning. This link cannot be avoided in any approach to valuation that has reality for management decisions.

The application can take account of liabilities as well as assets. In estimating the long-run cash flows of the concern as a whole, receipts and payments from the creation or extinction of liabilities and for servicing these would be included.

If the valuation is for the information and benefit of the equity shareholders of a company, it should presumably be based on the expected cash flows to them. For this purpose preference shares would be treated as a liability. In state undertakings where in effect the whole investment including all loan capital bears an equity risk, whatever the formal nature of the finance, debt capital owned or guaranteed by Government would be treated as part of the equity.

[11] See footnote 5 above.

4

What has been said above suggests that to report the current financial position of a concern in a way that conveys to its owners a realistic view of the economic value of the resources invested in it requires a subjective assessment involving a look into the future, and involves consideration of the concern as a whole (including assessment of its value as a whole) as distinct from an assessment obtained merely by summing values set on individual assets.

So far as reported profit is to be a measure of the improvement in the concern's economic value in the same sense (allowing for payments in or withdrawals of ownership funds and withdrawal of dividends), it must be based on comparison of successive assessments, using the same approach.

Such an approach to annual accounting in effect implies a switch to reporting based on management assessments of the best cash flows that can be expected from the existing organisation and conversion of these in some way to a present value, coupled with a study of the cost of replacing the existing organisation as a whole in the best possible way. This is hardly likely to be acceptable immediately as a normal basis for financial accounts in practice.

On the other hand, as noted above, it can be argued that such an assessment is, in principle, required by orthodox accounting rules, since it is needed to test whether the balance sheet as a whole overstates "net realisable value" in the sense of its ability to produce future cash return for its owners that will amount in aggregate to not less than the present balance sheet net assets.[12]

One can, however, go further than this. In simple cases, where cash-flow contributions can be closely identified with particular assets, as in, say, a taxi business, or a shipping business, or a chain store, clear significance can be attached to deprival value assessments of individual assets – taxis, ships, freehold premises, etc. – and the method provides in these cases what is lacking in present-day financial accounting, a principle of general application, the use of which would lead to better balance sheet interpretation.

Even in such cases, however, the application of the assessment to the concern as a whole cannot be dispensed with if a full view is to be given. The economic worth of a concern to its owners will depend in part on the way in which it is operated as a whole. One can put this another way by saying that the deprival value of the asset "goodwill" cannot be assessed independently of the concern as a whole.

This has some bearing on what, for accountants, is the troublesome problem of accounting for goodwill. No method of dealing with this question is likely to be of much use in conveying information unless it is based on an overall assessment of the concern's value. Deprival value has a clear application in this context.

[12] Consider this in relation, say, to the balance sheet of Rolls-Royce before the débâcle.

Where individual assets are of specialised nature and their operation demands the co-operation of other assets, as in the case of the power station example above, it is doubtful if any method of "valuing" the individual assets for balance sheet purposes can have a great deal of significance in assessing the quality of the undertaking as a continuing concern. The deprival value concept can, however, supply a basis of principle to the balance sheet valuation process in the simpler cases. Given that there is a continuous spectrum of business types, the principle could well be extended generally to all concerns. As one moved from the simpler to the more complex, individual asset values would in general become more arbitrary and more reliance would need to be placed on any overall assessment that could be provided. This seems unavoidable.

The deprival value approach has the particular merit of drawing attention to the relevance of replacement cost (adjusted in the way described above for the effect of delay, and differences in age and other characteristics between the existing and the hypothetical replacing asset) as an absolute limit to the worth to the concern of any asset, and to the replacement cost of the concern as a whole as an absolute limit to its value to the owners.

This has special relevance to stock inventory. The application of the deprival value approach to this would mean that the familiar formula "cost or lower net realisable value" would be replaced by "cost, net realisable value or replacement cost, whichever is lower." That this formula has greater management significance in some contexts can hardly be doubted. A fall in the replacement value of purchased stock may be of considerable significance to a concern – *e.g.* a tailoring chain – that is competing with others that, by delaying their purchases, have avoided the fall. The fall is also evidence of an error in purchasing, attributable to the accounting period in which it occurs, and in which it would seem sensible to record the effect.

Deprival value may have particular significance for a nationalised industry, where it is particularly important that the financial accounts should reflect the economic and management realities. This is because under present circumstances it is likely that these accounts will be used as a basis for financial directives, on such matters as financial targets to be attained, without a full understanding of the limitations of this kind of statement. This in turn means that the level at which tariffs are fixed may well depend to a large degree upon the financial accounts. The estimation of a deprival value for sections of the undertaking, and for the undertaking as a whole, could provide an important check on the economic significance of the conventional accounts, and could, for example, highlight a situation where the past depreciation policy had been inadequate, either because the rate of cost reduction through technological advance had been underestimated in the past, or because errors in investment had occurred.

A NOTE ON CAPITAL AND INCOME IN
THE LAW OF TRUSTS

John Flower

A common situation in a trust is that the person who is entitled to the income is different from the person who is entitled to the capital. For example, *A* may settle property so that *B* is entitled to the income during his life-time, and *C* is entitled to the capital on *B*'s death. *B* is known as the life-tenant, *C* as the remainderman. The courts have from time to time been faced with the problem of deciding whether a certain item is "income" and therefore belongs to the life-tenant, or "capital" which must be preserved for the benefit of the remainderman. In solving this problem, the courts developed a concept of capital which is fundamentally different from that used by the economist as exemplified by the famous definition of Hicks: "Income is the maximum amount the individual can consume in a week and still expect to be as well off at the end of the week as he was at the beginning."[1] Suppose that *X*'s capital at the start of 1972 is £20,000; under the Hicksian definition he will have maintained his capital, as measured by disposable wealth, intact if he finishes the year with assets worth £20,000 (given constancy of the general price level). Any increase will be income. The composition of the assets is immaterial – only their total value is taken into account.

The lawyer's normal concept of capital in the context of a trust is different. To him, if *X*'s capital at January 1, 1972 was 1,000 shares in a company, *X* will have maintained his capital intact if he finishes the year with the same 1,000 shares. If he sells some shares, the money that he receives in exchange is regarded as the equivalent capital asset. Any increase in the value of the assets whether realised or unrealised is not part of income. If a capital asset is sold for a value greater than its initial value, the extra value has indeed to be recorded, but it is called a "capital gain" to differentiate it from income.

Lawyers have thus tended to regard a capital asset as a *res* or a "thing." Seltzer in a fascinating chapter has traced this concept to the practice of entailing landed estates in eighteenth-century England.[2] The person to whom a life interest in the estate was granted, was entitled to receive the income of the estate but had no right to spend the capital. The courts often had to decide what was in fact the income of the estate and therefore belonged to the life-tenant, as opposed to what was capital. Not unnaturally

[1] J. R. Hicks, *Value and Capital*, Oxford, 1938, 172.
[2] L. H. Seltzer, *The Nature and Tax Treatment of Capital Gains and Losses*, New York, 1951, ch. 2.

they took the view that the capital was the land itself and the income was the annual harvest. The life-tenant was entitled to the annual harvest, which could be disposed of without affecting the physical existence of the land.[3]

Over the next two hundred years estates came to consist more and more of financial securities – shares, bonds, etc. – but the courts applied the same principles to these assets as to land. The capital to be maintained was the bond itself, not its money value. A rise or fall in the market value of the bond did not change the physical character of the bond; it was not therefore regarded as an element of income. If the bond were sold, the entire proceeds of the sale retained the character of a capital asset as did any assets acquired with the money. Any surplus arising on the sale was of course capital; the life-tenant had no right to it. It was described as a capital gain to emphasise this point. Thus the practice developed of recording capital gains when they were "realised," *i.e.* on the sale of the assets. Unrealised capital gains were ignored. The income of the bond was its annual "harvest" – that "which is periodically detached and periodically recurs," *i.e.* the annual interest payment.

The reason for the courts adopting the *res* principle seems to have been largely pragmatic. To have applied a Hicksian "value" principle consistently and accurately would have required regular revaluations of all the assets of the estate. This would not only have entailed considerable extra work but would have provided endless opportunities for disputes between life-tenants and remaindermen. Certainly it would have been necessary to keep the most detailed accounting records in which each asset would be listed and entries periodically made to record changes in the assets' values. The *res* principle could be applied with the most rudimentary accounting records – only a list of physical assets was needed. The principle is simple, straightforward and easy to apply. In most cases it will lead to a clearcut, unambiguous distinction between capital gains and income with the minimum of dispute and difficulty. The cost of this simplicity is that it may, on occasion, lead to decisions that offend one's natural sense of fairness and justice; for example, if a share is sold *cum div* the entire pro-

---

[3] This attitude of the courts is well illustrated by the case of *Hassell* v. *Perpetual Executors Trustees and Agency Co. Ltd.*, High Court of Australia (1952) 86 C.L.R. 513. A man left the income of his estate to his wife for her lifetime, with the stipulation that on her death, the capital was to go to residuary legatees. The man died on September 26, 1950. Included in his estate were a large number of sheep which were shorn shortly after his death. The wool was sold for £20,095 in November 1950. The court held that the whole sum was income to which the life-tenant was entitled, stating: "The reason why the proceeds of wool shorn and lambs dropped are brought into the accounts of a business as revenue items is to be found in the character in which wool and the lambs came into existence as independent subjects of the property. They come into existence, by severance in the case of wool and by birth in the case of lambs, as produce of the sheep from which they are derived, and, like crops of grain and fruit, they belong to that class of produce which is periodically detached and periodically recurs. They are by their very nature, a profit." This passage illustrates very clearly the attitude of the courts in regarding certain objects (sheep in this case) as being capital and other objects (shorn wool in this case) as being, by their very nature, income.

ceeds are treated as capital, whereas if it is sold *ex div* the dividend when it is received is regarded as income.

There is clearly a world of difference between the lawyer's and the economist's concept. The lawyer's realised capital gain would be classified by an economist as income if it were expected; it would be a capital gain from the point of view of economic analysis only in so far as it was unexpected, and this concept, unlike the lawyer's, would have nothing to do with respective property rights. Many of the lawyer's capital gains can be clearly shown to be expected. A person who in December 1972 buys £100 of 3 per cent Saving Bonds at 89 which are due to be redeemed at 100 in 1975 is clearly expecting to make a gain on redemption of £11. The economist would regard this as income, the lawyer would call it a capital gain.

However, despite these differences, in a number of special cases involving judicial decisions the legal concept has been brought closer to the economic concept. The courts long ago recognised that a strict adherence to the *res* principle could in certain circumstances lead to arbitrary and specially unfair treatment of persons entitled to the income of a trust. For example, *A* leaves the residue of his estate, worth £10,000, in trust so that *B* is entitled to the income and *C* to the capital on the death of *B*. The amount of income that *B* will receive will depend on the nature of the investments. If, at present prices, the capital were invested in $2\frac{1}{2}$ per cent. Consols, *B*'s income under the normal rules would be around £983. If it were invested in a highly speculative share, say of a South African mining company, the dividend could be twice as much. Equating the income of a share to its dividend (the basic *res* principle) ignores the risk and the strong probability of the eventual fall in market value of the shares.

The courts have recognised this inequity and in certain cases, where the investments consist of "wasting" or "hazardous" property, have attempted to alleviate it by the application, pending realisation and re-investment of the property, of a set of rules known as "equitable apportionments." These rules only apply, however, when the investments in question are not authorised by law or under the will, so that the testator cannot be assumed to have intended the apparent inequity to arise, and they do not apply to real property. The basic principle, known as the rule in *Howe* v. *Earl of Dartmouth*,[4] is that the investment's income is to be taken, not as the dividend received, but as an annual percentage (at present 4 per cent.) of the market value of the securities at the date of death (or in some cases at the end of one year from the death), subject to the proviso that the life-tenant may only be paid out of cash generated by the securities (either from dividends or from sales of shares). The annual rate of return was originally intended to be the normal yield from trustee investments.

On the assumption that the initial market value is based on perfect knowledge of future dividends and sales proceeds and that the market rate

---

[4] *Howe* v. *Dartmouth* (*Earl*) (1802) 7 Ves. 137.

of discount is 4 per cent., the application of this rule produces a figure for income that is not dissimilar from that which an economist might calculate. Suppose that a block of shares is held for three years and then sold, the expected dividends and final selling price being as given in Table 1. (Tables are in the Appendix.) Given perfect market foresight and a 4 per cent. market rate of discount the value of the shares at the beginning can be calculated as £9,538·57. The life-tenant would be entitled to an annual income of 4 per cent. of this figure, £381·54. Thus he would be entitled to only part of the dividends, the rest being credited to the capital of the trust. The equitable apportionment between capital and income is given in Table 2. If it were assumed that the capital portion of the dividends was invested in 4 per cent. bonds, the total income of the life-tenant in succeeding years would be £381·54, £406·27, £439·02 and thereafter £378·22 per year as shown in Table 3. This is not the same as the economist's income since the latter would be equal each year. However it is much closer to it than if income were taken as being the dividends received. The economist could also point out that after the first year, the shares are overvalued in the books, a point made clear when a book loss of £1,938·57 is recorded when they are finally sold (Table 3). This "capital loss" is quite different from the economist's idea of a capital loss: since the dividends and sales proceeds are exactly as planned there is no unexpected loss.

The court thus discarded the *res* principle and measured income according to a "value" principle. The approximate consistency of the rule with the Hicksian principle depends, evidently, on the assumption that the initial market value of the investment is equal to the net present value of future cash flows at a 4 per cent. discount rate. However, in measuring Hicksian income it is essential to make some assumption about the future and that made by the courts is perhaps as reasonable as any.

The discrepency as compared with Hicksian income could be corrected by a slight modification of the lawyer's rule. The amount of the dividend regarded as apportionable to capital instead of being added to capital could be deducted from the value of the shares, thus reducing the base on which the income of 4 per cent. is calculated in the following year. The effect of this modified rule is shown in Table 4. The income of the life-tenant is £381·54 per year every year, and the shares are always correctly valued in the books, eventually being sold for exactly their book value. If in the event the shares were sold for a figure other than their ultimate book value, £7,600, a capital gain or loss would be shown and would indicate that the pattern or amount of dividends and ultimate selling price was different from what had been initially expected: in the economist's use of the term, there would be a true capital gain or loss. If the income of 4 per cent. could not be paid to the life-tenant in any year because of insufficient cash, a similar principle would apply: the amount of the deficiency would be added to the capital value of the shares in that year.

An especially interesting equitable apportionment occurs when the investment generates no cash receipts at all before its final realisation so that the application of the normal rule would prejudice the life-tenant; for example, one asset of an estate may be a debt that does not bear current interest but is repayable at a premium at a future date. The rule, known as the rule in *Re Earl of Chesterfield's Trusts*,[5] is that the total sum finally received when the investment is realised is to be apportioned between capital and income: capital is to receive an amount equal to the present value calculated by discounting the final sum realised to the start of the trust at the appropriate rate of interest, less income tax; the remainder of the sum received is income. It is possible in this instance to make a precise calculation of Hicksian income because no action is taken until the investment is finally realised; the apportionment can be made with perfect knowledge of all the facts.

To summarise, the lawyer's basic concept of income in this context is different from that of the economist. Although the application of the rules of equitable apportionments tend to lessen this difference, they do not remove it completely: there are still differences in detail. Moreover, the area of application of these rules is very limited, and they do not apply where the investments are authorised.

APPENDIX

Table 1

Date	Cash flow	Present value at 1.1.72 £
31.12.72	Dividend £1,000	961·54
31.12.73	Dividend £1,200	1,109·46
31.12.74	Dividend £800	711·20
31.12.74	Sale of shares £7,600	6,756·37
		9,538·57

Table 2

Date	Total dividend £	Income £	Capital £
31.12.72	1,000·00	381·54	618·46
31.12.73	1,200·00	381·54	818·46
31.12.74	800·00	381·54	418·46

[5] *Chesterfield's (Earl) Trusts* (1883) 24 Ch.D. 643.

Table 3

Date	Transactions	ASSETS Shares £	4% Bonds £	Cash £	CLAIMS Income £	Capital £
1.1.72	Opening balance	9,538·57	—	—	—	9,538·57
31.12.72	Receive dividend	—	—	1,000·00	381·54	618·46
	Invest in bonds	—	618·46	618·46 —	—	—
	Pay cash to life-tenant	—	—	381·54 —	381·54 —	—
1.1.73	Balance	9,538·57	618·46	—	—	10,157·03
31.12.73	Receive dividend	—	—	1,200·00	381·54	818·46
	Receive interest	—	—	24·73	24·73	—
	Invest in bonds	—	818·46	818·46 —	—	—
	Pay cash to life-tenant	—	—	406·27 —	406·27 —	—
1.1.74	Balance	9,538·57	1,436·92	—	—	10,975·49
31.12.74	Receive dividend	—	—	800·00	381·54	418·46
	Receive interest	—	—	57·48	57·48	—
	Sell shares	7,600·00 —	—	7,600·00	—	—
	Write off capital loss	1,938·57 —	—	—	—	1,938·57 —
	Invest in bonds	—	8,018·46	8,018·46 —	—	—
	Pay cash to life-tenant	—	—	439·02 —	439·02 —	—
1.1.75	Balance	—	9,455·38	—	—	9,455·38 —
31.12.75	Receive interest	—	—	378·22	378·22	—
	Pay cash to life-tenant	—	—	378·22 —	378·22 —	—
1.1.76	Balance	—	9,455·38	—	—	9,455·38 —

Table 4

Date	Transaction	ASSETS Shares £	4% Bonds £	Cash £	CLAIMS Income £	Capital £
1.1.72	Opening balance	9,538·57	—	—	—	9,538·57
31.12.72	Receive dividend	618·46 —	—	1,000·00	381·54	—
	Invest in bonds	—	618·46	618·46 —	—	—
	Pay income to life-tenant	—	—	381·54 —	381·54 —	—
1.1.73	Balance	8,920·11	618·46	—	—	9,538·57
31.12.73	Receive dividend	843·19 —	—	1,200·00	356·81	—
	Receive interest	—	—	24·73	24·73	—
	Invest in bonds	—	843·19	843·19 —	—	—
	Pay income to life-tenant	—	—	381·54 —	381·54 —	—
1.1.74	Balance	8,076·92	1,461·65	—	—	9,538·57
31.12.74	Receive dividend	476·92 —	—	800·00	323·08	—
	Receive interest	—	—	58·46	58·46	—
	Sell shares	7,600·00 —	—	7,600·00	—	—
	Invest in bonds	—	8,076·92	8,076·92 —	—	—
	Pay income to life-tenant	—	—	381·54 —	381·54 —	—
1.1.75	Balance	—	9,538·57	—	—	9,538·57
31.12.75	Receive interest	—	—	381·54	381·54	—
	Pay income to life-tenant	—	—	381·54 —	381·54 —	—
1.1.76	Balance	—	9,538·57	—	—	9,538·57

OPPORTUNITY COST: THE LONDON TRADITION[1]

J. R. Gould

INTRODUCTION

A recent monograph[2] by Professor Buchanan has drawn attention to a group of economists associated with the London School of Economics whose work over the two decades from 1930 can be said to constitute a London tradition in the theory of cost. He sketches the historical background and development of this tradition, and he regrets that the important insights achieved by its members seem largely to have been neglected by the profession. The adverse consequences that Buchanan attributes to this neglect are illustrated in the second half of the book by examples from applied welfare economics.

While there is much in Buchanan's book which is informative and stimulating, I believe that his interpretation and evaluation of the contributions of the London tradition are misleading in some important respects. His review of the historical development of cost theory conveys the impression of successive writers moving gradually towards a more and more refined and accurate concept of cost. The Golden Fleece is the definition of opportunity cost as the decision-maker's subjective evaluation of the foregone alternative. This definition, whose shades of meaning he discusses at great length, is regarded by Buchanan as the key to a theory of choice.

In my view, Buchanan attaches far too much weight to this definition of opportunity cost, both in his historical review and in his discussion of aspects of economic policy. That is not to say, of course, that clarity about concepts is unimportant. But it is possible for an excessive concern with the meaning of words to distract attention from substantive problems.[3] This, I believe, has happened in Buchanan's review of the London tradition. By presenting each author as hardly more than a link in the chain of

---

[1] I would like to thank Kurt Klappholz and the editors for helpful comments on a first draft of this paper.
[2] J. M. Buchanan, *Cost and Choice: An Inquiry in Economic Theory*, Chicago, 1970.
[3] In the extreme case, words are regarded as having some "essential" or "true" meaning which is clouded over in casual, everyday, usage. The task of discovering the "fundamental nature" or "essence" of a word is regarded as an important task for philosophical inquiry. The contrasting view is that words are the tools of clear thought and communication, and that definitions should be framed to suit the purpose in hand. The essentialist and nominalist views are discussed by K. Popper, *The Open Society and its Enemies*, 3rd ed. London, 1957, vol. 2, ch. 11.

evolution of the concept of opportunity cost, he does less than justice to their substantive contributions.

However, my purpose is to present an alternative to Buchanan's account of the London tradition, rather than to review his book. Instead of emphasising concepts and definitions, I shall stress the substantive problems and the way in which they were formulated. I shall try to show how the concept of opportunity cost developed in economic theory; and I shall argue that, in this context, it should be viewed, not as a definition of cost to be used for the analysis of choice, but as characterising the general equilibrium approach associated with the Austrian school, an approach which directs attention to questions of efficient resource allocation. These general ideas diffused among specialists in accounting and administrative theory at LSE, who found the conception of the economic problem as the efficient use of scarce resources fruitful in their own fields. The justification for regarding these LSE writers on diverse subjects as a school or tradition lies, I believe, more in the manner in which they formulated their problems than in an attachment to a particular definition of cost.

Indeed, I shall argue that opportunity cost has a very limited, though important, role in the analysis of problems of choice. This role is to ask *questions*: to ask, "What is the opportunity cost?" of some proposed plan is to ask that the alternatives be spelled out, evaluated, and compared; it is a reminder, often necessary, that the problem should be carefully formulated.[4] However, the concept is of very little use in providing the *answers* to problems of choice; for the computation of opportunity cost will generally require the prior ranking of the alternative plans – that is, the *prior* solution of the problem of choice, Moreover, as I shall illustrate below, a misguided insistence on the primacy of the opportunity cost definition over all other definitions of cost has sometimes resulted in unnecessary obscurity in analysis and sometimes in downright confusion.

OPPORTUNITY COST AND THE LONDON TRADITION

Limitations of space debar an attempt at a comprehensive review; the purpose of this section is limited to illustrating the roles played by the concept of opportunity costs in the writings of some members of the London tradition in the related disciplines of economic theory, accounting, and administrative theory. In the first, and beneficial, role, by focussing attention on efficient resource allocation, it led to fruitful reformulation of some important problems. To bring this point out, I provide a brief sketch of the history of ideas in each subject as a background to the contributions of the London tradition. In its second role, opportunity cost appears as the definition that, it is believed, captures the essential nature of cost, and

---

[4] This point of view is argued by Krish Bhaskar and Peter Watson in an unpublished paper "Decisions with Opportunity Costs."

which is more fundamental and thus to be preferred to other concepts of cost. This role was to the detriment of clarity in analysis and exposition.

(i) Economic Theory

The central problem of the theory of value is to explain the relative prices of goods. The classical answer is well illustrated by Adam Smith's famous beaver-deer example. "If among a nation of hunters . . . it usually costs twice the labour to kill a beaver which it costs to kill a deer, one beaver would naturally exchange for or be worth two deer."[5] In more general terms, the values of goods tend to equal their relative costs of production defined in terms of factor units.

The classical theory left some important problems unresolved. Clearly relative costs of production cannot supply a satisfactory answer when goods, *e.g.* Rembrandts and Rubens, cannot now be produced. Intuition suggests that market values must be related to the subjective evaluations of buyers; but the classical economists found difficulty in relating consumers' preferences to market prices. Early explanations along the lines that value was related to the utility inherent in the good foundered on counter-examples, well illustrated by the diamond-water paradox.[6]

Secondly, the theory exemplified by the beaver-deer case loses its sharpness when goods are produced by combinations of more than one factor of production: if two goods use factors in different proportions, their costs cannot be unambiguously compared in terms of physical units of factors. The obvious method of dealing with this difficulty is to evaluate the factor costs of production in money terms. But this raises the further problem: what determines the prices of factors of production?

Satisfactory answers to these problems were not provided until the marginal revolution of the late nineteenth century. The subjective theory of value, in which prices are proportional to marginal utilities and unrelated to total utilities, resolved the diamond-water paradox. Similarly, marginal analysis provided the foundations for a theory of demand for factors of production: profit-maximising firms hire each factor up to the point where the price of the factor equals the value of its marginal product.

The treatment of the supply of factors of production developed along two different lines. In the Anglo-Saxon tradition, exemplified by Marshall, emphasis was placed on "real costs," and the "pain" of supplying labour to different occupations and on saving as abstinence from consumption. The Marshallian approach leads naturally to the consideration of such questions as the short-run responsiveness of the supply of a factor to its price, and the differences in wages as between occupations. In contrast, the Austrian school commonly assumed factors to be fixed in aggregate supply

[5] Adam Smith, *The Wealth of Nations* Modern Library ed., New York, 1937, 47.
[6] That is, that diamonds are more valuable than water, although water is more useful than diamonds. The example is ambiguous, since the quantities of the goods are unspecified, but it has served to bring out the point that the relative values of goods are not related to the relative usefulness in any simple and obvious way.

and indifferent between the non-monetary aspects of occupations. These assumptions diverted attention to rather different questions, the answers to which make up the opportunity cost doctrine.[7]

The Austrian analysis directed attention to the relation between the cost of producing one good and the values of other goods. In outline, the argument is as follows. Each firm in a perfectly competitive economy equates the price of factor X to the value of its marginal product. Equilibrium, given that factor owners have no non-monetary preferences as between occupations, requires that all firms pay the same price for a factor of production. Thus the cost of employing a unit of X to a firm in industry B is, in equilibrium, equal to the value of the marginal product of X in industry A.

The argument can be epitomised by statements such as: the opportunity cost of employing a unit of factor X in industry B is the value of the additional product that the unit of X would have produced had it been employed in industry A; or even more briefly as: opportunity cost is the value of the displaced product. Valuable as it is to have the results of a chain of reasoning summarised in a pithy phrase, there are dangers of misinterpretation; and in this case the danger is that the two summary statements be treated as definitions of cost. Clearly, if the statements are interpreted as summaries of the preceding argument, the word "is" should not be understood as "is by definition," but as "is in equilibrium equal to." In the theory of the competitive market economy, costs are payments by firms to owners of factors of production;[8] these payments are pulled into line with displaced products by maximising behaviour of individuals as constrained by competitive forces. Moreover, out of equilibrium, or in an imperfectly competitive economy, the theory says that costs are *not* equal to the values of displaced products.

The Austrian contribution is misinterpreted if it is understood to advocate the concept of opportunity cost as a definition to be used in the analysis of the behaviour of individuals or firms. Rather the concept is part of the description of a relation that holds when markets are in equilibrium, and which provides insight into the forces determining factor prices. By its stress on the interrelation between prices and costs in one industry and prices and costs in other industries, the opportunity cost doctrine is identified as a general equilibrium approach to economic theory.

That the opportunity cost doctrine was understood in this general sense at LSE is illustrated in a well-known paper by Lionel Robbins.[9] It is clear from the following quotations that Robbins distinguishes sharply between

---

[7] For an account of the opportunity cost doctrine and its relation to the real cost doctrine see Mark Blaug, *Economic Theory in Retrospect*, 2nd ed. London, 1968, especially 491–495.

[8] Or imputed payments when the owner of the firm employs his own factors.

[9] Lionel Robbins, "Remarks on Certain Aspects on the Theory of Costs," *Economic Journal*, 44, 1–18.

the money costs with which the individual entrepreneur is concerned and the relations which hold in general equilibrium.

> The entrepreneur . . . thinks of the prices he has to pay for factors of production. . . . All that he knows is the values of factors of production, which are, of course, reflections of the values of other products. . . It is only in equilibrium that . . . harmony exists. In a state of disequilibrium prices, costs and displacement ratios may all be different. If we do not keep these things conceptually discrete, we cannot understand the process of equilibrium.[10]

The importance of understanding the process by which general equilibrium comes about is made clear in Robbins's ensuing critique of some aspects of partial equilibrium analysis. While allowing that the apparatus of partial equilibrium analysis can be useful in supplying approximate answers, he stresses the limitations and dangers of the technique. He concludes that

> . . . experience of the controversies of the last twenty years does, I think, suggest that the use of supply curves rather than the apparatus of general equilibrium analysis, carries with it dangers which may entrap even the subtlest and acutest intellects.[11]

In addition to its contribution to positive economic theory, the Austrian doctrine has an important normative aspect. By directing attention to the values attached to alternative uses of given resources, the concept of opportunity cost raises questions about efficient resource allocation somewhat more effectively than does the Marshallian partial-equilibrium analysis which had largely dominated English-speaking economics.[12] If, at the margin, the opportunity cost of a product is less than its price, this immediately suggests that consumers could gain more than they lose if resources were transferred to this product from other industries. Although now much refined, this simple argument remains the essence of a fundamental theorem of modern welfare economics.

The LSE economics department of the 1930s was among the most receptive to the contribution of the Austrian school to positive general equilibrium theory; but it was possibly the connection between opportunity cost and efficiency which most influenced those members of the department who were inclined towards applied, rather than theoretical, economics.

(ii) Accounting

Within the economics department at LSE were a small group, under the leadership of Professor Plant, whose main interests lay in the field of business administration rather than in the classical problems of economic theory. This group devoted considerable attention to the relevance of

[10] *ibid.*, 5–6.
[11] *ibid.*, 10–11.
[12] See Blaug, *op. cit.*, 495.

orthodox accounting procedures to business problems, in particular, to the usefulness of cost accounting for business decisions.

As a guide to decision-making, current practice was open to serious criticism. The manifest deficiencies of cost accounting in this respect can be explained by its historical development,[13] of which a brief sketch follows. It is commonplace that the roots of much modern accounting practice can be traced to the evolution of double-entry bookkeeping in northern Italy in the fourteenth and fifteenth centuries, and that double-entry is an elegant and efficient system of recording financial transactions for purposes of stewardship and control. Originally applied to the activities of merchants and to financial transactions outside the firm, the techniques of double-entry were extended to cover the recording of the flow of materials through processes within the manufacturing firm. By the late nineteenth century, it is evident from contemporary textbooks that the technical bookkeeping problems of this extension to cost accounting had been largely solved. Although the practices advocated do not seem to have been at all widely adopted at that time, with the growth in scale and complexity of manufacturing firms and the attendant increasing difficulties of administration, the use of cost accounts gradually became more widespread.

Although cost accounts were installed primarily for purposes of administrative control, it was natural that businessmen should turn to their accountants for figures to aid decision-making: for example, the businessman concerned with selling price would ask what an article cost to manufacture. This seemingly straightforward question turned out to contain hidden difficulties, among which were the valuation of materials drawn from stock, the computation of depreciation, and the allocation of overhead expenses. By the 1930s little progress had been made towards the resolution of these problems, other than by patently arbitrary devices, and orthodox accounting was, to a perceptive critic, a manifestly unsatisfactory tool for decision-making.

In retrospect the explanation seems clear. The traditional system of recording transactions, as extended to costing, was being asked to solve problems for which it had not been designed. Most fundamentally, traditional accounting was concerned with recording what *had* happened, that is, with historic cost, while decisions are concerned with the future consequences of alternative plans. Moreover, apart from the inadequacy of the data, the manner in which it was presented – as average, or unit, cost – was inappropriate for decision-making. The concept of the unit cost of an item seems so natural and familiar that it requires some economic sophistication to realise that it is not a useful concept for profit-maximising decisions, and that in many common circumstances its very meaning is ambiguous. Thus where there are joint costs of production, the problem of

[13] For a detailed account of the development of cost accounting see David Solomons, "The Historical Development of Costing," in D. Solomons (ed.), *Studies in Costing*, London, 1952, 1–52.

allocating overheads is logically intractable: much fruitless controversy over methods of allocation stemmed from the failure to appreciate this point.

In short, orthodox cost accounting for decision-making was built on inadequate foundations. A new approach was needed starting from the question: what data are required for decision-making, and how should they be analysed and presented? But the orthodox cost accountant was so conditioned by the traditions of bookkeeping for past transactions that it was extremely difficult for him to approach the problem of accounting for decision-making with fresh eyes.

The group of young business economists under Plant suffered from no such inhibitions. Apart from a good fund of commonsense, they brought to the task the standpoint and analytical tools of economic theory: they were accustomed to thinking of economic problems as choices between alternatives; and they were accustomed to dealing with these problems in terms of marginal analysis. The following summaries of papers by Ronald Edwards, William Baxter, and Ronald Coase are intended to convey the analytical approach of the London tradition in accounting and the role played by the concept of opportunity cost.

Ronald Edwards practised as an accountant before turning to economics. "The Rationale of Cost Accounting"[14] focuses attention on accounting for decision-making. Edwards begins by asking what business data are worth collecting, and answers: only that which can influence policy. In his view ". . . the most important thing about costs is the extent to which they change with output . . .,"[15] and he illustrates the importance of data on "additional," or marginal, cost by showing how comparison of additional cost and additional revenue can determine profit-maximising prices, outputs, and the allocation of resources between departments. He points out that fixed costs should not affect policy decisions, and that many problems, such as the inclusion of interest in cost and the valuation of materials drawn from stock, become tractable if the marginal approach is adopted. The allocation of overheads is unnecessary because ". . . we compare increments to cost with increments to revenue, rather than totals or averages . . ."[16] He emphasises that ". . . data (on past costs) is useful only in so far as it is a guide to future costs; it is future variable cost which is important . . ."[17]

Two other papers by Edwards elaborate on the same theme of marginal analysis. In "Cost Accounting and Joint Production,"[18] Edwards criticises in detail the currently orthodox methods of allocating joint costs. He shows how, when proportions between the joint products are variable, marginal analysis can determine the most profitable proportions to produce without

[14] Published in Arnold Plant (ed.), *Some Modern Business Problems*, London, 1938, 277–299. Reprinted in Solomons (ed.), *Studies in Costing*, 87–104.
[15] *op. cit.*, in Solomons (ed.), *Studies in Costing*, 90.
[16] *ibid.*, 96.
[17] *ibid.*, 94.
[18] *The Practising Accountant and Secretary*, May 7, 1937, 481–485. Reprinted in Solomons (ed.), *Studies in Costing*, 310–320.

allocating joint costs. In "The Approach to Budgetary Control,"[19] he uses the Marshallian distinction between the long and the short runs, and the Chamberlin–Robinson diagrammatic analysis of the firm's output decision, to show what information is necessary for profit-maximising plans to be formulated, and how it should be analysed. He then goes on to discuss the complications that arise when the assumptions of his simple model are not met.

In none of these papers does Edwards make explicit use of the concept of opportunity cost. The key concept is that of additional (or incremental, or marginal) cost, and Edwards's main objective is to demonstrate that marginal cost, and not average cost, is relevant for choosing the best of alternative plans. There is no formal definition of the word "cost," but I do not believe that this would hamper someone wishing to apply the marginal analysis advocated by Edwards to a practical problem, if he used his own common-sense definition.

William Baxter's paper, "A Note on the Allocation of Oncost between Departments,"[20] was published nine years before he came to LSE. However it was stimulated by a problem discussed briefly by Edwards, is referred to with approval by Coase, and is clearly in sympathy with the London tradition.

The problem with which Baxter is concerned is whether a business's general overhead expenses should be allocated to departmental accounts. He describes the main uses of departmental accounts and, employing the same method of reasoning as Edwards, he quickly concludes that the practice of allocating overheads is without logical foundation. He then raises an interesting question. Why, if the practice of allocating overheads rests on such shaky logical foundations, is it so widely employed and approved by businessmen, when it should lead to poor results and thus to rejection? Two of the possible explanations he advances need not detain us here. It is the third hypothesis which is interesting in the present context.

Baxter suggests that the allocated overheads may correspond in a rough way to opportunity costs. If resources were not being used in one department, they might be earning revenue in another. Conventional accounting neglects this sacrificed revenue, although it is clearly relevant for decisions about the use of resources. It is conceivable that allocated overhead expenses turn out to be a reasonably close approximation to these opportunity costs.

> We should then have an interesting example of compensating errors; the error of omission (the leaving out of opportunity costs) would neutralize the error of commission (the putting in of overheads(. Needless to say, however, accountants ought not to rely on this

---

[19] *The Practising Accountant and Secretary*, July 23 and August 6, 1937. Reprinted in Solomons (ed.), *Studies in Costing*, 365–382.
[20] *The Accountant*, November 5, 1938, 633–636. Reprinted in Solomons (ed.), *Studies in Costing*, 267–276.

possibility, but should try to estimate the opportunity costs when working out the possible results of a change in policy.[21]

In the essay "Business Organisation and the Accountant," by Ronald Coase,[22] the concept of opportunity cost figures as a keystone in the argument. Coase begins, in a manner very similar to Edwards, by explaining the concepts of marginal and avoidable costs, and illustrating by example how they can be applied to business problems. He concludes this part of the discussion: "The practical problem which then arises is how far accountants can be expected to produce figures which enable estimates of avoidable and marginal costs to be made."[23] The major part of his essay is concerned with these problems of measurement.

In the section headed "The Nature of Costs," Coase prepares the ground for a detailed discussion of the measurement of cost. ". . . the notion of costs which will be used is that of opportunity or alternative cost. The cost of doing anything consists of the receipts which could have been obtained if that particular decision had not been taken." This statement is qualified a little further down the page: ". . . it is probably better to regard the cost of doing anything as the highest alternative receipts which could have been obtained. . . ."[24]

There is a clear resemblance between Coase's specification of opportunity cost and the statements I have used above[25] to summarise the determination of factor prices in general equilibrium theory. Unfortunately, Coase does not make it clear whether he intends this description of opportunity cost to be a definition of cost to be employed in computation, or something else.

In my view it should not be regarded as a definition to be used in computation; for that purpose it is of little use and, indeed, can be misleading. The point can be illustrated by a simple example. Suppose a property developer owns a piece of land and is considering three alternative plans for its use: to build a factory, a garage or a hotel. Suppose that in each case he intends to sell the completed building and that in each case the work of construction will be undertaken by a contractor. The estimated selling prices and prices quoted by the contractor are:

	Factory	*Garage*	*Hotel*
Selling Price	100	80	70
Contractor's Price	80	50	45
Net receipts	20	30	25

[21] *op. cit.*, in Solomons (ed.), *Studies in Costing*, 273.
[22] *The Accountant*, October 1–December 17, 1938. Reprinted in Solomons (ed.), *Studies in Costing*, 105–158.
[23] *op. cit.* in Solomons (ed.), *Studies in Costing*, 115.
[24] *ibid.*, 123.
[25] *e.g.* "Opportunity cost is the value of the displaced product." See p. 94 above.

Common sense indicates correctly that the decision should be to construct the garage. Further, it is obvious that the cost of the land is irrelevant to the decision about how it should be exploited.

Now consider a somewhat obtuse developer who persisted in the literal use of Coase's definition of opportunity cost in his calculations. Since the plot of land is a resource with alternative uses, it has an opportunity cost in any given use, that is the highest alternative receipts. He would cost the land to the factory at 80 (the highest alternative receipts are from building a garage), to the garage at 100, and to the hotel at 100. Deducting the opportunity cost of the land from net receipts in each case, he would compute losses of 60 for the factory, 70 for the garage, and 75 for the hotel. The absurd conclusion would be reached that none of the plans is profitable and that the factory, is the least unprofitable.

A less obtuse developer would interpret opportunity cost to mean highest alternative *net* receipts. On this interpretation, the factory would show a loss of 10, the hotel a loss of 5, and the garage a profit of 5. The correct decision would be made – but the concept of opportunity cost has played no useful part in the computations necessary to arrive at the decision. The net receipts of each plan must be worked out *before* the opportunity cost of any one plan can be computed; and once the net receipts are known the correct decision can be made without further computation.[26]

This simple example shows that Coase's specification of opportunity cost, if interpreted as a definition for use in computation, is at best superfluous, and at worst downright misleading. The key to a more useful interpretation of his section on "The Nature of Costs" is to be found in the sentence in which he justifies the concept of opportunity cost on the grounds that ". . . it concentrates attention on the alternative courses of action open to the businessman." It might be objected that it would seem superfluous so to direct a businessman's attention. But this would be to forget the context in which Coase was writing. The orthodox costing figure of unit historic cost was inadequate precisely because it was produced mechanically from the costing records, without regard for the nature of decision problems.

Indeed, in my view the main contribution of the London tradition to

[26] The preceding criticism of opportunity cost as a concept for use in computation is essentially the same as that in my paper, "The Economist's Cost Concept and Business Problems," in W. T. Baxter and S. Davidson (eds.), *Studies in Accounting Theory*, London, 1962, 218–235. Solomons disagreed with that argument, and sought to rescue opportunity cost by relating it to the best of the alternatives outside those being considered. David Solomons, "Economic and Accounting Concepts of Cost and Value," in M. Backer (ed.), *Modern Accounting Theory*, Englewood Cliffs, 1966, chapter 6. This attempt was rejected by Amey who describes it as ". . . an unnecessary attempt to bring opportunity cost into the accounting framework. Why bother to introduce this complication when the correct solution can be obtained more directly without it? . . ." Amey's paper seems broadly in sympathy with the view I express here, but with reservations: while the concept of opportunity cost is never necessary for decision calculations, it may in certain limited circumstances be a useful device for computational efficiency. Lloyd Amey, "On Opportunity Costs and Decision Making," *Accountancy*, July 1961, 442–451.

accounting for decision-making was to direct attention away from the standard conventions of accounting practice and towards the fundamental problem – the choice between alternative business plans. Once attention is focused in this direction, the appropriate concept of cost becomes, as a matter of common sense, a forecast of the diminution of net assets which will result from a given plan.

The emphasis on marginalism is, I believe, of secondary importance. If the total effect on net assets of each plan is evaluated, the plans under consideration can be ranked for decision purposes. Marginalism – which is essentially carrying out the computations in terms of the differences between two plans' effects on net assets – is not necessary for decision-making. Rather, its role is to cut down the amount of computation necessary to compare alternative plans.

To summarise, I think that the following view emerges of the role of opportunity cost in this group of papers on cost accounting. Edwards did not use the concept explicitly; Baxter used it solely and explicitly to draw attention to what was omitted from accounting for decision-making – that resources have alternative uses; Coase could be interpreted to have used it for similar purposes, but could also be interpreted to have advocated it as a definition to be used in computation. As I have argued, it is either misleading or superfluous for this latter purpose. The most important sense in which this group of writers can be described as following an opportunity cost approach to accounting for decision-making is that they focused attention on the underlying problem, the efficient use of resources.

(iii) Administrative Theory

G. F. Thirlby returned from Capetown University to teach at LSE, where he had previously been a student of Arnold Plant. Thirlby was extremely critical of an orthodox economic theory in which the firm was, in effect, represented as controlled by one omniscient decision-maker, when most firms are organisations whose actions are the resultant of the decisions of a group of individuals.

> . . . The neglect of this case in economic theory is due, I imagine, to some inhibition in economists against recognizing the existence of an organization of men . . . What . . . is distressing is that the organizational relationships should fall between two stools (economics and politics), and make it necessary to establish a new subject called administrative theory.[27]

Thirlby would not, I believe, claim that he had presented a fully-fledged administrative theory in the papers which I shall discuss below. Rather, the contribution of these papers is to show that even an embryonic theory of administration can be used to criticise effectively accounting practice and established propositions in economic theory and policy, and to suggest new and important areas for investigation.

[27] G. F. Thirlby, "The Economist's Description of Business Behaviour," *Economica*, 19 (1952), 148–167, at 149.

Before coming to Thirlby's substantive contributions, I must discuss Thirlby's concept of cost, a concept which he discusses at some length in all of his papers and plainly regards as his most important analytical tool. There are two aspects of his discussions which I would like to distinguish carefully, for I believe that one of these aspects was wholly detrimental to the clarity of his exposition, while the second is the key to understanding his contribution.

The first aspect is that Thirlby uses the concept of opportunity cost as, in some sense, the fundamental definition of cost.[28]

> . . . [C]ost [should] be understood to refer to the prospective opportunity displaced by the administrative decision to take one action rather than another. . . . The acts of discovering cost, which really means discovering which of the considered alternatives is to be rejected, inevitably involves valuation, . . . arranging the opportunities in order of preference. . . .[29]

I have already argued that, although this usage may be well-understood when its purpose is to state, or ask for, the results of the evaluations of alternative plans, it is useless or confusing for the purpose of computing those evaluations. Similarly, I would contend that, so defined, it is useless and confusing for Thirlby's purpose, that is, as a tool in the analysis of decisions; for a definition which merely conveys the results of evaluation of alternative plans does not help us to understand how these evaluations are arrived at.

The second, and more important, aspect of Thirlby's discussion of cost is his stress on the "subjective" nature of the decision process.

> The alternatives between which a final selection is made are themselves a result of personal discovery and selection . . . the very limitation on human capacity necessitates the selection for consideration of only a few of the (infinite) alternatives, and that selection might be different . . . if a different administrator made the selection. . . . The act of discovering which of the considered alternatives is to be rejected inevitably involves valuation. . . . This valuation necessarily involves estimates of happenings in the future about which the decision-maker can never be certain.[30]

Thirlby's decision-maker is in sharp contrast to the omniscient entrepreneur operating in the certain world of static equilibrium theory.

Thirby values an adequate conception of decisions, not simply for its own sake, but because it is a necessary tool of administrative theory. "The decision . . . is the logical starting point for any investigation which seeks an explanation of why production or the industrial structure is what

---

[28] In this he believed, erroneously as I have argued above, that he was following Robbins. See *e.g.* Thirlby, *ibid.*, 156. Quite possibly he was misled by phrases such as "the fundamental nature of costs" which Robbins used when discussing the Austrian opportunity cost doctrine.

[29] G. F. Thirlby, "The Subjective Theory of Value and Accounting Cost," *Economica*, 13 (1946), 32–49, at 33–34.

[30] *ibid.*

it is."[31] The actions of an organisation in which administrative powers are delegated should be viewed as the resultant of the subjective evaluations of individuals, with possibly conflicting opinions about the values to be attached to, and the likelihood of, the consequences of any given plan. This view of organisational decisions – which is obviously quite independent of his definition of cost as the value of the displaced alternative – should, I believe, be regarded as the keystone of Thirlby's arguments.

Of the following brief accounts of three of Thirlby's papers, the first two illustrate his use of simple administrative models to criticise administrative techniques of control, and the third sets out the main features which a more complete administrative theory of the firm should incorporate.

"The Subjective Theory of Value and Accounting 'Cost'"[32] is concerned mainly with a critique of the usefulness of orthodox accounting for the control of a decentralised firm. Thirlby begins by describing the process of thought of the owner of a one-man business deciding how much money to invest in stock, and how much of each line he should buy. He then constructs a simple model of how this composite decision might be decentralised – two departmental managers are subordinate to a merchandise manager, who in turn is subordinate to a finance director. He specifies the information that must be collected and the information that must flow between successive levels of the hierarchy, and he describes how the tentative plans of the administrators are co-ordinated and finalised in a set of budgets.

Thirlby then turns to examine accounting practice. It is concerned with the *ex post* recording of the outflow of money costs, as adjusted by conventional methods to allow for depreciation, stock valuation, and allocation of overheads. Using his previous analysis of the administrative process, Thirlby argues that accounts in this form have no relevance for testing the "efficiency" of subordinate administrators. Departmental accounts should be related to the discretion allowed by the firm's administrative arrangements, and to what the person with delegated powers undertakes to perform. He concludes with pleas to economists to devise more refined models of decision making in decentralised organisations, and to accountants to study administrative theory.

The next paper relates to similar problems, but comes to more pessimistic conclusions.[33] Can authority be effectively delegated to a manager to run an industrial enterprise according to some rule that relates revenues to costs (for example, that managers of nationalised industries should equate price with marginal cost)? Thirlby is not concerned with the theoretical justification for the rule, but rather whether some higher authority, the "Ruler," can ascertain if the rule has been carried out.

---

[31] *ibid.*, 35.
[32] *loc. cit.*
[33] G. F. Thirlby, "The Ruler," *South African Journal of Economics*, 14 (1946), 253–276.

In brief, Thirlby's answer is that he cannot. The costs and revenues relevant to the efficient administration of resources are those of the planning stage; they are necessarily subjective estimates of future possibilities. Observation of what a manager has done will not indicate what he might have done. For example, the *ex post* accounts might suggest that price was equal to marginal cost even though the manager was neglecting, through laxity, or simply because he was not omniscient, more efficient techniques of production. The difficulties are compounded in a decentralised organisation, where plans are the resultant of the co-ordination of separate individuals' forecasts.

In "The Economist's Description of Business Behaviour,"[34] Thirlby outlines the requirements for an administrative theory of the firm. He argues that, even for a one-man business, the orthodox economic model has serious shortcomings. To remedy these deficiencies, explicit recognition must be given to the time taken for production plans to be implemented, and to the necessarily uncertain estimates on which plans must be based. Important though this is for the one-man business, not to recognise it in the case of organisations is "to neglect more than half the problem." In organisations, the crucial problem is the co-ordination of the tentative plans of individual administrators, each of whom is presumed to have specialised knowledge of some aspect of the firm's environment, and whose (uncertain) judgment on those aspects must be trusted if the advantages of decentralisation are to be obtained.

Thirlby believes that the non-monetary objectives of businessmen have particularly important implications for organisational behaviour. The administrator may be swayed by his personal values, by identification with his department or his profession; value judgments which are in conflict with the policy of the organisation may intrude into his decision-making. Delegation is difficult even if administrators try conscientiously to follow official objectives, for it is not easy to see how to frame policy directives in such a manner that the administrators can give appropriate weights to non-monetary objectives.

These summaries are intended to convey the substantive issues with which Thirlby was concerned. In economic theory, the firm is represented by a highly abstract model and attention is focused on efficient resource allocation via markets: Thirlby pointed to the neglected problems of efficient resource administration *within* the firm. In formulating the problems of administrative theory in terms of the efficient use of resources, Thirlby was following lines characteristic of the London tradition. What cannot be easily conveyed – it would require inappropriately long quotations – is the obscurity and confusion in Thirlby's exposition caused by his insistence on his concept of opportunity cost as the *only* admissible definition of cost.

[34] *loc. cit.*

THE DEATH OF A TRADITION?

The concept of opportunity cost has been something of a double-edged weapon. On the other hand, it directed attention to the efficient use of resources. In cost accounting, this perspective led to a reformulation of the problem. The traditional problem had been to derive a figure of unit cost from the accounts by averaging historic costs. The new question was: what information should be collected, and how should it be analysed? This perspective also led Thirlby to call for a theory which dealt adequately with the problem of the administration of resources within the firm.

On the other hand, the concept of opportunity cost has sometimes proved a hindrance. It has sometimes been regarded as, in some sense, incorporating "the fundamental nature of cost"; *ipso facto* other definitions of cost must be rejected. Unfortunately, the opportunity cost definition turns out to be a poor analytical tool and, as a consequence, those who tried to cast their thoughts in this mould succeeded only in making communication with their readers more difficult.

Buchanan believes that the opportunity-cost tradition at LSE died sometime in the 1950s.

> The concept of opportunity cost which emerged from both the subjectivist–Austrian and the common-sense approaches – the concept that blossomed for two decades at LSE – seems to have lost its struggle for a place among the paradigms of modern economics. Along with other conundrums of intellectual history, this is not easy to explain.[35]

There would indeed be a conundrum if opportunity cost were the powerful analytical tool which Buchanan claims it is.[36] If, on the other hand, it is not, then that the term might be less used now is not difficult to understand. Moreover, if opportunity cost is thought of as no more than a useful phrase for focusing attention on the problem of the efficient allocation of scarce resources, then, though the slogan may be less used, the basic approach is very much alive and well in modern economics, nowhere more so than at LSE.

A thorough evaluation of the influence of the writers in the London tradition is beyond the scope of this paper. Nevertheless, if only to add a

[35] *op. cit.*, 35.
[36] In the second half of his book, Buchanan attempts to display the virtues of his concept of opportunity cost by exposing errors that he discerns in many current propositions in applied welfare economics. In my opinion this attempt fails. Buchanan's general accusation is that economists make *logical* errors because of their neglect of the opportunity cost doctrine. However, examination of his discussions of specific propositions shows that his criticisms turn on *empirical* questions. For example, many standard propositions in the literature are based on the assumption that the individual's welfare depends only on the goods and services which he consumes. Buchanan objects to some of these on the grounds that the individual's welfare may also depend on the welfare of other individuals. [See *e.g.* his discussions of drinkers (p. 54), foxhunters (p. 76), and thieves (p. 93)]. Which of these assumptions is correct is a question of fact, which cannot be settled by reference to a definition of cost or any other definition. Buchanan has some interesting things to say about applied welfare economics. Unfortunately, as in Thirlby's case, his points are obscured by his over-enthusiasm for the concept of opportunity cost.

counterweight to Buchanan's somewhat depressing evaluation quoted above, the following tentative suggestions may be useful.

I have associated the concept of opportunity cost with a general equilibrium approach to both positive and normative economics. Since the war, the balance has swung towards general equilibrium analysis, and the undue dominance of Marshallian partial equilibrium analysis has to a large extent been corrected. Mathematical economists are asking fundamental questions about the nature of equilibrium models of the market mechanism, and in the specialised fields, such as international trade, public finance, and labour economics, two-sector general equilibrium models are frequently used to re-examine the conclusions of partial-equilibrium analysis. At a minimum, it can be claimed that the London tradition was very much in sympathy with this emerging trend.

The group of papers which I have selected to exemplify the London tradition of opportunity cost as applied to accounting were all published within a brief period in 1937–38. As a group, they accomplished two major tasks: they showed that current cost accounting practice was quite inadequate for decision making; they laid the foundations for improvements in the estimation and analysis of data for decisions by emphasising that the fundamental problem is that of choice between alternative plans.

It is probable that the influence on contemporary practice was slight, relative to the long-run effects. Established practitioners who have spent their professional lives following well-established procedures are not easily persuaded to rethink the foundations of their art – especially at the behest of a few papers by young academics.

In the longer run, the influence may have been considerable. No student could pass through the LSE Accounting department without becoming familiar with the opportunity cost approach to decision-making, interpreted broadly as directing attention to the alternative uses of resources. At a minimum, he would emerge with a critical attitude towards current professional orthodoxy. More important, he would not be trained in some alternative dogma, but in a more valuable approach – that problems should be formulated clearly and the answers thought out from first principles.

The LSE Accounting department, with an annual intake of some twenty to thirty students, is, of course, small in relation to the accounting profession. Nevertheless, its influence is magnified by diffusion. First, many of its students have gone on to acquire professional qualifications and have secured responsible posts in large accounting practices, which themselves are training grounds for other generations. Second, when university teaching of accounting expanded in the 1960s, LSE graduates formed a readily available pool of potential teachers who combined academic and professional expertise. By this process of diffusion, the London tradition may have played an important role in releasing cost accounting from its historical shackles.

The work of George Thirlby seems never to have captured the imagination of his LSE colleagues. However, his appeal for a theory which takes account of the organisational structure of the firm has been answered elsewhere by the recent vigorous development of the so-called "behavioural" and "managerial" theories. Many of the issues raised by Thirlby, for example, the importance of managers' non-monetary objectives, the possibility of conflict between the objectives of the manager and those of the firm, the "limited rationality" of decision-makers, have now been incorporated in more fully-elaborated models.[37]

Thus the substantive contributions of the writers in the London tradition cannot be said to have fallen on stony ground. It is true that the phrase "opportunity cost," then so much part of the jargon, is now somewhat out of fashion. But I believe that there is a very good reason for this. The analysis of optimal decisions in terms of costs and benefits has, to some extent, been superseded. Nowadays, even those who, like myself, are not mathematicians are inclined to think and speak in terms of maximising an objective function subject to constraints. And this new jargon is not used solely to "snow" the uninitiated; for it offers a more elaborate and more refined apparatus for structuring decision problems.

Dissatisfaction with the rather untidy way that the word "cost" is used in several different senses in everyday speech can lead to a bogus, and completely fruitless, intellectual inquiry into the "true meaning of cost." It is far better to recognise that each of the everyday meanings may be useful, and to coin a terminology which distinguishes them carefully for the purpose of rigorous scientific discussion. Thus, we do not ask whether costs are "really" monetary, or physical, or psychological magnitudes, but we distinguish money outlays from marginal rates of transformation in production and marginal rates of substitution in consumption. To insist that our thoughts be cast in terms of opportunity cost would be to turn back the clock, and analogous to requiring modern astronomers to describe all phenomena in Newtonian terms.[38]

[37] See *e.g.* Richard M. Cyert and James G. March, *A Behavioural Theory of the Firm*, New Jersey, 1963.

[38] James M. Buchanan and G. F. Thirlby (eds.), *L.S.E. Essays on Cost*, London, 1973, includes most of the papers referred to above, together with an introductory essay by Buchanan. It appeared after my paper had been set up.

LAWRENCE DICKSEE, DEPRECIATION, AND THE DOUBLE-ACCOUNT SYSTEM[1]

J. Kitchen

LAWRENCE Robert Dicksee was the first man to hold a chair of accounting in a British university. He was also the first holder of a chair of accounting in the University of London; and he was the first teacher of accounting at the London School of Economics and Political Science. He was, in addition, the first British chartered accountant to write a book on depreciation.[2]

Dicksee was articled in London in 1881, and wrote his first book *Auditing*[3] in 1892. Most of his ideas on depreciation had taken shape by that time, and *Auditing* incorporated them. This essay aims to consider Dicksee's approach to depreciation in the light of developments relative to that subject which were taking place in the accountancy profession and elsewhere in the dozen or so years prior to 1892. It pays attention to the so-called "double-account system" of preparing accounts for certain Parliamentary and other companies, particularly railways, which significantly influenced Dicksee's thinking – and that of accountants and lawyers generally – during those years.

Dicksee was born in 1864, and he tells us[4] that he qualified by examination for membership of the Institute of Chartered Accountants in England and Wales (ICA). The Institute had been incorporated by royal charter in 1880. When Dicksee became an associate in 1886, there were about 1,400 members.[5]

Dicksee set up immediately in practice in London on his own account. But in 1889 he joined Peter Price of Cardiff in partnership in that town under the style of Price and Dicksee. A London office was maintained for a while. Price died in 1892, and Dicksee left the firm in 1894, after allowing time for Price's son to complete his articles. In September 1894, Dicksee

---

[1] I am greatly indebted to Mr. Percy F. Hughes, Editor-in-Chief of *The Accountant*, for facilitating reference to volumes of that publication dated prior to 1912; and to Miss K. M. Bolton, the Librarian of the Institute of Chartered Accountants in England and Wales, and to the staff of the National Library of Wales for assistance with other material. The Editors and I are also indebted to Lord Justice Buckley and to Messrs. Gee & Co. (Publishers) Ltd. for permission to reproduce extended passages from copyright works.

[2] *Depreciation, Reserves and Reserve Funds*, London, 1903. At this date, terminological distinction was not made between "provisions" and "reserves."

[3] London, 1892. Dicksee appears on the title-page as "formerly Lecturer on Book-keeping at the Technical Schools of the County Borough of Cardiff."

[4] Presidential address to the Birmingham Chartered Accountant Students' Society, November 10, 1904. *The Accountant*, November 19, 1904, 626–9.

[5] *The Accountant*, May 7, 1887, 265.

went into partnership in London with Arthur Sellars. Together they founded the firm of Sellars, Dicksee and Co. which Dicksee headed from 1898 until he died in 1932.[6]

Auditing was an immediate success. The book ran to fourteen British editions in Dicksee's lifetime. An eighteenth edition was published in 1969. Dicksee's was not the first book on auditing. The distinction of writing the first such work seems to belong to F. W. Pixley, who published his *Auditors: their Duties and Responsibilities under the Joint-Stock Companies Acts and the Friendly Societies and Industrial and Provident Societies Acts*[7] early in 1881. But Dicksee's book was, as its subtitle claimed, "a practical manual for auditors," and though Pixley's *Auditors* ran to a dozen editions by 1922, it was not a serious competitor. Pixley's book included a brief reference to depreciation, which we shall note later.

After Cardiff, Dicksee had some further teaching experience in London, where he ran the coaching classes of the Chartered Accountant Students' Society of London. In 1901, the University of Birmingham announced that they proposed to set up a Faculty of Commerce. A part-time chair in Accounting was advertised in 1902, and Dicksee was appointed. *The Accountant* announced the appointment with satisfaction, noting that it was Dicksee's intention to continue his practice in London.[8] When, a couple of months later, LSE issued its sessional programme for 1902–1903, an optional course was included of sixty lectures over two years on "Accountancy and Business Methods," framed to meet the requirements of the University of London's degree of Bachelor of Science. Professor Dicksee was named as the lecturer. He was to teach at LSE (always on a part-time basis) for the next quarter of a century.

Dicksee contrived to limit his visits to Birmingham to one day a week, though work on the Birmingham courses occupied a substantial portion of his time. All the indications are that Birmingham University and its students were well pleased with the accounting courses. The University conferred an M Com on Professor Dicksee at its degree congregation in 1903.[9]

Dicksee published *Depreciation, Reserves and Reserve Funds* later in 1903, eleven years after the first edition of *Auditing*. He had not, however, been idle. Apart from lectures and articles, and unsigned contributions to periodicals including *The Accountant*, Dicksee had published *Book-keeping for Accountant Students* in 1893 (which ran to eight editions before Dicksee died); *Comparative Depreciation Tables* in 1895 (the third edition appeared in 1925); *Bookkeeping for Company Secretaries* in 1897 (six editions at Dicksee's death); *Goodwill and its treatment in accounts* also in

[6] *The Accountant*, February 20, 1932, 236.
[7] London, 1881. Francis William Pixley was a member of the Council of the ICA from 1888, and President in 1903–1904.
[8] *The Accountant*, August 2, 1902, 758.
[9] *The Times*, July 6, 1903. See also *The Accountant*, November 19, 1904, 626; and an extract from the (Birmingham) *University Engineering Journal* quoted in *The Accountant*, April 13, 1907, 502–503.

1897 (which, with F. Tillyard, ran to four editions before Dicksee died); *Bookkeeping Exercises for Accountant Students* in 1899 (the fourth edition was current when Dicksee died); *Auctioneers' Accounts* in 1901; *Gas Accounts* and *Solicitors' Accounts* both in 1902; and a major book on *Advanced Accounting* in 1903 (which ran to seven editions before Dicksee died).

Dicksee resigned from the Birmingham chair at the end of 1906 in order to concentrate on his work at LSE, where he was made Reader in Accounting in 1912, and given the title of Professor of Accounting and Business Methods in 1914. This he held to 1919, when the London commerce degree was introduced and he was appointed to one of the newly-established Sir Ernest Cassel chairs as Professor of Accounting and Business Organisation in the University of London.

DEPRECIATION BEFORE THE 1880s

By coincidence, the formative years of Dicksee's career (1881–92) were almost exactly the years in which some of the most important developments took place in ideas about depreciation in the minds of businessmen and engineers, accountants, and lawyers.

Some general concept of depreciation – by whatever name it was called – had been familiar from the earliest times, and there is a good deal of evidence of the evolution of depreciation accounting dating back into the seventeenth century and earlier.[10] But, as William Baxter rightly observes in his own *Depreciation*,[11] "there is little point in worrying over asset values and the exact timing of costs ... [unless] ... these ... affect practical issues."

Depreciation did not become important for the accountancy profession until invention and the increasing pace of change in tastes and techniques brought about substantial business investment in relatively short-lived fixed assets. Even that was not sufficient, for concomitment development was required in the markets for investment finance, and in new forms of business organisation, before depreciation became significant in the calculation of the annual profit figures necessary for reasonable justice to be done between different categories of investor and between investors present and future. Railway development, mainly between the 1830s and the 1870s, brought all these things – massive industrial investment, a transformation of the capital market,[12] and the development of the company form of business organisation together with the divorce, on a new scale, of ownership from control. But the railways were a special case, by virtue of the

[10] See, *e.g.* A. C. Littleton, *Accounting Evolution to 1900*, New York, 1933, or Perry Mason's "Illustrations of the Early Treatment of Depreciation," *Accounting Review*, September 1933.
[11] London, 1971, Preface.
[12] See, *e.g.* M. C. Reed, "Railways and the Growth of the Capital Market," in M. C. Reed (ed.), *Railways in the Victorian Economy*, Newton Abbot, 1969, 162.

peculiar circumstances attending their development and financing. Because of these circumstances, and also as a result of the application in the Regulation of Railways Act of 1868 of the double-account system,[13] the railways generally did not furnish early direct precedents for depreciation accounting. None the less, they provided considerable opportunity for the discussion of depreciation problems, and railway experience was widely relevant to the ideas about depreciation which emerged in the 1880s.

Up to that time, besides British and Indian government securities, foreign and colonial government and other loans, the loan stocks of municipal and other corporations, and the share and loan capital of railway companies, investors were principally concerned with banking companies, insurance and life assurance companies, docks, gas, and water companies, and collieries and mining ventures at home and overseas. For banks and other finance and similar organisations, depreciation was not an issue, though properties and other assets might be written down, mainly to provide secret reserves. Standard forms of account incorporating the double-account system were prescribed for gasworks under the Gasworks Clauses Act 1871. Docks and water companies had characteristics in common with railway undertakings.

Like the railways (though for different reasons) mines were another special case. It was common for the proprietors of mining undertakings to agree to have regard to the once-for-all character of their investment and the geological uncertainties and other contingencies to which it was subject, and to accept the paying away of net earnings as dividends after allowing for maintenance (and perhaps depreciation of some machinery) but without provision for amortisation of the costs of establishing the *corpus* of the mine. Single-ship companies were most commonly operated on similar lines.

DICKSEE'S GENERAL APPROACH TO DEPRECIATION IN 1892

It will now be convenient to turn to Dicksee's basic approach to depreciation, as he himself set it out in the first edition of *Auditing*. Paradoxically, Dicksee excluded from *Depreciation, Reserves and Reserve Funds* the discussion of general principles relative to depreciation which he included in *Auditing*, and later in *Advanced Accounting*, and which constituted his basic views about profit estimation and asset values for balance sheet purposes.[14] We should remember that for publication in 1892 Dicksee

[13] See Appendix.
[14] *Depreciation* begins with some paragraphs about the importance of a regular and adequate provision for depreciation, and proceeds straightaway to a consideration of methods in relation to different categories of assets. Dicksee includes some three pages on the double-account system near the end of his book. At the beginning, when he is making the case for regular direct charges for depreciation, Dicksee puts the weight of opposition on what he calls the special pleading of those who would inflate profits by arguing that no direct charge is necessary because "such provision as might under normal circumstances be proper in this connection" has been effected "by other means" (p. 2).

would have been writing soon after the decision of the Court of Appeal (February 1889) in *Lee* v. *Neuchatel Asphalte Co.* (*infra*) which had taken the accountancy profession aback. There was a relationship between the *Lee* judgment and the logic underlying the double-account system which Dicksee must have been aware of, though he does not seem to have seen it very clearly.

Dicksee introduced his discussion with the warning that

> As the points now about to be discussed are the most important, so are they also the most debatable, accountants of the highest repute being by no means agreed as to the principles involved . . .

At the same time he seems to have felt impelled to assert that "the acute observer" would be able to discern that "much of this apparent difference is . . . merely verbal," adding that ". . . it is . . . not unreasonable to suppose that, in any particular case . . . there would not exist among our leading practitioners any radical difference of opinion as to what the profit of a company had really been. . . ."[15]

Dicksee went on to consider the "Principle in Valuation of Assets" in the following terms:

> It being the primary object of most ordinary undertakings to continue to carry on operations, it is but fair that the assets enumerated in a Balance Sheet be valued with that end in view; before this subject is pursued any further, however, it is well to acknowledge two *essentially different features* obtaining to different classes of accounts. Certain Parliamentary Companies, constituted for the purposes of undertaking certain definite public works are, on account of the peculiar circumstances under which they were called into existence, required to render their accounts in a manner radically different from that of all other undertakings: the system they are required to adopt is called the DOUBLE-ACCOUNT SYSTEM. It being required that all capital raised by these companies shall be expended in the construction of the public works (for the construction of which they were called into existence), care was taken by the Legislature to see that this provision is duly complied with: hence a special form of account, in which all monies expended in the construction of the works is separated from the General Balance Sheet. Now, in order that this account (the Capital Expenditure Account) might perpetually show that – and how – the capital authorised to be raised had actually been spent only upon the authorised purposes – except a small margin for working capital or contingencies – it was necessary that the actual amount expended on the works alone be debited to the account, regardless of any fluctuations in value that might afterwards occur. It would, of course, have been easy for the Legislature to have provided that any fluctuation that might occur should be duly allowed for in the General Balance Sheet; but, having regard to the fact that no such fluctuation could in any way practically affect the company, so long as it carried on business, and bearing in mind also the fact that it was contemplated that the company should *permanently* carry on business, it would

[15] *Auditing*, 1892, 117.

appear that all consideration of these fluctuations was considered superfluous. With an eye to the future, however, and doubtless also with a view to – so far as possible – insuring the business being permanently carried on, it was provided that the company's works (which were required to be kept perpetually at the amount of their initial cost, regardless of their after value) be continuously kept in a state of efficiency, and that the cost thereof be borne out of Revenue. It will thus be seen that the *form* of the Double-Account system arose from the statutory requirement that all capital raised should be used for the carrying out of the works for the execution of which the company was created; and that the principle that, so long as the works were maintained in a state of efficiency their actual value need not be periodically reconsidered, arose from the circumstance that it was contemplated that the work authorised would be permanently carried on.

How far – if at all – these considerations need affect one's judgment concerning the valuation of the assets of undertakings not specifically covered by [such statutes] it will now be necessary to enquire; but it may be mentioned that, inasmuch as Auditors are not compelled to regard the Legislature as the highest possible authority in the matter of accounts, they are still free to discuss the principles involved upon their merits, even if a sense of logic compels them to admit an analogy between the accounts of Parliamentary companies and those of other undertakings.[16]

Dicksee then turned to the case of private traders, "whether *sole* or firms," noting that "as no man can . . . hope to live for ever, the business of such an one is ephemeral . . . compared with that of a parliamentary company." None the less, since such businesses often outlived their founders, a revaluation of assets was likely to be involved upon a change of proprietorship, and it must be expected that the basis of valuation in such case would be "as a going concern." To this term, Dicksee attributed a somewhat "elastic meaning" implying "at such a value as [the assets] would stand in the books if proper depreciation had been provided for" – the term "depreciation" being taken to represent "the amount by which the value of an asset has become reduced by effluxion of time or wear." Having also commented that it was "not really practicable so to maintain the efficiency of assets that no depreciation" should "ever exist", and that private firms were "under no statutory requirement to *retain* the whole of their undertaking intact," Dicksee concluded that the double-account system did not apply to the accounts of private traders.

Considering registered companies, Dicksee noted that they had a perpetual succession and "consequently the Double-Account system of stating values might be employed." But he argued that it should not, because companies in practice were generally shorter-lived than private businesses; because registered companies were under no obligation to retain any particular one of their assets; and because in any case it was

---

[16] *Auditing*, 117–118.

impracticable to divide the assets into two balance sheets on the basis that some were permanent and others not. Dicksee concluded: "The amount, therefore, at which *all* assets are stated in Balance Sheets, except where a special statutory provision to the contrary obtains, should be regulated by the value of such assets."[17]

However, it is not certain that Dicksee was able to dismiss the influence of the double-account system (with its emphasis on different treatment for capital and non-capital items) as readily from his mind as his arguments above might lead us to suppose. Thus, he turned almost immediately to consider the "Valuation of so-called Permanent Assets,"[18] arguing:

> The points to be borne in mind here are that wasting may reduce their value, and that fluctuation may increase or reduce their value. So far as wasting is concerned, inasmuch as it has directly contributed to the profit earned, it is clearly an expense with which profit may be fairly charged. On the other hand, fluctuation is something altogether apart from profit and loss, being merely the accidental variation (owing to external causes) in the value of certain property owned, but not traded in: to carry the amount of such variation to Profit and Loss Account would be to disturb and obscure the results of actual trading, and so render statistical comparison difficult if not impossible. On no account, therefore, should the results of fluctuations affect the Profit and Loss Account . . .[19]

A few pages later Dicksee repeated the same point and added:

> The author is not prepared to admit that this distinction is contrary to the various legal decisions that have occurred from time to time; but in any case, he would remind readers that, whatever deference or obedience is owing to the Courts, they cannot be regarded as indisputable authorities upon matters of account.[20]

As to depreciation methods and individual asset values, Dicksee's consideration proceeded for about a dozen categories from freehold buildings to furniture. Fixed instalments, and fixed percentages on reducing balances (with or without interest adjustments), were based specifically or by implication on original cost.[21] Obsolescence received appropriate treatment, but Dicksee clearly thought much plant and general machinery ran "comparatively little risk of becoming obsolete." For assets like plant or furniture and fittings, Dicksee thought "an occasional revaluation [would] be desirable."[22]

Dicksee mentioned two other categories which should be noted:

[17] *ibid.*, 120.
[18] Dicksee called these fixed assets in later editions of *Auditing*.
[19] *Auditing*, 121.
[20] *ibid.*, 126.
[21] *ibid.*, 126–128. Prices in general had fallen steadily from about 1873 to 1886, whereafter a less noticeable decline in prices continued to about 1896.
[22] *ibid.*, 130. In the first edition of *Depreciation*, 1903, Dicksee said of shafting that ". . . within reasonable limits it may perhaps be said that there is practically no risk of [its] becoming obsolete . . ." (p. 31), though he included a caveat about light machinery and small electric motors. These observations remained unchanged into the fifth edition of *Depreciation*, 1926.

Investments need not be depreciated unless of a wasting nature, such as shares in Single Ship Companies . . .

Mines undoubtedly depreciate in direct proportion to the amount of mineral extracted. By a singular inconsistency of the law, however, no depreciation need be provided for by a mining company before declaring a dividend.[23]

VIEWS ON DEPRECIATION, 1881–86

Students of Professor Yamey's "The Case Law relating to Company Dividends"[24] know well that a "single unifying idea runs through the decisions . . . before the year 1889"; and that the case decisions up to 1882 were

premised on the view that the provisions of the Acts regarding the capital of a company, and more especially its reduction, make it clear that the legislature would . . . [frown] upon any dividend payment which would . . . [leave] the company with a sum of assets less, in value, than its nominal paid-up capital . . .

They know too that there was ". . . no hint in the . . . decisions as to which 'value' of the assets . . . had to be maintained." [25]

This was exactly the position taken by Pixley, in his *Auditors* in 1881, and he was able to dismiss the principle very simply (though he too was silent on the meaning to be attributed to "value") thus:

The Auditor should also require a proper amount written off for depreciation of plant, machinery, &c. This is usually a percentage on the cost, and small or large according as it has to be seldom or frequently replaced, the object being to charge the Revenue Account of the period with a proper sum for the usage of the plant, and for the balance to represent its present value.[26]

By contrast, the following paragraph from a lecture given in November 1882, by a Birmingham chartered accountant, imports the flavour of practice in a centre of industry:

The cost of the property should be stated, and for the leasehold property a sinking or redemption fund should be established and accumulated at compound interest, in order to provide for the extinction of the asset which naturally ensues at the expiration of the lease, *or else, as is more commonly done, the cost is reduced from time to time out of profits.* . . .

[A] very good plan, *when it can be carried out*, is to establish by means of a yearly percentage a fund to which the cost of renewals may be charged, and against which the value of obsolete or worn out and unrenewed property may be debited. *A more general practice is to*

[23] *Auditing*, 128–129. The "singular inconsistency" must refer to the *Lee* v. *Neuchatel Asphalte* case of 1889.

[24] In W. T. Baxter and S. Davidson (eds.), *Studies in Accounting Theory*, London, 1962, 428–442.

[25] Yamey, *ibid.*, 429–430.

[26] Pixley, *Auditors*, 118.

write off out of profit lump sums from time to time, but in my judgment
the plan I have indicated is decidedly the preferable one.[27]

The italics are mine. The lecturer, Joseph Slocombe, prominent in Birmingham accountancy circles, was addressing the Birmingham Accountants'
Students' Society (formed in that year) on Auditing, and had chosen the
1862 Table A *pro-forma* balance sheet as his model – "I think we
cannot do better than take up the form of Balance Sheet laid down in
Table A . . . because it is based upon sound principles and is a very good
general pattern."[28] It will be recalled that the Table A Balance Sheet listed
various asset-headings (including stock) adding: "The cost to be stated
with Deductions for Deterioration in Value as charged to the Reserve
Fund or Profit and Loss."[29] Uncertainty as to whether depreciation should
be treated as (to use twentieth-century terminology) an appropriation or a
charge against profits appears in the Table A form and is evident throughout Slocombe's paragraph. This uncertainty was at the heart of the
depreciation problem at the beginning of the 1880s.[30]

In the last quarter of 1883, Ewing Matheson published four articles in
The Engineer on "The Depreciation of Factories." Matheson wrote as an
engineer (MICE) and a former factory owner with more recent experience
in the professional examination of machinery in other factories. His
articles gave rise to some interesting correspondence in *The Engineer* from
engineers and factory owners, and Matheson published them in book form
in 1884.[31] *The Accountant* received a copy of the book late in 1884, and it
provoked no less than six leading articles (but no correspondence – other
than Matheson's letter) in *The Accountant* in the weeks that followed.

We may wonder why, in the early 1880s, there was this apparent eruption
of interest in depreciation of industrial plant. We have, however, already
observed (footnote 21 above) that prices in general had been falling
steadily since their high-point around 1873, and they were to continue to
fall into the mid-1890s. The rate of growth of industrial production was
also low around 1880, at any rate well below the average for the latter half

[27] *The Accountant*, December 16, 1882, 9.
[28] *The Accountant*, December 9, 1882. When Slocombe died, *The Accountant* May 13,
1899 referred to this as "the earliest lecture on auditing."
[29] See the Companies Act 1862, or Edey and Panitpakdi, "British Company Accounting
and the Law, 1844–1900," in A. C. Littleton and B. S. Yamey (eds.), *Studies in the
History of Accounting*, London, 1956.
[30] For lack of space, I do not deal here with Edwin Guthrie's lecture on "Depreciation
and Sinking Funds," printed in *The Accountant*, April 21, 1883, 6–10. Guthrie was in
no doubt that depreciation required treatment as a cost, and argued clearly for a
"going concern" basis for (fixed) asset values. He presented a full range of methods
related to original cost. Periodic revaluation he favoured "for purpose of check,"
but he warned that "[m]atter and things fixed in a permanent working position must
not be treated in accounts as following the fluctuations of the market . . ."
[31] In a letter published in *The Accountant*, January 3, 1885, 6–7, Matheson said: "It was
the entire absence, as far as I could find, of any treatise whatever on a subject which
I, in common with other engineers, often sought information about, that prompted
me to write mine." The book was *The Depreciation of Factories and their Valuation*,
London, 1884.

of the nineteenth century. Profits were relatively hard to make and price setting was a delicate exercise. These factors may have been relevant, in addition to the factors of most direct concern to the accountancy profession (*e.g.* the spread of the company form of business organisation) which we have already noted.

The Accountant gave Matheson's book a cool reception. Nevertheless, with six leading articles the depreciation problem got a good airing and Matheson some good publicity. His second edition (1893) had a glowing foreword by a Council member of the ICA – William Charles Jackson – which ended by recommending the book especially "to those who, untrained in . . . auditing, are confronted with unfamiliar and specious pretexts for avoiding [this] unwelcome charge against profits."[32]

Matheson's first edition ran to around 100 pages, and we must confine our attention to one or two aspects only. For an assessment of the book's overall importance, we may note that Littleton in his *Evolution* . . . referred to Guthrie's lecture, observing that the application of depreciation to industry received further impetus in 1884 from Matheson's book, which, in Littleton's eyes, formed, with Pixley's *Auditors* . . ., "the foundation of the technical literature of professional accounting" (p. 237). We may go further and suggest that Matheson's remarkable book probably exceeded in its grasp of the nature of the depreciation problem, and especially in the clarity of its presentation and its handling of the related technical, financial and accounting aspects, anything that was to appear on depreciation in the world of business and accountancy in Britain before the 1930s.

Matheson began by saying that for depreciation, "no fixed rules or rates can be established for general use, because not only do trades and processes of manufacture differ, but numerous secondary circumstances have to be considered in determining the proper course."[33] Matheson sought, if possible, "to lay down some general principles which will always apply, or which, at any rate, may with advantage be held in view in deciding particular cases."[34]

Matheson then turned to a consideration of the relationship of depreciation to maintenance which he made central to his argument for the necessity of a direct provision for depreciation, and which also led into a discussion of railway practice. The railways used the double-account system, and what Matheson said is therefore of particular interest to the present paper, thus:

> The question of depreciation cannot be separated from that of maintenance, and in theory one may be said to balance the other. In

[32] *The Depreciation of Factories*, 2nd ed., London, 1893, vii.
[33] *The Depreciation of Factories*, 1. Page references are to the second (1893) edition of Matheson's book. The material quoted appeared in Matheson's original articles in *The Engineer*, except where indicated.
[34] *ibid.*

practice it is only in certain cases that this can be acted on. In any particular building, machine, or appurtenance, decay or wear of some sort must take place in the course of time, and repairs, in order to compensate fully for the decline in value, must take the form of renewal. This being the case, the absolute replacement of some portion of the plant every year may thus maintain an average aggregate value. *In only two kinds or classes of plant, however, can such an exact balancing of loss by repairs and renewals be ventured on; one, where the plant wears out so quickly as to need replacement at short intervals, affording constant proof, by the mere continuance of working, that not only the earning power of the factory is maintained, but also the capital value; and in a second class, that of undertakings so large and permanent as to afford a wide average of deterioration and renewal over the whole plant.*[35]

Matheson then went on to deal with railway renewals and railway accounts in the following terms:

... on a Railway the deterioration of the fixed and moving plant is supposed to be fully and properly met by the expenditure for repairs and renewals, and so long as the working of the railway is maintained, no regard is had to a future valuation such as might disturb the accounts of a manufactory subject to a change of ownership or cessation of trade. When a railway has been in operation for many years, and an average rate of expenditure in relation to revenue has been arrived at, such a method may be sound, but there is a risk that in the earlier years of working the gross revenue may not be sufficiently charged with due depreciation.

Railway companies in England have to publish annual accounts in a form prescribed by law, but these accounts seldom fully disclose the deterioration of the plant, partly because the expenditure of a particular year for repairs or renewals may not represent the deterioration due to the traffic of that year, and partly because expenditure necessary for maintenance may be mixed up with the capital expenditure for extensions. ...

The omission of any provision in the earlier years for future renewals is often excused by the small earnings, but the wear and tear necessary to such earnings must sooner or later be paid for out of revenue or from new capital; and though in course of years the expenditure for repairs and renewals must almost of necessity balance the deterioration if the traffic is to go on, there is room for much error in the accounts of particular years; and in the case of constantly changing shareholders, of an unfair allotment of charges. ...

The temptation to treat as Profit the Surplus of Income over Expenditure, without sufficient allowance for Deterioration, appears to be often irresistible. ...

There are railways where the dividend income and the corresponding value of the shares have fluctuated considerably, not according to

[35] *ibid.*, 2. The italics are mine. In this paragraph, and in his reference to his "second class," Matheson recognised the function of the double-account system, which was based upon a complete segregation of all so-called capital expenditure, and which, by providing for all repairs and renewals to be charged to revenue, left the question whether or not there should be any charge for depreciation entirely to the discretion of the directors, bearing in mind that the adequacy of the standard of maintenance was intended to be established by the engineers' certificates which were part and parcel of the form of accounts prescribed (*e.g.*) by the Regulation of Railways Act, 1868. See Appendix.

alterations in the real earnings, but according to alternate neglect and attention in regard to plant.[36]

Matheson referred also to water companies and gas companies where a similar state of affairs might be found. He also noted that certain Parliamentary companies were allowed, under statute, to set aside out of profits at the discretion of the directors a reserve to equalise dividends in any future years when current profits might not permit the payment of the maximum dividend permitted by the Act. Though such reserves could only be applied to the prescribed purpose of equalising dividends, Matheson commented: ". . . it is obvious that if the earnings of a particular year are burdened with some heavy expenditure for renewals, the latter are really paid for out of the fund nominally applicable for dividend."[37]

Perhaps the aspect of greatest interest to us is Matheson's view on the object of depreciation. He wrote:

> There are various methods of estimating the Depreciation of a Factory, and of recording alteration in Value, but it may be said in regard to any of them that the object in view is so to treat the nominal capital in the books of account, that it shall always represent as nearly as possible the real value. The most effectual method of securing this would be, if it were feasible, to Revalue everything at stated intervals, and to write off whatever loss such valuations might reveal without regard to any prescribed rate. By such a plan the deterioration due to a period of arduous working, or to any average or idle year, would be properly allotted.[38]

But he added:

> The plan of valuing every year instead of adopting a depreciation rate, though it is the more perfect, if strictly carried out, has some disadvantages. The two leading considerations in such an appraisement are generally the condition of the machine or other appurtenance, and its earning power. In both these respects there may be absolutely no sign of deterioration; a machine may appear and for all practical purposes be as good as new, and may show proof of it by actual earnings. Yet none the less its working life is shortening every year, and unless some provision is made for a replacement a severe loss will fall on the future. And if, with this in view, something is written off the value, though no alteration is apparent, then the plan of a depreciation rate is really adopted.
> For the above reasons, and because of the time, trouble and expense it would involve, a system of annual valuation is seldom strictly maintained. . . . The next best plan, which is that generally followed, and which it is intended now to investigate, is to establish average rates which can, without much trouble, be written off every year, and to check the result by complete or partial valuation at longer intervals.[39]

Matheson had no difficulty in putting forward suggestions for depreciation rates – usually a range of rates – for different types of assets, and he was at home with diminishing balance, straight-line, and interest-adjusted

[36] *ibid.*, 3–5.   [37] *ibid.*, 7.   [38] *ibid.*, 14.   [39] *ibid.*, 14–15.

methods. The book included interest and annuity tables. But our concern is with what Matheson meant by the "real value" which was to be represented as nearly as possible in the accounts. The following extract from his chapter on "Valuation: different kinds of value defined" gives some answer:

> "Value" is a term which has different significations according to the circumstances in which it is used. Thus, there may be the value to a vendor of a property taken by Compulsory purchase; there is the value as between Partners of a factory or business in full operation, or of the same factory as a "Going concern" to a purchaser who will have the advantages of the established management and connection; there is the Rateable value; there is the value of the factory as a whole if it has Stopped working; the value of what has been destroyed by Fire may have to be appraised; there is again the value of the Land, Buildings, and Plant if dismantled, and sold separately; and finally there is the value, generally the lowest of all, obtainable by a Forced sale . . .
>
> The value of anything is sometimes defined as that which it will fetch: and in the sale of a factory, the price at any particular time will, if there be freedom on both sides, depend not on the original cost or on any arbitrary standard of value – although of course the cost at which a similar factory could be built and equipped is an important consideration – but on the competition either of buyers or sellers, in other words on the supply and demand. . . .
>
> The real basis of value, however, which generally guides a purchaser, is the estimated earning power, or the net revenue past, present, and prospective, so far as it can be ascertained. From this point of view there is often more scope for difference of opinion than would at first sight appear. The rate of profit in the past is a primary basis, but this is not conclusive. A purchaser may see his way to improved methods, to an extended trade, or to a better utilisation of the plant, and so to greater profits. On the other hand, past profits may have been largely due to special knowledge of the proprietors, and much may really have been owing to skilled management, which, if obtainable at all in the future, may involve the payment of considerable salaries taking precedence of profits.[40]

Matheson approaches a view on "cost of capital":

> There is no fixed rule for the percentage of profit which will induce capitalists to embark in a manufacturing trade. The regularity of the trade, the chances of occasional high profits, the accompanying risks of loss, the locality in which the business is carried on, and the indirect advantages or drawbacks attending it, are all circumstances which may tempt or repel different persons.[41]

For a general working basis, however, there seems little doubt that Matheson intended to apply his depreciation rates to original cost, in

---

[40] *ibid.*, 71–72. These paragraphs were not included in Matheson's articles in *The Engineer* in 1883, but we have no reason to doubt that they appeared (at least in substantially this form) in the 1884 edition of his book.

[41] *ibid.*, 73.

default of satisfactory alternative valuation data. This impression emerges from his articles, and his book included a chapter of Examples and Tables in which the calculations are based on original cost.

Matheson had a lively grasp of financial and accounting aspects. He speaks of the "capital rendered free by a system of depreciation,"[42] and asks whether money set aside "may properly be employed in the business itself, or whether it should be invested outside . . ." He gives his answer:

> If the object of the reserve be to provide ready money for some sudden call, the latter plan may be expedient, but in a manufacturing business the reserve may generally be best employed in it. Money can seldom be safely invested so as to be immediately available and yet at a rate of interest as high as that which a manufacturer could afford to pay for the use of it . . .[43]

DEPRECIATION, PROFITS AND DIVIDENDS, 1887–92[44]

Emile Garcke and John Manger Fells paid Matheson the compliment of quoting extensively from his book in their famous *Factory Accounts: their Principles and Practice*.[45] At the conclusion of their section on depreciation, however, they went a step further and noted:

> . . . a periodical valuation of the assets, as the basis of a depreciation rate, raises considerations of very great significance, such as the question of the interdependence of the revenue and capital accounts, and the question of how far a loss or profit on capital account . . . should affect the profit and loss account.[46]

Garcke and Fells then reproduced the views of "a leading authority on the law relating to joint-stock companies." This was Henry Burton Buckley, Q.C.[47]; and they quoted from the fourth edition (1883) of his *Law and Practice under the Companies Acts*. We shall now turn to Buckley's views (which we shall take from his third edition of 1878) because they were prophetic of the decision in *Lee* v. *Neuchatel Ashphalte Co.* which governed the further development of ideas on depreciation in the second half of our period, namely 1887–1892.

Table A to the 1862 Companies Act had followed the 1856 legislation in requiring (where the model Articles applied) that "No dividend shall be payable except out of the profits arising from the business of the Company" (clause 73). Likewise, the Companies Clauses Consolidation Act of 1845, which applied similarly to Parliamentary companies, including railways,

---

[42] *ibid.*, 5.
[43] *ibid.*, 21–22.
[44] I do not deal in this essay with O. G. Ladelle's interesting lecture "The Calculation of Depreciation" which appeared in *The Accountant*, November 29, 1890, but, owing to Ladelle's untimely death, was never delivered. See *Journal of Accounting Research*, 5, 1967, 27 and *e.g.* 173; and 6, 1968, 149.
[45] London, 1887.
[46] *ibid.*, 102.
[47] Buckley J. from 1900; Buckley L. J. from 1906; and Lord Wrenbury from 1915.

provided (121): "The Company shall not make any dividend whereby their Capital Stock will be in any Degree reduced. . . ."

Commenting on clause 73 in the third edition of his book (1878), Buckley noted that if directors paid dividends out of capital, they might be liable for the whole amount misapplied. He continued:

> The question is believed to be as yet entirely open whether a company under the Companies Acts, which has lost part of its capital, can continue to pay dividends until the lost capital has been made good.
>
> The writer has always understood the true principle to be, that capital account and revenue account were distinct accounts, and that dividend was properly payable whenever revenue account was in credit. If this is not so, it is difficult to say how some companies could ever safely pay dividend at all. For instance, a tramway company lays its line when materials and labour are both dear, both subsequently fall, and the same line could be laid for half the money, and as an asset (independent of deterioration from wear) is worth only half what it cost. Is the company to make this good to capital before it pays further dividend? If so, then it would seem to follow, that if the cost of materials and labour had risen after the line was laid, the company might have divided as dividend this accretion to capital.
>
> Upon such a principle dividends would vary enormously, and sometimes inversely to the actual profit of the concern.
>
> If revenue account be treated as a distinct account, these difficulties disappear, and subject to the difficulty, which must be encountered, of discriminating between revenue charges and capital charges, a safe and intelligible principle is arrived at. The creditors of the company are entitled to have the capital account fairly and properly kept; but, *quaere* whether they are entitled to have losses on capital made good out of revenue. It is no doubt true, that before arriving at revenue at all, there are payments which must be made good to capital, on account of capital wasted or lost in earning the revenue. For instance, in the common case of leaseholds, which are a wasting property, the whole of the rental will not properly be income; or in the case of colliery properties, the difference between the price at which the coal is sold, and the cost of working and raising it, will not all be income, for there must also be a deduction made in favour of capital representing the diminished value of the mine by reason of its containing so many less tons of coal. But when all proper allowances have thus been made in favour of capital, the balance it is submitted is revenue applicable for payment of dividend.[48]

In the *Lee* case, Buckley was one of the Q.C.s appearing for the various defendants in the Chancery court. Stirling J. gave his judgment in their favour in February 1888, and the appeal against his decision was dismissed in February 1889. At appeal, the principal judgment was given by Lindley L.J.[49]

[48] *ibid.*, 415.
[49] Lindley's own *Treatise on the Law of Partnership* (including its application to Joint-Stock and other Companies) first published in 1860, was itself a precedent (especially from the third edition, 1873, 812–813, though not clearly in the earlier editions) for Buckley's views; see *e.g. in Verner* v. *General and Commercial Investment Trust* [1894], 2 Ch. 239, at 262.

Accountants are familiar with the *Lee* case, and it is not necessary to rehearse all the facts here. We may note that as Yamey has said, "before 1889 . . . [there] was no clear-cut case before the courts where a dividend was paid out of the excess of current receipts over current payments despite a decline in the value of the company's assets."[50] In the lower court, Stirling J. relied on evidence for the defendant company that the value of its principal asset (the right, under a concession, to mine bituminous rock in a certain area) had increased, because the term of the concession had been recently extended; moreover, it now covered a larger area, and was held on more favourable terms than had originally been the case. Accordingly, to quote Yamey again, Stirling J. "merely reaffirmed the earlier series of decisions. . . ." Capital remained intact, current receipts exceeded current expenditure, and the court had no power to interfere with the directors' decision to pay a preference dividend.

The well-known *Lee* rule, which emerged from the judgment of Lindley L.J. in the Court of Appeal, and which supported the decision in the lower court, was however based on a different argument, and in fact the appeal judgments were made "on the assumption that there *had* been a decline in the value of the [defendant company's] asset,"[51] as was indeed alleged by plaintiff's counsel. Lindley L.J. gave a convenient summary of the *Lee* rule five years later (in *Verner* v. *General and Commercial Investment Trust*, 1894) which was, as Yamey says, "to become the classic and always-quoted pronouncement of the doctrine," *viz.*

> Perhaps the shortest way of expressing the distinction which I am endeavouring to explain is to say that fixed capital may be sunk and lost, and yet that the excess of current receipts over current payments may be divided, but that floating or circulating capital must be kept up, as otherwise it will enter into and form part of such excess, in which case to divide such excess without deducting the capital which forms part of it will be contrary to law.[52]

Though it does not have the force of Lindley L.J.'s pronouncement, the head-note to the *Verner* Report gives a slightly revised but more understandable version of the last few lines of the rule: "though where the income of a company arises from the turning over of circulating capital no dividend can be paid unless the circulating capital is kept up to its original value, as otherwise there would be a payment out of capital."[53]

In the *Lee* case, Lee's counsel had contended that the Neuchatel directors were in effect proposing to pay the preference dividend out of capital because the property of the company was of a wasting nature and had depreciated in value by reason of the bituminous rock extracted. And no such depreciation had been allowed for in arriving at the profit out of which the dividend was to be paid. At appeal, Lindley L.J. said that the court were being invited "to lay down certain principles, the adoption of

---

[50] Yamey, *op. cit.*, 431.   [51] *ibid.*, 432.   [52] [1894] 2 Ch. 239, at 266.
[53] [1894] 2 Ch. 239, at 240.

which would paralyse the trade of the country;" and later in the course of his judgment he said, *inter alia*:

> Now we come to consider how the Companies Act is to be applied
> to the case of a wasting property. If a company is formed to acquire
> and work a property of a wasting nature, for example, a mine, a
> quarry, or a patent, the capital expended in acquiring the property
> may be regarded as sunk and gone, and if the company retains assets
> sufficient to pay its debts, it appears to me that there is nothing what-
> ever in the Act to prevent any excess of money obtained by working
> the property over the cost of working it, from being divided amongst
> the shareholders, and this in my opinion is true, although some portion
> of the property itself is sold, and in some sense the capital is thereby
> diminished. . . .
> As regards the mode of keeping accounts, there is no law prescribing
> how they shall be kept. There is nothing in the Acts to show what is
> to go to capital account or what is to go to revenue account. We know
> perfectly well that business men very often differ in opinion about
> such things. It does not matter to the creditor out of what fund he gets
> paid, whether he gets paid out of capital or out of profit net or gross.
> All he cares about is that there is money to pay him with, and it is a
> mere matter of bookkeeping and internal arrangement out of what
> particular fund he shall be paid. Therefore you cannot say that the
> question of what ought to go into capital or revenue account is a
> matter that concerns the creditor. The Act does not say what expenses
> are to be charged to capital and what to revenue. Such matters are
> left to the shareholders. . . .[54]

For our purposes, we may note Lindley L.J.'s apparent emphasis on the concept of separate capital and revenue accounts; and also that this emphasis appears to accord, in particular, with Buckley's view (of at least ten years earlier) that capital account and revenue account were "distinct accounts." And we may remind ourselves that it was of the essence of the double-account system embodied in the Regulation of Railways Act of 1868 that it provided a separate account for capital (i.e. comprising receipts from the issue of shares and long-term loan stock on the one hand, and actual expenditure on the fixed assets representing the capital works of the undertaking on the other) and a separate "General Balance Sheet" made up of the assets and liabilities of a current or circulating nature, in addition, of course, to the residual balance – under-spent or over-spent – of the so-called "Receipts and Expenditure on Capital Account."

Clearly the *Lee* rule "legalised" the practice of dividing the net receipts (before depreciation) of single-ship companies (which, as it happens, were probably not, for the most part, incorporated companies) and certain colliery and mining companies or undertakings. And it rationalised (if it did not stem from) the policy of the 1868 Act which left open the question whether or not depreciation should be provided on the capital assets of

---

[54] 41 Ch. D. 1, at 24–25.

railway companies, bearing in mind that repairs and renewals were to be charged to revenue and that standards of maintenance were subject to control.

That the *Lee* decision took the accountancy profession aback in 1889 none the less we need have no doubt. *The Accountant* found the principles "simply startling,"[55] and Yamey has noted that the decision met with a storm of disapproval from accountants.[56]

Although the *Lee* decision in the court of first instance (February 1888) had involved no departure from the simple doctrine of capital maintenance, accountants were already disturbed in 1888 by the knowledge that there was a major difference of opinion among leading company lawyers as to what constituted profit. Ernest Cooper delivered a lecture in November 1888 under the title "What is Profit of a Company."[57] His audience was nominally the Chartered Accountant Students' Society of London, but the chair was taken by the immediate Past-President of the ICA, F. Whinney, and there were also present the Institute's Vice-President and about a dozen members of the Council.[58]

Cooper was concerned to bring out the difference between the opinion of Buckley (with which he did not agree) and that of F. B. Palmer (later Sir Francis) who was Buckley's contemporary, and was in some respects his rival for reputation among company lawyers not already serving on the Bench. Cooper quoted Buckley's views (already noted above) and continued:

> From these extracts it is seen that Mr. Buckley adopts as applicable to companies registered under the Companies Acts 1862 to 1886, what is known as the "double account" system as distinguished from the "single account" system, and further – in adopting the double account view – he bases upon the supposed separation of capital and revenue the very important doctrine, that although capital may have been lost as he describes it on capital account, dividends may perhaps still be paid. . . .
>
> Mr. F. B. Palmer, on the other hand, after describing what he calls the double account view [i.e. Mr. Buckley's view] adopts [what he refers to as] the single account view, which he states thus:
>
>> ". . . profit is to be ascertained as in an ordinary partnership, namely, by a balance sheet, showing the general result of the company's operations to date. That is to say, the capital account and revenue account are to be treated as one continuous account, . . ."

[55] *The Accountant*, February 23, 1889, 89–91.
[56] Yamey, *op. cit.*, 433.
[57] *The Accountant*, November 10, 1888, 740–746. Ernest Cooper was senior partner of Cooper Brothers for some thirty years before he retired in 1923.
[58] The President in 1888 was W. W. Deloitte, who had already accumulated some fifty-six years' experience in the profession, was "well advanced in years," and had been ill during the previous weeks.

Mr. Palmer adds, "Ninety-nine companies out of a hundred under the Act of 1862, ascertain, or purport to ascertain, their profits in accordance with this view."

Further Mr. Palmer says, "It has generally been assumed that the double account system can only be adopted where the adoption of that system is specially prescribed by the legislature, as in the case of railway and tramway companies . . ." [On the other hand] the single account view is in accordance with the practice adopted by the commercial world in ascertaining the profit or loss of an ordinary partnership; and it may, no doubt, be asked with some reason, "How can that which in the case of an ordinary partnership would not be profit be profit in the case of a limited company . . . seeing that the creditors have only a limited fund to look to?"

Cooper was quoting from Palmer's *Company Precedents* (fourth edition, 1888, p. 258), and he proceeded to a very able examination of these two conflicting views in what he chose to describe towards the end of his lecture as "wearisome length." He concluded this part of his lecture by saying: "I need not refer to Mr. Palmer's views further than to say that so far as they go, I consider that they state accurately the way in which profits should be, and are by general usage, ascertained." Cooper ended with the disclaimer that he did not pretend to express final opinions.

CONCLUSION

William Baxter says at page 27 of his *Depreciation*:

If depreciation is a matter of fall in an asset's value over time, then the primary step in measuring it must be to establish the successive value figures. When these figures have been found, the depreciation costs emerge as a by-product.

This is another way of suggesting that accounting must not try to measure cost *in vacuo*, leaving asset value as an unimportant and possibly meaningless residual. The tail should not wag the dog: the value is the thing that matters, and the cost is the residual. If the accountant declines to treat his asset figures as part of a valuation process, then he divorces his values and costs from the reality that he is striving to measure and reduces them to empty abstractions.

If we are to reckon it a measure of the failure of Dicksee and the other accountants of his generation that they effectively abandoned the attempt to erect a better basis than original cost for the valuation of fixed assets in accounts, we must see to it that in our generation we achieve the needed improvement. At least we are well aware of what is unsatisfactory in our present situation.

That Dicksee was satisfied, by and large, with original cost we need not doubt, though he did not announce his unqualified adherence to it as did some of his contemporaries and immediate successors. We need to bear in mind the general experience relative to price level changes during the latter half of the nineteenth century and up to the First World War. It does seem possible, however, that Dicksee and his generation were further influenced in favour of original cost, even than they might otherwise have been, as a result of the emphasis placed upon it by the double-account system.

Overall, we may note that Dicksee's views changed comparatively little between 1892 and 1928 when the fourteenth edition of *Auditing* appeared. Dicksee did, however, insert some additional material under the heading of "Principle in Valuation of Assets" before turning to the "Valuation of Fixed Assets" in the fourteenth edition of *Auditing*, *e.g.*

> In the great majority of cases there can be no doubt that the position of affairs can be more readily and clearly disclosed by a single Balance Sheet than by accounts kept upon the Double Account System.[59] In the case of companies, however, there is a further point to be considered, namely, that there are increases which are not divisible profits, and losses which (as a matter of law) need not be made good before dividing profits in the form of dividend. The Profit and Loss Account must obviously be framed so as to show the divisible profits, and the question thus remains . . . how profits and losses that do *not* affect Revenue – or, to put it another way, capitalised fluctuations – are to be treated. . . . [It] is clear that two courses are open. Either the capitalised items must be disregarded in the Balance Sheet by misstating the value of an asset or a liability, or some account must be raised to record the profit or loss that is not taken to Revenue. . . . If, however, a profit has been made which is not available for distribution, it is often considered unnecessary to modify the accounts so as to disclose the circumstance. . . . As a general rule, the amount at which *all* assets are stated in the Balance Sheet – except where a special statutory provision to the contrary obtains – should be regulated by the realisable value of such assets on the basis of a going concern.

The "general rule" was, however, plainly vulnerable, for in the next paragraph (anxious to register the distinction between realisable value in a forced sale and the balance sheet's normal concern with the affairs of a continuing business) Dicksee asserted that the function of the balance sheet was:

> chiefly to prove the reasonableness of the apportionment of income and expenditure as between one year and another, and also to show the financial position of the business – *i.e.* the resources it has available to meet its current liabilities. . . . [So] far as [fixed] assets are concerned, so long as it is reasonable to assume the continuity of the business, the correct thing is not to attempt to show the realisable value (which may be considerably more, or very considerably less, than the original cost) but rather to show such expenditure *as* expenditure, subject to the fact that in so far as it will not last for ever its cost must be apportioned as fairly as possible, and charged against the profits earned in successive years, in order to arrive at the true working expenses and the true net profit of each year.[60]

[59] It may be interpolated here that Dicksee had, from 1903, continually stressed that the difference between the double-account and the single-account need be no more than one of form only. But the difference of form did invite a different attitude to depreciation.

[60] *Auditing*, 14th ed., 1928, 196–198.

The similarity is marked between this latter statement and the view conveyed at the time of its issue by (*e.g.*) paragraphs 3 and 4 of Recommendation N.18 (Presentation of balance sheet and profit and loss account) published by the Council of the Institute of Chartered Accountants in England and Wales in 1958.

APPENDIX

THE REGULATION OF RAILWAYS ACT 1868

Forms of Account: Extract from First Schedule to the Act

(No. 4)   RECEIPTS AND EXPENDITURE ON CAPTIAL ACCOUNT.

Dr.   Cr

	Amount Expended to	Amount Expended during Half Year.	Total.		Amount Received to	Amount Received during Half Year.	Total.
	£ s. d.	£ s. d.	£ s. d.		£ s. d.	£ s. d.	£ s. d.
To Expendtiture— On Lines open for Traffic (No. 5) ... On Lines in course of Construction (No. 5) ... ... Working Stock (No. 5) ... ... Subscriptions to other Railways (No. 5) ... ... Docks, Steamboats, and other special Items (No. 5) ...				By Receipts— Shares and Stock, per Account No. 2 ... ... Loans, per Account No. 3 ... ... Debenture Stock, per Account No. 3 ... ... Sundries (in detail) ...			
„ Balance							

(No. 13.)   *Dr.*   GENERAL BALANCE SHEET.   *Cr.*

£ s. d	£ s. d.
To Capital Account, Balance at Credit thereof, as per Account No. 4	By Cash at Bankers — Current Account ....
„ Net Revenue Account, Balance at Credit thereof, as per Account No. 10	„ Cash on Deposit at Interest
	„ Cash invested in Consols and Government Securities ....
„ Unpaid Dividends and Interest	„ Cash invested in Shares of other Railway Companies not charged as Capital Expenditure ....
„ Guaranteed Dividends and Interest payable or accruing and provided for	
„ Temporary Loans	„ General Stores — Stock of Materials on hand ....
„ Lloyd's Bonds and other Obligations not included in Loan Capital Statement, No. 3.........	„ Traffic Accounts due to the Company ....
„ Balance due to Bankers.........	„ Amounts due by other Companies..................................
„ Debts due to other Companies	„ Do. Clearing House ....
„ Amount due to Clearing House	„ Do. Post Office ....
„ Sundry Outstanding Accounts	„ Sundry Outstanding Accounts
„ Fire Insurance Fund on Stations, Works and Buildings	„ Suspense Accounts (if any)...
„ Insurance Fund on Steamboats	*To be enumerated.*
„ Special Items......................	„ Special Items ....
£	£

Form of Engineers' Certificates Appended to Accounts

CERTIFICATE RESPECTING THE PERMANENT WAY, &c.

I hereby certify that the whole of the Company's Permanent Way, Stations, Buildings, Canals, and other Works, have during the past Half-year been maintained in good working condition and Repair.

Date   18 .   *Engineer.*

CERTIFICATE RESPECTING THE ROLLING STOCK.

I hereby certify that the whole of the Company's Plant, Engines, Tenders, Carriages, Waggons, Machinery, and Tools, also the Marine Engines of the Steam Vessels, have during the past Half-year been maintained in good Working Order and Repair.

Date   18 .   { *Chief Engineer or*
                                          Locomotive Superintendent.

CORPORATE SOCIAL PERFORMANCE: A NEW DIMENSION IN ACCOUNTING REPORTS?

David Solomons

TRADITIONALLY, financial reporting by accountants has meant, above all else, profit reporting. Recent emphasis on earnings per share has focused even more attention on profitability, and this in spite of all the academic criticism which has been directed to accounting profit as a measure of performance in the business sector.

It is easy enough to see why profit occupies the position of primacy that it does. If profit maximisation is the principal goal of business, then performance ultimately must be measured in terms which relate directly to the attainment of that goal; and even if profit is not what the businessman is trying to maximise, profitability is a condition of survival for the business so that some minimum required level of profit becomes a constraint to be satisfied, whatever other maximand may have taken profit's place. And no other single figure comprehends so many different facets of business performance. No other single figure captures not one or some but *all* of a firm's capacities: to select or develop product lines that consumers want; to obtain orders for those products; to produce or procure them in volume; to maintain satisfactory selling prices; to get its products to customers; to keep its costs, including selling and collection costs, under control; and to handle its finances satisfactorily. All of these functions impinge on profit, and a satisfactory performance in all but one of them is not good enough to produce a profit if there has been a serious failure in only one. That single failure will trip the profit switch, so to speak. No serious failure in this quite broad range of activities can pass unnoticed so long as someone has his eye on the profit signal.

Yet, lest this song of praise for profit as a measure of performance sound strange from someone who, ten years ago, went on record as thinking that "the next twenty-five years may subsequently be seen to have been the twilight of income measurement,"[1] one or two reservations should be noted.

If the principal strength of profit as a measure of business performance is that it is a reflection of many different aspects of performance, it has one great weakness, besides many lesser ones. Its great weakness is financial myopia. It does not reflect in current earnings what today's managers are doing or failing to do to affect the company's future well-being. Of course these activities today, though their effects may not become visible for some

[1] David Solomons, "Economic and Accounting Concepts of Income," *Accounting Review*, 36 (1961), 383.

131

time, are indeed part of today's performance. But our present profit-measurement techniques are not capable of handling them.

It is because we cannot handle them that income measurement presently rests on the concept of realisation. But because unrealised benefits are not included in income, methods of quantifying them are neglected. No doubt this could be changed if accountants wanted to badly enough. The outlook in this respect today is, as a matter of fact, much brighter than it has perhaps ever been. The Accounting Principles Board in the United States made some movement in this direction, notably in its discussion of investments.[2] Arthur Andersen & Co. have wholeheartedly embraced the view that values should replace costs as the primary basis of reporting in future. "What we are urging is a basic change in attitude that will acknowledge value as a goal so that cost will be regarded as a means of conveying information about value, rather than being viewed as an end or objective in itself."[3] After years of apparently fruitless discussion, there seems to be some movement at last.

A second weakness of profit as a measure of performance, not as fundamental as the first, and not as difficult to correct, is that profit can be the result of good luck as well as good judgment, and our traditional methods are not designed to separate the two. Another way of putting this is to say that an enterprise can be successful, in profit terms, in spite of poor managerial performance as well as because of good management, and no doubt sometimes management performance can be neutral. Anything which improves our capacity to distinguish between *enterprise* performance and *managerial* performance cannot fail to increase the contribution which accountants can make to economic efficiency. But it is not the purpose of this paper to pursue that line of thought further.

PRIVATE AND SOCIAL COSTS AND BENEFITS

The term "myopia" which was used just now was chosen carefully, for it referred to accounting shortsightedness in the literal sense that distant benefits and losses are blurred or, quite commonly, ignored altogether. "Similarly," said the American Accounting Association's 1970 Committee on Non-Financial Measures of Effectiveness, "there are social benefits (*e.g.* contributions of research and development activities to basic research and training of researchers) and social costs (*e.g.* environmental costs of pollution) which are not reflected in a traditional income statement."[4] One may question that "similarly." There is an important difference between the ignoring by accountants, when measuring business

[2] For some comments by a member of the APB on the Board's readiness to depart from historical cost, see Charles Horngren's remarks at the 39th International Conference of the Financial Executives Institute in October 1970, *Financial Executive*, February 1971, 62–64.

[3] Arthur Andersen & Co, *Objectives of Financial Statements for Business Enterprises*, 1972.

[4] Report of the Committee, *Accounting Review*, Supplement to 46 (1971), 165.

income, of long-run costs and benefits *to the business itself*, and their ignoring divergences between private and social costs and benefits. These externalities are not unimportant, and much of this paper is concerned with them. But they present a different kind of problem.

The distinction is in danger of being blurred, also, by a much-quoted question put by Paul Lazarsfeld: ". . . will the accounting profession study the business enterprise in order to measure enterprise effectiveness only in terms of profit or loss or will it study the development of measurements of effectiveness in terms other than profit or loss such as worker happiness or consumer satisfaction?"[5] Of course worker happiness and consumer satisfaction are important to the long-run welfare of the business itself, and to ignore them is to that extent an aspect of the myopia already referred to. But there is a danger of confusion when one uses a phrase like "enterprise effectiveness" in a context like this, without making it clear whether "effectiveness" is being viewed from the stockholder's standpoint or from society's.

The more important causes of divergence between private efficiency and social efficiency are discussed by Lloyd Amey in *The Efficiency of Business Enterprises*.[6] Abbreviated and paraphrased, they are as follows:

1. Economic efficiency implies perfectly competitive conditions. In imperfectly competitive conditions, a firm which optimises its own position will not achieve maximum efficiency from the social point of view. For instance, it will normally get more profit from a smaller output than it is socially desirable that it should produce.

2. There will normally be external economies and diseconomies to which the firm contributes which will give rise to discrepancies between its private costs and benefits and its social costs and benefits. The social cost of pollution and the social benefits of corporate philanthropy are perhaps the most often cited of these.

3. A different kind of divergence between private and social cost may arise because of disequilibrium elsewhere in the system. For example, unemployed labour has no opportunity cost and ought to be employed so long as its productivity, however small, is positive. But minimum wage legislation and the enforcement of trade union rates of pay will make it impossible for an individual firm to provide what may be socially efficient employment without diminishing its own business efficiency.

4. The effects of taxation will cause private and social efficiency to diverge. Indirect taxes cause the market prices of resources used by the firm to differ from their factor cost, and are likely to distort its choice of inputs from what is socially most desirable. Direct taxes, because they do not bear evenly on all kinds of activity, may lead firms, in seeking to maximise after-tax profits, to operate in a way which is not socially most

[5] Paul F. Lazarsfeld, "Accounting and Social Bookkeeping," in R. R. Stirling and W. F. Bentz (eds.), *Accounting in Perspective*: *Contributions to Accounting Thought by Other Disciplines*, Cincinnati, 1971.
[6] L. R. Amey, *The Efficiency of Business Enterprises*, London, 1969.

productive. For example, favourable depletion allowances to extractive industries may lead to over-investment in them.

5. Imperfect knowledge on the part of the firm about present conditions, let alone the future, may cause what it *perceives* to be efficient behaviour to be less efficient than it thinks it is.

This is not an exhaustive list of the causes of divergence between private efficiency and social efficiency, but it covers the main points; and it should now be easy to see why no measure of private *business* performance, whether it be accounting profit or some derivative thereof such as earnings per share or return on investment or residual income, or some non-financial measure such as output per man-hour, can be used as anything more than a very approximate measure of social performance. If we wanted to make the measure of social performance a little less rough, one and only one of the above factors which cause private and social performance to diverge would offer any promise of being susceptible to correction by accounting or statistical means. This is the "externalities" factor. The others seem to call for statistical corrections of such a hypothetical character that to make them is quite beyond us. They would also be less useful for action, even if they could be made.

The possibility of recognising external costs and benefits in assessing a company's performance is now receiving some attention. It is not clear yet whether social performance can be measured. Perhaps it can only be described and assessed subjectively. It is already too late to conclude, however, that corporate reporting had better stay out of this area altogether. The recognition that corporations have responsibilities beyond those to their stockholders is here, and it is here to stay. Only if we lived in a world of perfect competition, if wealth were distributed equally and if business were made to feel the full weight of all its costs and could not inflict them on society as our imperfect tax system now allows it to do in certain respects would it be easy to agree with that often quoted statement of Milton Friedman that "Few trends could so thoroughly undermine the very foundations of our free society as the acceptance by corporate officials of a social responsibility other than to make as much money for their stockholders as possible."[7] For then there would be few important differences between social performance and that business performance which the firm would want to optimise for its own purposes, and we could then say, with much more confidence than we can today, "what is good for General Motors is good for the country."

It is the main assertion of the Committee for Economic Development's Report on Social Responsibilities of Business Corporations that, taking a sufficiently broad and long-range view, "it is in the 'enlightened self interest' of corporations to promote the public welfare in a positive way."[8] Thus the company which is sensitive to the needs of society by minimising

[7] Milton Friedman, *Capitalism and Freedom*, Chicago, 1962, 133.
[8] Committee for Economic Development, New York, June 1971, 27.

pollution, by training minority group workers, by fostering good community relations, by supporting good causes and the like will in fact be promoting the long-run interests of its stockholders by gaining governmental and community goodwill, by increasing its supply of trained personnel, and by anticipating and therefore circumventing unwelcome forms of interference by government.

But it is clear that some of these benefits are not appropriable by the company that spends money on them. Minority workers trained by Company A may leave to work for Company B, grants by B to the University of ——————— may help to educate graduates who go to work for C. Who can say that concern for social performance is really in the interests of the stockholders of a particular company?

This question is examined by Henry Wallich and John McGowan in a paper written in connection with the above CED study;[9] and they argue that since most stockholders hold more or less diversified portfolios, either directly or through pension funds and the like, to a greater or less extent they have a much broader stake in the corporate sector than is implied by any single stockholding. Thus non-appropriable benefits paid for by any one corporation nevertheless redound to the advantage of its stockholders in so far as the benefits are shared by other corporations in which they hold stock, or at a minimum because these benefits contribute to the health of the corporate sector generally.

This in an ingenious argument which will comfort management that is "looking not so much for guidance as to what it ought to do, but for an economic justification of what it already wants to do on compassionate and other grounds."[10] Yet the argument is not entirely convincing. Though there is obviously some validity in the view that not all non-appropriable benefits are lost to the stockholders of companies that spend money on them, there is surely much force in the view of Mr. Abbott, of 3M Company, who, in a note of reservation to the CED Report, says, "I believe that very few investors in considering whether to purchase or retain a stock consider the effect of that company's social outlays upon his other investments."[11]

CAN SOCIAL PERFORMANCE BE MEASURED?

Before accountants can seriously confront the challenge of measuring social performance, the crucial question to which an answer has to be found is: what is the criterion of social performance? If enlightened self-interest is indeed the correct motivation for corporate social expenditure, then

[9] Henry C. Wallich and John J. McGowan, "Stockholder Interest and the Corporation's Role in Social Policy," in *A New Rationale for Corporate Social Policy*, Committee for Economic Development, Supplementary Paper No. 31, New York, 1970, 39–59.
[10] *op. cit.*, 39.
[11] *Social Responsibilities of Business Corporations*, 70.

presumably some long-range DCF calculation is an appropriate way to judge them. But another view would be that any corporate activity motivated by *self*-interest is really not distinguishable from any of the corporation's ordinary business activities, except that the benefits may take longer to accrue and be harder to trace. And in that case, corporate *social* performance would seem to disappear as anything different from corporate private performance. All we would have to do, in that case, would be to quantify and compare the costs and benefits *to the company*, as for any other activity. Bad performance would mean a failure to recognise the company's self-interest, or a failure to pursue it actively enough. If there really is something different about corporate social performance, there must be some other criterion by which to judge it, though the criterion need not be – indeed, should not be – entirely unrelated to the normal criteria of business performance.

There are at least two different reasons why a corporation itself might want to get an objective measure of its social performance. First, there is the defensive aspect. Corporations are coming increasingly under fire for actual or alleged anti-social conduct, and rebuttal would be more effective if it could be based on hard facts, especially those that can be quantified. But, second, some objective measure of the results obtained from expenditures laid out for social purposes would seem to be necessary if a corporation is to be able rationally to make decisions as to the amount and direction of such expenditures. How much should it spend on pollution control, how much on community relations, how much on corporate philanthropy? Even if "enlightened self-interest" is the only criterion to be taken into account, there is still the question of how it is to be used. A company may not even know that it is behaving anti-socially, and it is even more likely to be unaware of how much benefit has been lost to society by its failure to act in some particular manner. "Information of this type could have an important effect on many business decisions," says James B. McComb of the Dayton-Hudson Corporation (U.S.A.). "I'm convinced that most businessmen do not consciously set out to increase costs to society; the problems occur because the businessmen do not have adequate information as to the impact of their operations on society."[12]

Moreover, without such measurements, how are governments to know when and where to take action to prevent or to correct corporate anti-social behaviour? It does not make economic sense to lay down standards of conduct which are more costly to follow than the costs they are intended to prevent. Cries of distress have already been heard from many United States industries, notably automobiles, asserting that excessively high standards of emission control and other anti-pollution standards will cost more than the benefits are worth. Without measurements, these arguments cannot be rationally resolved. They can only be decided on the basis of

[12] *Social Measurement*, AICPA, New York, 1972, 17.

subjective judgments. But to say that it is desirable to measure something does not make it possible. On that it may be easier to form an opinion when we have asked how, if at all, a measure of corporate social performance might be obtained.

Perhaps the first thing to note about corporate social performance is that the most important component would seem to be the production of goods and services that the company is in business to supply. "Value added" would seem to be the best point of departure for developing a measure of social performance. It gives the company credit for the value of goods and services provided for society's enjoyment, and the incomes generated within the company during this process are properly not deducted, so that the employment provided by the company is treated as part of, not a diminution of, its social performance. Yet even as a starting-point, this measure has many imperfections. For instance, a successful monopoly which cornered the market in a product, pushing the price up, could appear to be generating more value added while in fact it was diminishing welfare. But if market prices are not accepted at their face value, the project had better be abandoned at the outset, for we shall then have to ask whether consumers would not be better off without some of the things they spend money on – tranquilisers, say, or cigarettes. This point will be taken up again shortly.

To get from the private performance represented by value added to a measure of social performance it would be necessary to add the unappropriable benefits generated by the company and to deduct the external costs which it inflicts on others but does not feel or only partially feels itself. The most obvious example of unappropriable benefits is those resulting from corporate philanthropy, though such philanthropy is seldom "pure" in that it usually produces a mixture of appropriable and unappropriable benefits. Thus university scholarships which a company finances will usually bear its name and so may help its recruiting. Gifts to a local hospital may raise the level of health care of its workers and therefore their efficiency. It is only the benefits which are not recaptured which would need to be added to value added. In any case, the total amount involved is modest – in the United States, about one billion dollars a year or roughly 1 per cent of corporate pre-tax profits, and in Britain almost certainly less. But for some companies the figures will be much more significant.

Some expenditures producing unappropriable benefits are even more complex. Thus, a company takes over a piece of land which was formerly an eyesore and builds on it a head office which is an outstanding piece of architecture and adorns it perhaps with the work of a famous sculptor. Much of this expenditure will help to produce "value added" simply through use as office space. Some of it raises the morale of the office workers but does not make them more productive. Some of it provides enjoyment for passers-by. Using a cost basis of valuation for want of anything better, the excess of the cost of the building over the hypothetical cost of a no more than adequate building might be regarded as the (capital) cost of the unappropriable benefits flowing from the building.

But already, this example shows how thin the ground is. There is no way to place a value on the aesthetic pleasure from the building and sculpture, because we are outside the realm of market prices. There is no way, therefore, of determining objectively whether the extra cost was worth while. The same thing is true of the benefits of corporate philanthropy. The benefits of philanthropy to the donor can only be judged subjectively, though the benefits to the donee might usually be equated with the amount given away. Even this will not always be true, for philanthropy can be misdirected. If there really is such a thing as "benign neglect," it presumably has an opposite, "malign concern."

Turning from external benefits to the external costs generated by a company and imposed on other people, these, if they could be suitably quantified, would have to be deducted from value added. Pollution, in the broadest sense, is the example which has been most discussed. One way which has been suggested for quantifying the deduction to be made from private net product to give social net product is by reference to the cost of the equipment which a company would need to install in its premises or on its products (cars, for example) to reduce pollution to the lowest level currently attained by the industry. This would not set an impossibly high standard, and the computation is capable of being made. But of course it has no value as a guide to action, for to assess the cost of pollution prevention is only a part of the computation – the easier part – needed to determine whether that expenditure ought to be incurred.

The benefits to others which result from expenditure on pollution prevention are rarely capable of measurement. For one thing, the costs imposed by pollution itself are so diverse in nature. They may take the form of money costs, as when soot in the atmosphere increases laundry bills. They may change industrial location, by keeping business away from a heavily polluted area. They may take the form of reduced human efficiency or longevity. They may show up simply as loss of aesthetic satisfaction. Diverse in their nature and with incidence widely diffused, the external costs imposed by pollution, and therefore the benefits yielded by its prevention, may never prove capable of measurement.

But now let us return to cigarettes. It was argued earlier that we had better not look behind the fact of market prices, for once one begins to question whether a product is worth the price it commands in the market, one is on a slippery slope indeed. But can we ignore the lethal element in cigarettes in assessing the social performance of companies that market them? Of course a negative answer to this question will bring a hundred other products into the dock; but in the case of few legally marketed products – this excludes addictive drugs – is the product so clearly a "bad" as well as a "good."

Though the law does not shrink from placing a money value on human life, we had better do so. There is no prospect in the foreseeable future of being able to quantify the social cost of cigarette consumption for inclusion in the report on social performance of an individual tobacco firm. But it would not be impracticable to require tobacco companies to give relevant information in their annual reports in non-financial terms – information about mortality and morbidity rates attributable to their products, for example. Most of it is available at the macro level already. To bring it down to the micro level might introduce an interesting new dimension into the discussion.

Another interesting example of a good which is also a bad, less dramatic than cigarettes but perhaps more amenable to analysis, is the non-returnable container. Should the social performance of a business which sends out its products in containers which the community has to dispose of be debited with the cost of disposal? The private cost-cutting which motivates the switch from using returnables to non-returnables is one of the most clear-cut examples of a transfer of cost from the private to the public sector. In part, of course, it is transferred back in the local taxes which a company pays to cover, among other things, refuse disposal. But for some companies operating nationally this tax contribution must fall far short of the social costs. An estimate of this shortfall could be made and could be brought into the computation of "social value added" as a deduction. The question which this leaves is this: how should responsibility be allocated between producer and consumer for the disposal of waste material? If all consumers had a keen social conscience and always deposited waste in litter bins, disposal costs would be reduced, though they would still not be negligible. A similar question relates to the disposal of abandoned automobiles, which in the United States plagues city governments. The point has been recognised by proposals to tax the first owner of a car to pay for its ultimate disposal, but nothing has come of this yet. Similar proposals have been made for taxes on non-returnable containers, proposals which have naturally been resisted by their producers.

This difficulty could be resolved, if somewhat arbitrarily, by accepting the consumer as he is. The whole of the excess cost of waste disposal could then be treated as a social cost of production, to be deducted in determining the producer's "social value added." But this solves one problem only to reveal another. Which producer is to be charged with this cost, the one that produced the container or the one that filled it and sold it to the public? In some cases both operations will be in the same hands, but often responsibility for them will be divided. Where they are, the question just posed seems to be one of moral philosophy, not accounting or economics. It illustrates rather well the nature of the quicksands that lie between us and the goal of social measurement.

The measure of corporate social performance which has been discussed – social value added seems to be a good short name for it – starts with value added and then calls for appropriate additions and deductions.

There are good reasons for doubting whether most of the adjustments called for can be made. The pluses and minuses mentioned above are only a few of those which in a practical exercise would have to be taken into account. The social effects of operating heavy trucks, which add to congestion and damage roads; the reduction of peak-hour pressure on public transportation systems which some companies achieve by staggered working hours; the reduction in recidivism which others have helped to bring about by employing ex-convicts; further examples could easily be found. Some of them lend themselves to measurement but most do not, either because the resulting costs and benefits cannot be expressed in terms of market prices or because those costs and benefits are too widely diffused to be traceable.

Where does this leave the accountant if he still wants to help the corporate sector to report on its social performance? First of all, he had better distinguish between objectivity and quantification. Raymond Bauer illustrates the point well in relation to this very subject of social measurement. "Let me make a flat assertion: the proposition 'Thirty per cent of a cross-sectional sample of American adults 18 years and over said they are very happy' is just as objective as the statement that the GNP of the U.S. is one trillion dollars. It may also, in fact, be more accurate."[13] This is a salutary reminder of an important truth. Nor should we dismiss the lengthy descriptive statements, found as yet more commonly in the United States than in Britain, in which corporations report to their stockholders (and others) in their annual reports how many minority group employees they have hired and trained, how much they have spent on conservation of resources and on anti-pollution devices. We would not think much of financial statements that were equally fragmentary and disjointed; but the moral to be drawn from that, perhaps, is that this kind of descriptive reporting should be made more comprehensive and that quantities (not values, usually) should be reported wherever they appropriately can be.

But to describe social performance with a high degree of objectivity is still a long way from evaluation. For reasons which have already been sufficiently explained, it does not seem likely that that can be done objectively. Personal judgments in this field are not soon going to give way to accounting procedures, and they probably never will.

THE SOCIAL AUDIT

In 1971, Dr. Howard McMahon, president of Arthur D. Little, Inc., was reported as predicting that "corporate managers will soon have to submit to social as well as fiscal audits . . . such self-imposed audits will emerge as corporations become convinced that accountability to their employees, customers and the community at large is as crucial to corporate survival

[13] Raymond Bauer in *Social Measurement*, AICPA, New York, 1972, 10.

as profits."[14] This is by no means a new idea. A social audit seems first to have been suggested by Howard Bowen in 1953 in his book, *Social Responsibilities of the Business Man*.[15]

> Just as businesses subject themselves to audits of their accounts by independent public accountant firms, they might also subject themselves to periodic examination by independent outside experts who would evaluate the performance of the business from the *social* point of view. The social auditors would make an independent and disinterested appraisal of a company's policies regarding prices, wages, research and development, advertising, public relations, human relations, community relations, employment stabilisation, etc. They would then submit a comprehensive report to the directors and to the management with evaluation and recommendations. Such a report would be for the information of responsible officials and not a public document. Social audits might be made every five years rather than annually, as is usually the case with the accounting audit.[16]

The social audit teams, which might be private firms organised for profit or independent co-operative organisations created by groups of business corporations, would, said Bowen, be made up of persons "technically trained in fields such as law, economics, sociology, psychology, personnel, government, engineering, philosophy, and theology."[17] Not, it will be noted, in accounting. This is a striking and rather sobering omission for accountants. Bowen's proposal, bold as it was for 1953, is too timid for the 1970s. In the age of Ralph Nader, accountability and disclosure are here to stay. The social audit *will* result in a public document, contrary to Bowen's prediction. His suggestion of an inter-disciplinary audit team is a good one, though it will be surprising if there is not room on the team for persons with accounting skills. The social audit might, as he suggests, well be conducted at intervals of several years. How long it will be before this kind of audited report is a routine part of corporate disclosure it is impossible to say. To judge from the cautious approach of the Securities and Exchange Commission to this matter in America,[18] it will not come soon there, and Britain has even further to go. But in any case there are so many technical problems yet to be solved that a period for private experimentation will be no bad thing. It will be time enough, when more experience has been gained in this field – we have a little already – to start talking then about placing an obligation on corporations to report their social performance as they now report their financial performance.

[14] *New York Times*, February 14, 1971. For a more recent discussion see "What *is* a corporate social audit?" by Raymond A. Bauer and Dan H. Fenn, Jr., in *Harvard Business Review*, January–February 1973, 37–48.
[15] New York, 1953, especially 155–158.
[16] *op. cit.*, 155.
[17] *op. cit.*, 156.
[18] See William Casey, formerly chairman of the SEC, on "Corporate Responsibility as seen from the SEC," in *Business and Society Review*, Spring 1972, 27.

PIOUS INSCRIPTIONS CONFUSED ACCOUNTS; CLASSIFICATION OF ACCOUNTS: THREE HISTORICAL NOTES

B. S. Yamey

I. PIOUS INSCRIPTIONS IN EARLY ACCOUNT-BOOKS

IN the first published work in which bookkeeping is treated, the author, Luca Pacioli, advised merchants that the name of God should appear at the beginning of every document. He also recommended that all true Catholics should mark the first of a series of journals (or ledgers) relating to their business with the sign of the cross "from which all our spiritual enemies flee and at which all the infernal pack justly tremble." Succeeding journals were to be marked with the successive letters of the alphabet.[1]

In giving his advice Pacioli was not merely expressing his own religious feeling: he was also describing contemporary practice in Italy. It was customary to begin business contracts with some expression such as "In the name of the Lord." Extant examples include the overseas-trade contracts of the Medici of Florence which often begin with the words "Col nome di Dio e di Buonaventura" (with the name of God and of Good Fortune) – a combination of invocations which has been seen as an illustration of the reconciliation in the early Renaissance of "medieval" faith and Renaissance self-confidence and of the co-existence of the Christian and the pagan.[2]

Fifteenth-century (and earlier) Italian account-books almost invariably begin with a pious inscription invoking the name of God. The more elaborate inscriptions appealed also to the Virgin Mary and to named saints or all the saints collectively, and often besought the merciful granting of good health, long life and profits. Three examples follow.[3]

An elaborate example is that of the *libro vermiglio* (1332–37) of the Florentine company of Jacopo Girolami, Filippo Corbizzi and Tommaso Corbizzi. The first paragraph of the lengthy inscription reads:[4]

---

[1] Luca Pacioli, *Summa de Arithmetica . . .*, Venice, 1494; P. Crivelli, *An Original Translation of the Treatise on Double-Entry Book-keeping by Frater Lucas Pacioli*, London, 1924, 4, 16.

[2] See A. Warburg, *Gesammelte Schriften*, Leipzig, 1932, vol. 1, 151. For earlier Italian (and other) documents, see R. S. Lopez and I. W. Raymond, *Medieval Trade in the Mediterranean World*, London, 1955, *passim*.

[3] Further Italian examples are to be found in, *e.g.* A. Sapori, *Mercatores*, Milan, 1941, 104; T. Antoni, *Il Libro dei Bilanci di una Azienda Mercantile del Trecento*, Pisa, 1967, *passim*.

[4] M. Chiaudano (ed.), *Il Libro Vermiglio di Corte di Rome e di Avignone del Segnale del C. . . .*, Turin, 1963, 1. The inscription continues with details about the partnership. The adjective "vermiglio" refers to the colour of the original binding and served to

> Al nome di Dio e de la beata Vergine Madre Madonna Santa Maria
> e di messer Santo Giovanni Batista Evangielista e di tutti Santi e
> Sante di Paradisso, che per loro santa pietà e misirichordia ne choncie-
> dano grazia di santa e di lungha e buona vita, chon acrescimeto di
> buone persone e di guadagnio, cho salvameto delle nostre anime e di
> chorpo.

A simpler inscription is placed at the beginning of the ledger of the
Venetian merchant, Giacomo Badoer, opened in 1436[5]:

> Al nome di Dio e de bon guadagno, libro de mi Jachomo Badoer. . . .

The third example of an inscription is that of a surviving account-book
(*libro di ricordanze*) of the Florentine sculptor, Lorenzo Ghiberti, relating
to expenditures on his property some six miles outside Florence[6]:

> Mccccxxxxi a di xxvi daprile. Al nome di dio e della sua madre
> madonna Sancta Maria e di tutta la corte del paradiso e del beato messer
> sancto Piero e del beato messer sancto Pagliolo e del beato messer
> sancto Giovanni Batista e del bato sancto Giovanni vagielista e di tutti
> li sancti e sante di paradiso. . . . Al nome di dio e chiamasi Libro
> di ricordanze segnato A.

According to the Italian economic historian, Armando Sapori, the
tradition of religious inscriptions persisted in Italy until the eighteenth
century, although it became progressively more a matter of mechanical
repetition rather than (what it had been in the medieval period) an expression or reflection of intense religious feeling. Sapori illustrated the per-
vasiveness of such religious sentiment in commercial affairs by the fact
that some companies in the fourteenth century opened accounts in their
ledgers for and in the name of God (accounts "per Dio" or "per messere
Domeneddio"). These accounts were credited with a share of profits when
the ledger was closed, and were debited with donations to charities.[7]

It may be suggested, further, that the pious inscriptions and invocations,
which conferred a certain gravity on the contents of the account-books,
may have served to increase the value of these books as evidence in courts
of law. Some title-page inscriptions included specific details which could
have been helpful to a third party attempting to interpret the contents
of the accounts or to determine their reliability – details such as number

---

distinguish the particular account-book from others. The letter "C," written large on
a leaf of parchment with which the account-book begins, shows that the account-book
was third in a series (or fourth, if the first in the series was marked with the sign of
the cross).
[5] U. Dorini and T. Bertelè (eds.), *Il Libro dei Conti de Giacomo Badoer*, 1956, 1.
[6] Sotheby and Co., *Catalogue of Sale, July 9, 1969*, 30.
[7] Sapori, *Mercatores*, 106–107; A. Sapori, *Le Marchand Italien au Moyen Age*, Paris,
1952, xviii–xix.
  For some German examples, see W. von Strömer, "Das Schriftwesen der Nürn-
berger Wirtschaft vom 14. bis 16. Jahrhundert," *Beiträge zur Wirtschaftsgeschichte
Nürnbergs*, Band II, 1967, 771; and G. von Pölnitz, *Die Fugger*, Frankfurt, 1960,
297–298 (referred to in von Strömer, *op. cit.*), where the account was opened in the
name of Augsburg's patron saint, St. Ulrich.

of pages, scope of the records, arrangement of the entries, and names of those who would make the entries. For example, the inscription in the ledger of the banking company of Filippo Borromei, kept in London, 1436 to 1439, explains that the contents would cover the firm's debtors and creditors as well as the merchandise it was to buy and sell and relevant expenses. The first page of an account-book of Americo Benci of the year 1459 informs the reader that it is named "secret book signed A, of 100 leaves," and that it "will be kept in the Venetian manner, that is to say, on one page the debits and on the other the credits, beginning with the name of God and good fortune."[8]

The use of pious inscriptions at the opening of account-books spread from Italy to the rest of Europe, together with the practice of heading pages and accounts with the words "Laus Deo."[9] The use of such inscriptions was recommended in early English textbooks. Thus the title-page of the specimen ledger in Peele's *Maner and Fourme . . .* of 1553 reads as follows:

> Anno M.D. LIII./Maie the xxiiij. daie./+/The Quaterne or/greate booke of accomptes, belongyng to/me Fraunces Bonde of London/ Grocer, dwellyng in the Parishe of sainct Olifes in/Marke Lane./ The name of GOD be our helpe./F.B.

Weddington, writing in 1567, included the following among the "rules very necessarie to be observid by all marchantis, In the kepinge of ther accomptis": "and at the beginninge of their writingis to put fyrst the name of God, makinge the signe of the crosse the wiche is most commonli usid amongst all Christen men."[10]

These various usages are shown very clearly in the inscription in the surviving journal (1546–52), designated as the "cross" (that is, first) journal, of Sir Thomas Gresham:[11]

> +Laus. Deo. 1546./26. Apryll./In the name of God Amen./This present boke shalbe the/Jornall called + apperteyning to me Thomas Gresham/of London mercer for therin to wryte with my owne hande/ or els with the hand of my prentys Thomas Bradshawe/alle my hoole trayne and doynges and out of the/saide Jornall, to wryte it into the greate/booke called the Leger which shalbe/holden by poundes shillinges and/pence of money of Englonde/ Pleaseth God to geve me/ profytt and prosperitye/to defende me from/evell fortune/losse and/ domage./Amen.

---

[8] F. Besta, *La Ragioneria*, Milan, 1929, vol. 3, 326 and 329 (also 328).

[9] For interesting examples of inscriptions in account-books in Finland, see A. Grandell, *Äldre Redovisningsformer i Finland*, Helsingfors, 1944, 180–181. An example of 1698, in German, asks, *inter alia,* for divine protection from "bad and deceitful debtors."

[10] John Weddington, *A Breffe Instruction . . .,* Antwerp, 1567. See B. S. Yamey, H. C. Edey and H. W. Thomson, *Accounting in England and Scotland: 1543–1800,* London, 1963, 48. A cross is printed at the top of each page of Weddington's text.

[11] See Peter Ramsey, "Some Tudor Merchants' Accounts," in A. C. Littleton and B. S. Yamey (eds.), *Studies in the History of Accounting,* London, 1956, 189. The upper part of the title-page is reproduced in the same book, plate VI.

Below this inscription appears Gresham's merchant's mark. From the distinctive lay-out, the words and phrases used and their ordering, it is apparent either that Gresham took as his model the inscription in the specimen journal in Jan Ympyn's *Nieuwe Instructie. . .* published in 1543 in Antwerp, a city with which Gresham was well acquainted, or else that both drew from a common source.[12]

Another English example is the extant "Leager or greate Booke of accomptes of Letter A appertayninge" to William Hoskins, begun in 1655, and with the words "In the name of God Amen" at the head of the title-page inscription.[13]

The use of pious inscriptions seems to have declined much earlier in England than in Italy, although terms such as "Laus Deo" continued to be used occasionally in the eighteenth century. Roger North explained why a person had to begin a set of accounts by means of an inventory, and then proceeded: "For this Reason the Merchants (having a Form of Godliness) write first, LAUS DEO, and then, an Inventory of all their wordly Estate, under such Heads, as they judge, will make proper Accompts in their Books. . . ."[14] Even where inscriptions were not used, words to the effect that "God be praised" are occasionally to be found in entries of profits in surviving English account-books of the seventeenth century.[15] Thus on successive pages of Robert Loder's account-book entries of profits are accompanied by the following: "The Lorde my God his aboundant mercies be magnified and exalted therfore Amen."; and "The Lorde be praysed for it. Amen."[16] This sentiment is reminiscent of that of the words at the end of Ympyn's illustrative journal, just after the profit for the period covered had been transferred to the capital account: "Praise and honour to almighty God who has given me this, Amen."[17] It is interesting to compare these expressions with the headings of the debit and credit sides, respectively, of the profit-and-loss account of an early (1383) ledger of Francesco Datini of Prato: "Here will be entered, God forbid, losses

---

[12] The title-page of Ympyn's specimen journal is reproduced in *De Comptabiliteit door de Eeuwen heen*, Koninklijke Bibliotheek Albert I, Brussels, 1970, 31.
 The model set of account-books is missing from the only known surviving copy of the English version of Ympyn's book, published in 1547.
[13] William Hoskins, Ledger A, Goldsmiths' Library, University of London, MS. 265.
[14] A Person of Honour [Roger North], *The Gentleman Accomptant . . .*, 2nd edition, London, 1715. The attribution of the authorship of this work to Roger North is due to David Murray, *Chapters in the History of Book-keeping Accountancy and Commercial Arithmetic*, Glasgow, 1930, 262. Mr. R. B. Grassby, Jesus College, Oxford, is of the view, based on a study of the North literary MSS. in the British Museum, that parts of the *Gentleman Accomptant* are based on unpublished work of Sir Dudley North. It is clear that Dudley taught his brother, Roger, most of his accounting.
[15] For example, see Yamey *et al.*, *Accounting in England*, plate IX. For another example, see B. S. Yamey, "Some Topics in the History of Financial Accounting in England 1500–1900," in W. T. Baxter and S. Davidson (eds.), *Studies in Accounting Theory*, London, 1962, 23.
[16] G. E. Fussell (ed.), *Robert Loder's Farm Accounts 1610–1620*, Camden Third Series, LIII, London, 1936, *e.g.* 118, 119, 122, 125.
[17] The words in the French version of Ympyn's book are: "Louenge, & honneur a Dieu le tout puissant que ce ma donne. Amen."

incurred on merchandise"; and "Profits on merchandise will be entered here, God grant us health and profits, Amen."[18]

Whether or not English merchants continued to have "a form of godliness," in eighteenth-century textbooks there are occasional exhortations for them to keep their books, like their consciences, clean and tidy and in a constant state of preparedness: ". . . A Tradesman's Books, like a Christian's Conscience, should always be kept clean and neat; and he that is not careful of both, will give but a sad Account of himself either to God or Man."[19]

II. A CASE OF "INTRICATE AND CONFUS'D ACCOUNTS," 1691[20]

The translator into English of Jan Ympyn's *Nieuwe Instructie . . .* (Antwerp, 1543) wrote in his preface "To The Reder":

> The whiche maners of kepyng bokes I have seen and knowen sondry and diverse marchantes so grosly, obscurely, and lewdely kept, that after their desease nether wife, servaunt, executor nor other, could by their bokes perceive what of right ether apperteigned to them to be received of other, nether what justly was due by them unto other.[21]

About a century later Richard Dafforne, on returning from Holland to the land of his "breaths first drawing," was appalled to observe "the small love that a great part of our merchants bear to this science [of book-keeping]."[22] One imagines that many account-books were poorly kept. It is known that some persons, skilled in accounts, offered their services to disentangle and adjust account-books and accounts which were in a muddle. Hustcraft Stephens, the author of a highly original text in 1735, described himself as one who taught "Italian Book-keeping, either at Home or Abroad," and "likewise all Kinds of intricate and confus'd Accounts justly made up."[23]

Seventeenth- and eighteenth-century ledgers have survived which can properly be described as being in confusion and disarray. It is rare, however, to find documents which represent the results of the labours of an accountant who tried to clear up errors and bring order into a "lewdely kept" set of books. Hence there is some interest in a set of records, a journal and a ledger, relating to the accounts of two partnerships of English merchants trading in Turkey in the last quarter of the seventeenth century.[24]

[18] E. Peragallo, *Origin and Evolution of Double Entry Bookkeeping*, New York, 1938, 26.
[19] *The Universal Library of Trade and Commerce . . .*, London, 1747, Part VI, "A Compendious System . . .," 13.
[20] I am grateful to Mr. R. B. Grassby for advice on several points. His forthcoming study of the life and works of Sir Dudley North includes information on the trading activities of Montagu North, who was a partner in the two partnerships with which this Note is concerned.
[21] Jan Ympyn, *A Notable and very excellent woorke . . .*, London, 1547.
[22] R. Dafforne, *The Merchants Mirrour . . .*, London, 1635.
[23] H. Stephens, *Italian Book-keeping, reduced into an art . . .*, London, 1735.
[24] Kent Archives Office, U 471 A 252, 253.

The background is well set out in a long statement at the beginning of the journal:[25]

> This Journall with it's Leiger are a Suppossititious Supplement to 3. Pair Books of which 2 pair the one beginning aprill 1678. the other aprill 1684 belong to Mr. Mount. North & Richard Hampden, The 3d. pair begin Nov. 1684. & belong to said Sig.¹. [Signori] North and Hampden with James ffairclough, all remaining open and containeing various accounts obscure & Difficult to be closed, & Different Interest's to be ajusted & requireing a true division to be made to each concerned his particular share of the Proffitt or Losse therein, all which, through the multitude of Errors of said Books not being capable to be shewn with that clearnesse & certaintie as ought, Our Design therfore here, is for the Satisfaction of the Concerned to give them all the open accounts in the foresaid Books with our most probable conjecture how ought to be shut up, our best opinion of the Severall Debt's whither Good or Bad & bring all to such a head that the Interested may a little more or lesse see the State of their concerns.

The first 36 pages of the journal, which was drawn up in 1691, relate to the first two pairs of account-books, and concern the partnership between Montagu North and Hampden. Seven further pages relate to the pair of books concerning the enlarged partnership of North, Hampden and Fairclough. There are two corresponding sets of ledger accounts in a single volume: the opening entries in these accounts are the balances taken from the original ledgers. In this Note references in brackets are to numbered pages in the journal, differentiating between the first and second sets by a prefixed numeral.

Montagu or Montague North was a younger brother of the well-known Turkey merchant, Sir Dudley North. After some years as factor in Aleppo, Montagu joined his brother as business partner in his commission house in Constantinople. Montagu remained in Constantinople after Dudley returned to England in 1680 where he continued in trade on his own account, married, and entered politics. Montagu visited England in the late 1680s, and on his return journey was incarcerated by the French, for suspected espionage, for more than three years in the castle at Toulon.[26] His enforced absence from Constantinople may partly explain the sorry state of the account-books of his two partnerships. He was not in Constantinople when the adjustment journal was compiled. Nothing has been discovered about Richard Hampden. James Fairclough began his business career as apprentice to Sir Dudley North after the latter's return to England. He was "the son of a Presbyterian old usurer." He later went to join Montagu in Constantinople.[27]

The adjustment journal and ledger are kept in double-entry, in form

---

[25] The numerous contractions (other than the ampersand) are spelled out fully here, but punctuation is left as in the original.

[26] On Montagu North, see Roger North, *The Lives of the Norths,* Augustus Jessopp (ed.), London, 1890, vol. 2, 159, 225, 244.

[27] On Fairclough, see North, *Lives,* 175 and 225.

corresponding to the best contemporary practice. The original account-books must also have been in double-entry, however badly they were kept. The money entries are in terms of the dollar and the asper. The dollar was the "Dutch rix-dollar, or a debased version of it, called the lion dollar in the Turkish dominions after the Lion of Zealand which appeared on its face."[28] The full-bodied dollar was worth a crown, but debased specimens were worth as little as three shillings. Aspers were Turkish currency which, in the present account-books, were taken as eighty to the dollar. Amounts stated in square brackets in the text of this Note are the amounts of entries expressed to the nearest dollar.

The entries in the adjustment journal are often furnished with lengthy explanations. The compiler (or compilers, since the first person plural is used) made use of the information in the original ledgers; he scrutinised notes and documents of the two partnerships and referred also to a "blotting book"; and he was able to consult Fairclough (but neither North nor Hampden) as well as traders and others who knew some of the debtors.[29] He appears to have been patient, endowed with commonsense, and well-versed in accounts and in the frailties of those who kept them.

It is abundantly clear that the original account-books had been badly kept. At one point in the adjustment journal the compiler's patience came near to breaking-point: ". . . indeed when Books are so very full of Error's as these little is to be proved out of them especially those R. Hampden made are soe many and so very grosse . . .". He describes one error "in the very first line he wrote in Cash [in the cash account], & this also in his own prejudice . . ." He should have carried down a balance on the cash account to the debit of a new cash account; instead, he closed the cash account and debited his own capital account "as if he had taken soe much out of Cash to Trade." Fortunately the compiler had earlier discovered this particular error "by accident"; but the error was "soe unhappily made" that "a very nice inquisition might have mist" it (2/4–5).

In the seventeenth century (and also later) it was customary to open separate ledger accounts for each parcel or lot of merchandise handled, especially but not only where the firm in question was acting as agent on behalf of a principal. The first of the two partnerships had been engaged in the cloth trade, as principals and also as agents; and it in turn employed shopkeepers as agents. It appears that there was great confusion among the

---

[28] On currency problems in the Levant, see Ralph Davis, *Aleppo and Devonshire Square*, London, 1967, ch. 11. The quotation is from p. 190. I am grateful to Professor Davis, for determining the currency units used in the account-books.

[29] In a few entries there are references to what "the Jews of the house" said to the compiler (*e.g.* 1/20, 1/22). Dudley North, through Roger North, explained how individual Jews attached themselves to foreign traders: "When a fresh merchant or factor comes to Constantinople, the first Jew that catches a word with him marks him for his own as becoming his peculiar property, and calls him his merchant; and so he must be as long as he stays." He adds: "It is not a little convenience that is had by these appropriated Jews; for they serve in the quality of universal brokers, as well for small as great things," North, *Lives*, 145.

entries to the various cloth accounts. The presence of errors was revealed
by the fact that the entries in the quantity columns of some cloth accounts
showed that more had been disposed of than had been available for disposal, while in others the reverse was true. A long "Note" to one entry
(1/10) explains this:

> In these Books are Diver's Cloth accounts which want Creditt
> for severall Cloths that is have not Credditt for the whole number of
> Cloths as they ought but want severall Cloths of their Complement
> which doe not appear how were disposed, other Cloth accounts also
> there are just contrary, which have Creditt for a greater number of
> Cloths then the whole parcell was at first.

The compiler suggests various ways in which these mistakes could have
been made: entries could have been made in the wrong cloth account;
a cloth account could have been wound up before the whole parcel had
been disposed of, and without a suitable accounting adjustment having
been made; and there could have been failures to record the return of
cloths from shopkeepers who acted as agents. The adjustment he made
was: "& all Cloths wanting or abounding in Cloth accounts of Principall's
wee carry accordingly in Debt or Creditt of Cloth Sundry Accounts"
(1/11).[30] The small balance [397] on the latter account, "which seeme to
gaine," was finally transferred to the profit and loss account (1/29).[31]

The most frequent entries in the adjustment journal concern the account
titled "Debts Bad or Erronious." Into this account the compiler transferred
all debit balances on personal accounts when he had reason to suppose
either that it represented a valid but irrecoverable debt or that it was the
result of an error in accounting. Thus, as an example of category of Debts
Erronious, there were the accounts of those shopkeepers "who we believe
stand Debtors only through" errors affecting the cloth accounts, that is,
shopkeepers whose accounts had not been credited for cloths they had
returned (1/11). Another example concerning an erroneous debtor is the
following: " . . . we have good reason to believe he owes not an asper . . .
because he's lookt on as an honest man & say's soe as also because since
this debt there have 20 accounts and more been made up with him & fairly
ajusted in the 3rd pair Books, soe Esteeme this an Error. . . ." (1/7). A
further example concerns a large balance [2698]: " . . . we have an Hogett
or Turkish acquittance wherby he & Richard Hampden confesse to have
ajusted all accounts with Each other & there remained noe demands
between them"(1/12).

---

[30] Thus in one such entry (1/12) we read that the particular cloth account "stands Creditor
through 5½ Cloth's being here past [=passed] more than ought . . . carry all [such
cases] to Cloths Sundry Account where at last 'twill appear how all bear's one with
another."

[31] In the first part of the adjustment ledger, covering the two earlier sets of books, there
are a Profitte & Losse account and also a Losse & Gain account – reflecting the different terms used in the two earlier ledgers. In the adjustment process, the balance on
the former is closed into the latter (1/16).

But there were many more genuinely bad debts. The narratives of a selection of the transfer entries in the journals follow: "being a person Long since Dead in Prison soe is nothing to be received" (1/1); "the Ballance stands Debtor but deny and are a Couple of Knaves" (1/1); "noe where to be found or heard of suppose Dead" (1/3); "are fellow's Broke & gon away" (1/6); "he is a troubsome [sic] intriguesome Person & fear scarce any thing will ever be gott . . ." (2/2–3).

The total of Debts Bad or Erronious in the first pair of ledgers was very large. It was reduced somewhat by the introduction into the adjustment ledger of a "Goods remaining" account representing the value [4284] of pawns known to have been given by particular debtors and of "all those other goods [in possession] which suppose may have been taken in discharge of some of those Debt's with which Debt's Bad are charged . . ."[32] The corresponding credit was to Debts Bad (1/34). The balance of the latter account was further reduced greatly by the transfer to it of the whole of the credit balance on "Losse & Gain" [27,550]: "the gaine by these Books which carry to help Ballance this heavy Account of Debts Bad" (1/34). Nevertheless, a debit balance persisted; and this amount [7664] was divided equally between the two partners: "seeme to loose by this account more than all the gaine by these Bookes" (1/35). In the second adjustment journal the balance remaining on the bad debts account was large [8485], and was carried to Proffitt & Losse: "from which if hereafter any thing happen to be got in must be carryed in Credditt of concerned by those receiving it" (2/6).

The debts judged to be sound, on the other hand, were gathered together in a Debts Good account. Thus a debt in favour of the partnership was transferred in this manner, with the explanation: "Esteem as good & hope will pay it shortly as promises" (1/12). Another debt was treated similarly, although the compiler had some doubts about it: ". . . for which is his house in pawn which is reported to be worth more though the Debtor is Broake & undone, twill be a very troublesome business to procure the Sale of the house & gett the money, so look on this as a Debt more doubtfull then good" (1/10).

The Debts Good account was also the repository of debts owed by the partnership. Thus an amount owed to Sir Dudley North was transferred to the credit of Debts Good, "the Ballance which this Ragione [commission house][33] appears to owe him" (1/28). However, the biggest single credit made to Debts Good account in the adjustment journal of the first partnership was a less straightforward matter.

An account "Voyage from England" showed a large credit balance [18,048]. The compiler judged that this balance was not a measure of the

---

[32] Appended to the journal proper there is an inventory of these goods.
[33] Other than the "Signori" in the opening inscription, the word "ragione" is the only Italian word used in the adjustment journal. The word was used as a term for commission house. It is used (in the form "ragion") in North, *Lives*, e.g. 37, 48, 225.

profits of voyages from England. He believed that the voyage account should have been debited with "Diver's Considerable Sumes made good from Messina Mars[a] [Marseilles] &c . . ." Apparently the partnership had shipped goods from Turkey, but had "all along" carried their "Proper Trade" [*i.e.* trade on their own account] "only to the first place whither [=whether] to Messina or else where & there left it never minding how it gott from those Places to England . . ." The partners did not know – so it seems from the explanation given – who in England had bought the return cargo on their account, and the voyage account was left "without that Debt it ought to have . . ." (It is perhaps more likely that the partners had this information but failed to record it.) On the other hand, for the same reason sums owing to third parties for the omitted purchases and expenses in England – the compiler thought Sir Dudley North "or some other friend in England" had acted for the partners[34] – had also been omitted from the accounts of creditors of the partnership. The adjusting entry made by the compiler was to close the Voyage account by a debit, and to make a corresponding credit to the account "Trade partable MN & RH," a sort of partnership trading account in the ledger. The author explains that all the voyage accounts "will center in the account of trade partable"; and also that if it should appear that a sum was owing to someone who had "invested from England or else where for this Ragione," that person "must have Creditt & this account Trade partable Debit for said sume" (1/13–14). Towards the end of the process of account adjustment a substantial credit on Trade Partable [14,534] was transferred to Good Debts (1/29):

> because [we] suppose if not the whole yett some part of these Debt's [i.e. debit balances on personal accounts] may have been discharged, by Cost &c of some part of said Trade partable nott brought to account which time will show, but if prove otherwise, the Proffitt & Losse will be as well carryed from this account Debt's as directly from that account Trade partable as we should now Ballance [i.e. to Profit & Loss] were it not for the above regard which makes us think it better here.

Both parts of the adjustment journal disclose carelessness in the use and recording of cash. The cash account in the ledger of North, Hampden and Fairclough had a large credit balance [23,022], an anomalous situation noted by the compiler: ". . . makes paid in these Bookes more than received which can't be . . ." The compiler inferred that either moneys received from debtors had not been entered (and their accounts subsequently treated as bad), or the partnership ". . . must have made use of old Ragione's Cash [*i.e.* the cash of the other partnership, of North and Hampden alone] which fall's short about this sume . . ." He therefore debited the cash account to close it, and credited the account of Old

---

[34] It is probable that towards the end of his life Sir Dudley North continued in trade partly to help his brother and former apprentice. North, *Lives*, 225.

Ragione (2/5).[35] This latter account was one which was opened to transfer ledger balances from one adjustment ledger to the other; for example, the individual accounts of North and Hampden in the second ledger were transferred to the first ledger (2/6), a tidying-up operation designed to show more clearly the net position of the three principals. (There is an equivalent but reversed New Ragione account in the first ledger. Thus the cash adjustment, described above, is recorded in the first part of the adjustment journal as a credit to cash and a debit to New Ragione, "which Summe it's supposed said Ragione may have made use of belonging to this which fall's short, as that comes over about the above Summe" (1/28).) Other small adjustments are made to the cash account in the first part of the adjustment journal. The account ends up with a credit balance [968], which is then expunged by transfer to Debts Bad: "the Ballance [of cash] stands Creditor though never could unlesse were first received & we suppose is part of that large Summe, of Debt's Bad, in discharge of which these moneys have been received though not entered" (1/34).

Each of the two parts of the adjustment journal concludes with two notes, the first listing the outstanding debit balances, and the second the credit balances. In the first part, the debits are: one debt [14,860] and two categories of "Good's &c remaining" [totalling 19,308]. The credits are: Debts Good "which doe appear to be owing by this Ragione" [3,566]; each partner "for his Estate which he appear's to have in these Books" [12,624 and 17,691]; and, the very last entry [287]: "The Difference in the Ballance of these Books which is a disagreement we have not found out & is none of our makeing" (1/36). Having put right so much, the pains-taking and patient compiler had at last to admit defeat by "what we find soe obscure & Intricate" (as he expressed his view elsewhere, 1/11). A small inequality is also recorded, but without comment, in the closure of the second part of the adjustment journal (2/7).

III. ACCOUNT-CLASSIFICATION AND THE LOGIC OF DOUBLE ENTRY

In Malachy Postlethwayt's *Universal Dictionary of Trade and Commerce,* first published in 1751, we read that in the journalising of the waste book "lies all the difficulty of account-keeping," because it is in the journal that "the debit and credit are rationally fixed and settled, according to the principles of accountantship."[36] Roger North, who has been identified as the "Person of Honour" who wrote *The Gentleman Accomptant,* first published in 1714, expressed the matter in his characteristic style as

[35] In the narrative for this journal entry, the compiler explains that Fairclough reserved "to himselfe the power of making himselfe good any such share as may be coming to him by any part of these Debt's past [=passed] as bad which shall appear in all probability to have been paid though not made received."

[36] M. Postlethwayt, *The Universal Dictionary of Trade and Commerce,* London, 1751, article "Mercantile Accountantship."

follows: "The making true *Drs.* and *Crs.* is the greatest Difficulty of Accompting, and perpetually exerciseth the Judgment. . . . For this Reason the entring Matters formally in the Books, is a Business that will not be done in haste, no more than calculating Propositions in Arthmetick and Geometry; and an Error of that Kind spoils all."[37]

Accordingly, in many textbooks published up to (say) 1850 much space and ingenuity were devoted to the instruction of the reader in the art of distinguishing, for each of a variety of transactions, the appropriate ledger accounts to be debited and credited respectively. A common method was to present, in various forms, a detailed enumeration of what was to be done for each type of transaction, sometimes prefaced by a statement of more or less elaborate generalised rules, which often were more likely to have confounded than enlightened the newcomer to the subject. Alexander Malcolm was referring to a popular form of exposition when he wrote (in 1731) of "our *English* Writers on this Subject": "They reduce all their other particular Instructions and Rules to certain Heads, and Branches of Business (which is so far right:) And then, in the Way of Question and Answer, they shew what Accounts are to be made Debtors, and what Creditors, in the various Cases and Transactions that most commonly occur under each of those Heads." He said that such a method, though it "seems to be very plain, and adapted to Learners," was in fact "both unreasonably tedious and obscure"; and he argued that "a very few general Rules comprehend all those Cases, in such a Manner as to make the Sense and Reason of what's to be done much more clear and obvious."[38]

The principal difficulty in framing such rules, which to be satisfying should not only give clear guidance to their users but should also reflect the logic or rationale of the double-entry system, is one which no doubt today still puzzles beginners and also lures newspaper leader-writers into ambiguity: from the point of view of the owner of a business, whether a debit is favourable or unfavourable depends upon the nature of the account in which the debit is recorded. Beginners who have difficulties with this problem may take comfort from the fact that Prince Maurice of Orange had similar difficulties when he was being instructed in double-entry bookkeeping by the celebrated mathematician and man of affairs, Simon Stevin, at the end of the sixteenth century.[39] In their dialogue about "bookkeeping questions," the Prince asked: "The entries in the ledger are in debit and credit, which of each are to my advantage and which to my disadvantage?" Stevin replied: "Debit to advantage, because Peter who owes me a lot, that augments my capital. Thus also does much pepper in the warehouse, much money in cash, which all stand in debit; but credit does the opposite." When the Prince asked whether there were any exceptions, Stevin at first replied that he could think of none. The Prince

---

[37] A Person of Honour [Roger North], *The Gentleman Accountant.*
[38] Alexander Malcolm, *A Treatise of Book-Keeping . . .*, London, 1731.
[39] Simon Stevin, *Vorstelicke bouckhouding op de Italiaensche wyse . . .*, Leiden, 1607.

remained puzzled. A profit balance shown on the ledger account for cloves represented an advantage to the owner and yet was a credit; and he gave other examples. Stevin conceded the point; and enunciated the further rule that debit is adverse and credit is favourable in all entries in the capital account or in other accounts representing the capital account (such as profit-and-loss account). The persistent Prince then wanted to have this class of exceptions explained. One may doubt whether he could have been satisfied with the answer given him: "For the reason that capital debit means the same as if the master [owner] says, I, *N.*, *am debit*: but the more a man is debtor to himself, the more it is to his disadvantage, and the more creditor, the more to his advantage, in which way these must be the opposite of the others [*i.e.* the other ledger accounts]."

The removal of the Prince's difficulty "in such a Manner as to make the Sense and Reason of what's to be done" (to quote Malcolm) called for an appropriate classification of ledger accounts; and Stevin's general discussion went some way in this direction. But the first fully satisfactory account-classification was to be presented in a book which was published some eighty years later. The credit for its devising and exposition belongs to a Dutch author about whom nothing is known apart from the publication in 1681 of his *Kort begryp.* . . .[40]

Van Gezel's book differs radically from the great majority of those of his predecessors and contemporaries in that it does not include worked examples or detailed lists of types of transactions. Instead, having observed that no soundly-based published exposition was known to him, he presented an analytical treatment of the subject at a level which aimed at general applicability; and he promised that, if spared by God, he would publish further works with illustrations and applications. (No further work of his is known.) His originality is manifest, although he may have derived some inspiration from Steven's rather sketchy observations. He obviously knew the work of Stevin, to whose account of the antiquity of bookkeeping he referred.

At the most general level of classification, he wrote, there are only two classes of accounts: "own" accounts (*eigene*) and "contrary" accounts (*tegengestelde*). An own account is one "whose debit means the merchant's [owner's] debit, and whose credit means the merchant's credit." The contrary accounts include accounts for other persons, for cash and for goods. A contrary account is one "whose debit means the merchant's credit, and whose credit means the merchant's debit." This somewhat cryptic explanation is elucidated immediately. The own accounts are kept so that the owner can know how big his initial capital (estate) is, and why and by how much it increases or decreases in a period of trading. The contrary

---

[40] Willem van Gezel, *Kort begryp van 't beschouwig onderwijs in't koopmans Boek-houden* . . ., Amsterdam, 1681. The novel character of van Gezel's exposition is fully recognised in O. ten Have, *De Leer van het Boekhouden in de Nederlanden tijdens de zeventiende en achttiende eeuw*, Delft, 1933, 28, 72–84.

accounts, on the other hand, are necessary to show how the owner "stands with each person, and money, and goods, with whom or which he trades." Together the own and the contrary accounts are also necessary "to provide the proof of each other in the making of the balance account." The rules for debiting and crediting ledger accounts are then derived. The author distinguishes three classes of transactions or events (*posten*):[41] advantageous (*voordeelig*), disadvantageous (*nadeelig*), and indifferent (*middelmatig*). Transactions of the first class are those which (taken by themselves) increase the owner's capital; the second are those which decrease it; and the third are those which leave it unchanged. It follows that for an advantageous transaction an own account must be credited and a contrary account debited; that the converse applies for a disadvantageous transaction; and that an indifferent transaction affects contrary accounts alone.[42]

In his rules for making debits and credits, van Gezel placed the emphasis on the nature of the accounts and not, as was customary, on the type of the transaction. After the publication of his book – although it is doubtful whether it had any direct influence[43] – attention was increasingly given in textbooks to the classification of accounts, although rarely, until the nineteenth century, along the lines laid down by van Gezel. Moreover, there was the very occasional attempt at exposition of the "theory" of the double-entry system. The earliest example in English of such an analytical exposition is Hustcraft Stephens's *Italian Book-keeping, reduced to an art* . . ., first published in 1735, which covers some of the same ground as van Gezel.[44]

Van Gezel's bi-partite classification of accounts is not encountered widely until the nineteenth century. On the other hand, a tri-partite classification, associated with another Hollander, Matthieu de la Porte, had more adherents (though again, direct influence is difficult to establish). He presented this classification in his *La Science des Negocians et teneurs de*

[41] Van Gezel distinguishes a fourth category of mixed (*vermengde*) transactions; the issue under discussion is not affected.

[42] In a passage in his textbook of 1610, the Venetian Giovanni Antonio Moschetti discussed the nature of transactions affecting the capital account in a manner which suggests some familiarity with Stevin's writings and also corresponds with van Gezel's later (and independent) treatment: Giovanni Antonio Moschetti, *Dell' universal Trattato di libri doppii* . . ., Venice, 1610; quoted in F. Melis, *Storia della Ragioneria*, Bologna, 1950, 675.

Zambelli, in 1671, wrote that ledger accounts had to be in one or the other of two classes: "private" (*privati*) and "open" or "long" (*aperti* or *longhi*). A somewhat enigmatic paragraph suggests that the author had in mind a bi-partite classification corresponding to van Gezel's "contrary" and "own" accounts – but that he arrived at it by a different route. However, his intentions are further obscured by the fact that he subsequently placed the cash account among the open accounts and said that the bank account could be private or open "secondo il caso occorrente." Andrea Zambelli, *Il Ragionato* . . ., Milan, 1671.

[43] Unlike several of its contemporaries or near-contemporaries, van Gezel's book did not go into a second edition.

[44] Hustcraft Stephens, *Italian Book-keeping, reduced into an art* . . ., London, 1735. A part of the theoretical discussion is reprinted in Yamey *et al.*, *Accounting in England and Scotland*, 135–142.

livres . . ., of which the first known edition is of 1704, and which was frequently reprinted and also translated into German.[45]

De la Porte divided ledger accounts into three classes:[46] the accounts of the owner (*le chef ou le négociant lui-même*), the accounts of "natural" assets (and liabilities) (*les effets en nature*); and the accounts of the persons with whom the owner trades (*les correspondans*). The first class includes the capital account and the profit-and-loss account and its sub-divisions; the second includes cash, goods, bills receivable and payable, and ships, houses, etc.; and the third comprises debtors and creditors.[47] The exposition of the treatment of various kinds of transaction is arranged in terms of the account-classification.

A similar tri-partite classification became common in English textbooks of the eighteenth century and early nineteenth century. Besides personal and real accounts, the texts refer to a third class of "fictitious" or "imaginary" accounts, which correspond to de la Porte's accounts for the owner. A typical definition or description of imaginary accounts is that of an early American text: "Imaginary Accounts are fictitious titles invented to represent the merchant himself, or to supply the want of real or personal titles, in recording such gains or losses as cannot be ascribed, or with propriety placed to real or personal accounts."[48]

By the early nineteenth century this tri-partite classification had become commonplace in English textbooks. It was sharply criticised by Cronhelm, writing in 1818,[49] who castigated it as "one of the most ludicrous that ever enlivened the gravity of the scientific page." Its nomenclature was inept, but more seriously it reflected a neglect of the "great essential principle of book-keeping," *i.e.* the principle of the equality between the value of "the whole capital" (in the owner's stock or capital account), and the "sum of all its [capital's] parts" (in the remaining accounts) "whatever variations they undergo, and whether the whole capital increase, diminish, or remain

[45] Matthieu de la Porte, *La Science des Negocians et teneurs de livres . . .*, Paris, 1704.
   One direct adoption of de la Porte's scheme is in Pietro Scali, *Trattato del modo di tenere la scrittura dei mercanti. . .*, Leghorn, 1755. The treatment is hopelessly confused, Scali having misread a tabular presentation in de la Porte.
[46] De la Porte, *La Science des Negocians*, "nouvelle edition," Paris, 1753, 181–182. De la Porte had a penchant for trichotomies and triads. In some introductory "Remarques sur les comptes en général," he listed ten tri-partite subjects. These include the three "sortes de négociations," *i.e.* to buy, to sell, to barter; and the three ways in which accounts can finish, *i.e.* with profit, with loss, and with neither profit nor loss. The classification of accounts is one of the triads.
[47] A somewhat similar tri-partite classification appears in an earlier book, also by a Hollander, the second edition of which (the earliest now known) was published in 1688: Abraham de Graaf, *Instructie van het Italiaens Boek-houden . . .*, Amsterdam, 1688. The two systems of classification differ in detail. It seems that de Graaf and de la Porte arrived independently at their schemes of classification, and ten Have speculates that both might have drawn from a common source. Ten Have, *De Leer van het Boekhouden*, 120.
[48] James Bennett, *The American system of practical book-keeping . . .*, New York, 1820. For earlier examples, see Yamey *et al.*, *Accounting in England*, 57–58, 62, 65–67.
[49] F. W. Cronhelm, *Double entry by single . . .*, London, 1818; extracts from this book are reprinted in A. C. Littleton, *Accounting Evolution to 1900*, New York, 1933, 168–170; and in Yamey *et al.*, *op. cit.*, 145–152.

stationary."[50] From this "clear and simple principle of the equality of the whole to the sum of its parts" (which he mistakenly claimed had "never before been laid down as the basis for Book-keeping"), Cronhelm proposed a bi-partite classification of accounts: "Parts of Property" (with sub-division into "personal," "money" and "merchandise") and "whole Property" (the stock account with its "branches" such as the profit-and-loss account).[51] This is an unwitting return to van Gezel's scheme of "contrary" and "own" classes of accounts.

A different scheme of bi-partite classification had been introduced meanwhile. In a book published in 1721 but written before the author's death in 1703, Bertrand François Barrême (whose surname furnishes the noun in French for ready-reckoner) enunciated the division of all ledger accounts into two classes: the general accounts (*les comptes généraux*) and the particular accounts (*les comptes particuliers*) which he opens for each of his debitors and creditors (his *Correspondans*).[52] This division has no basis in terms of the logical structure of a set of double-entry accounts (although it may be a sensible basis for the splitting-up of the ledger where this is desirable for administrative or clerical convenience). Hence in his exposition of the rules for the debiting and crediting of accounts, Barrême, in common with many who had preceded him and many more who were to succeed him, had recourse to the personification of accounts.[53] Thus, to give one example, he treats the cash account as follows: "Cash is a cashier to whom Capital has entrusted the management of his money."

Barrême's account-classification was taken up by several later writers, including, for example, the authors of the first two treatises on book-keeping in the Portuguese language.[54] His influence was further disseminated by the work of Edmond Dégrange, senior, whose principal book,

[50] For earlier criticisms, see J. W. Fulton, *British–Indian Book-keeping . . .*, London, 1800. Extracts are reprinted in Yamey *et al., op. cit.*, 142–145.

[51] A similar bi-partite classification of accounts into "whole property" and "parts of property" is to be found earlier in C. Morrison, *A Complete System of Practical Bookkeeping*, the first edition of which was published in 1815. See also, for example, Andreas Wagner, *Buchhalterei für das gemeine Leben . . .*, Leipzig, 1810.

[52] Bertrand François Barrême, *Traite des parties doubles . . .*, Paris, 1721.

The term *comptes généraux* to cover all accounts other than those of accounts with persons was also used in Samuel Ricard, *L'Art de bien tenir les livres de comptes . . .*, Amsterdam, 1709.

Much earlier, in 1540, Manzoni had divided accounts into two groups: "live" (*vive*) and "dead" (*morte*) accounts. The former were those which referred to "all animate creatures," and the latter to "merchandise or every other thing." But Manzoni's division had no purpose other than the arrangement of the entries in the index to the ledger, the live accounts being entered on the right-hand and the dead on the left-hand side of pages of that book. Domenico Manzoni, *Quaderno doppio . . .*, Venice, 1540, part 1, ch. 13. See Melis, *Storia della Ragioneria*, 648–649.

The earliest German textbooks, those of Schreiber and Gottlieb, described the splitting of the ledger into two separate books, one for goods accounts and the other for the remaining accounts. This division had no pegadogic significance, and presumably reflected considerations of practical convenience.

[53] On the personification of accounts in English textbooks, see J. G. C. Jackson, "The History of Methods of Exposition of Double-Entry Book-keeping in England," in Littleton and Yamey (eds.), *Studies in the History of Accounting*, 295–302.

[54] See B. S. Yamey, "Early Portuguese Treatises on Book-keeping and Accounts," *Accountancy*, August 1969, 581–582.

La tenue des livres rendue facile, had a "prodigious success."[55] It was first published in Paris in 1795, was reprinted nine times during the author's lifetime, and was translated into several languages. Dégrange was "professeur et arbitre en matières de commerce" and a member of the Société Academique des Sciences of Paris.

Dégrange began by explaining that in the single-entry system of accounts the ledger is confined to accounts of the persons with whom one trades (although he notes that some merchants also included a cash account). He went on to say that bookkeeping by double-entry had for a long time appeared to be unintelligible and confused because it was not based upon any firm rule ("parce qu'elle ne reposait sur aucune règle fixe"). Today, he claimed, we had such a unique principle. Double-entry differs from single-entry in that the former comprehends the general accounts (*comptes généreraux*) which "represent the merchant" whose accounts are being kept. These general accounts he divided into five sub-classes, the "cinq comptes généraux," which correspond to the "cinq objets principaux" which serve commerce increasingly as "moyens d'échange." The five sub-classes are accounts of merchandise, of money, of bills receivable, of bills payable, and of profits and losses. These general accounts are to be regarded as those of the merchant whose books are being kept: a debit to a general account is to be conceived of as a debit to the merchant himself, "under the name of the particular account."[56]

Dégrange's fivefold division of the general accounts was the foundation of much writing about and discussion of the accounting system, and "enjoyed a greater influence than it deserved."[57] It was taken up with enthusiasm by the *Cinquecontisti* in Italy, the more extreme of whom limited the number of general ledger accounts to five, although Dégrange had allowed in his scheme for further account subdivision of each of his five sub-classes.

The question of account-classification, commonly within the framework of a theory of the structure of a system of accounts, continued to occupy writers throughout the nineteenth century. Old ideas were rediscovered and presented afresh. Theorising, speculation and controversy flourished. However, one is inclined to believe that most teaching in practice proceeded on the basis of the drilling of pupils in rules for the debiting and crediting of ledger accounts which had nothing to commend them except

[55] J.-H. Vlaemminck, *Histoire et Doctrines de la Comptabilité*, Brussels and Paris, 1956, 142.
  Dégrange's fame rested in part also on his contribution to the development of systems of columnar accounts.
[56] Edmond Dégrange, *La Tenue des Livres rendue facile . . .*, 6th ed., Paris, 1806, 5–9.
  The initiation of the notion that the general accounts represent the owner of the business is usually attributed to Dégrange. But the notion had been expressed in Pierre Giraudeau, *Le Banque rendue facile . . .*, the first edition of which was published in 1749. See Besta, *La Ragioneria*, vol. 2, 365–366, where it is noted: "Dégrange, however, was more explicit."
[57] Peragallo, *Origin and Evolution of Double Entry Bookkeeping*, 100.

that they achieved results. But, taking a longer perspective, the various attempts at systematisation and classification did serve to deepen understanding of the logic of the structure of accounts in the double-entry system and to pave the way for improved methods of exposition. These attempts are indeed a far cry from the earlier mnemonic incantations, rules and rationalisations which were supposed to help the beginner in the initial stages of his mastery of double-entry—of which perhaps the most fanciful and least helpful is Johan Gottlieb's explanation (in 1531) why debts owed to third parties had to be entered on the right-hand side of the ledger: it reflects a "natural process," because "trust and faith *(trew und glauben)* are signified by the right hand."[58]

[58] B. Penndorf, *Geschichte der Buchhaltung in Deutschland*, Leipzig, 1913, 115.

INDEX OF NAMES